City Steeple, City Streets

City Steeple, City Streets

Saints' Tales from Granada and a Changing Spain

CANDACE SLATER

University of California Press

BERKELEY   LOS ANGELES   OXFORD

The publisher wishes to acknowledge with gratitude a publication
subvention from The Program for Cultural Cooperation between
Spain's Ministry of Culture and the United States Universities.

University of California Press
Berkeley and Los Angeles, California

University of California Press, Ltd.
Oxford, England

Library of Congress Cataloging-in-Publication Data

Slater, Candace.
    City steeple, city streets: saints' tales from Granada and a
changing Spain / Candace Slater.
        p.   cm.
    Includes bibliographical references.
    ISBN 0-520-06815-7 (alk. paper)
    1. Leopoldo, de Alpandeire, Fray, 1864–1956—Legends.
2. Leopoldo, de Alpandeire, Fray, 1864–1956—Cult—Spain—
Granada.   3. Granada (Spain)—Religious life and customs.
4. Granada (Spain)—Social life and customs.   5. Granada (Spain :
Province)—Religious life and customs.   6. Granada
(Spain : Province)—Social life and customs.   I. Title.
BX4705.L5485S42   1990
282'.4682—dc20   89–27995
                                                                 CIP

Printed in the United States of America

1 2 3 4 5 6 7 8 9

The paper used in this publication meets the minimum requirements
of American National Standard for Information Sciences—Permanence
of Paper for Printed Library Material, ANSI Z39.48–1984. ∞

For Hortensia, Loli, Paco, Alfonso, Trini,
Ana, Carmela, Strelli, Felipe, José María.
And, back home, for Paul.

Para mí, antes de venir a Granada fray Leopoldo era una leyenda, una cosa del pasado. Pero la gente de aquí lo tiene muy presente.

(For me, before coming to Granada, Fray Leopoldo was a legend, something from the past. But the people here have him very much at hand.)

Young radio announcer from Melilla.

Pregúntale a cien personas por fray Leopoldo y vas a tener cien respuestas diferentes. Todo el mundo tiene algo que contar de él. ¿Y yo? Bueno, ¿quién sabe? Puede ser que yo también.

(Ask a hundred people about Fray Leopoldo and you'll get a hundred different answers. Everybody has something to tell about him. And I? Well now, who knows? It could be that I do too.)

Egg vendor, age sixty-two, Bib-Rambla Plaza.

Contents

Acknowledgments

The initial fieldwork for this study of the Fray Leopoldo stories, conducted between January and August of 1984, was funded by the Joint U.S.-Spanish Committee for Educational and Cultural Affairs, with a supplemental grant from the University of Pennsylvania Research Foundation. The University of California at Berkeley provided airfare for a subsequent research trip to Granada during the summer of 1986 and supplied the word processor on which this book was written.

I am grateful to William A. Christian, Jr., who first told me about Fray Leopoldo and who later offered useful comments on this book. I also appreciate the suggestions and encouragement of Encarnación Aguilar Criado, David Alvarez, Ruth Behar, Robert Bellah, Stanley Brandes, George Collier, Alan Dundes, Nancy Farris, Richard Herr, Brother Ronald Isetti, Anne Middleton, and Randolph Starn.

A conference at Berkeley during April 1987 on saints and sainthood in Islam and two lectures on contemporary Moroccan-Israeli holy figures by Harvey Goldberg in spring 1988 provided a useful comparative perspective. Conversations with Honorio Velasco, Luís Díaz, and João de Pina-Cabral that grew out of a seminar on Iberian identity held on campus in May 1987 were similarly helpful. I also benefited from the interchange with my fellow participants in a session on Iberian / Ibero-American cultural transfers at the American Anthropological Association meetings in Chicago in November 1987 and from discussions surrounding a conference on anthropology and modernity held at Berkeley in April 1989.

In Granada, Domingo Sánchez-Mesa Martín and José Cazorla Pérez generously provided personal contacts as well as valuable insights into Andalusia and Spain. Robert Black and his students in the Beloit College

Spanish Program introduced me to many of the city's most appealing nooks and crannies. I appreciate the goodwill of Fray Leopoldo's biographer, Fray Angel de León (1920–1984), who, though well aware that my goals and orientation were very different from his own, nonetheless went out of his way to help me. My greatest debt, of course, is to the many persons who shared with me the stories and observations on which this book is based.

Doris Kretschmer of the University of California Press offered her usual good counsel. David Staebler painstakingly developed the pictures that I took in Spain. Theresa O'Brien provided the sketch for the title page. I thank my parents, Frank Slater and Adelaide Nielsen Slater, for their encouragement; and my husband, Paul Zingg, for his support.

Introduction

The following study focuses on narratives concerning Fray (Brother) Leopoldo de Alpandeire (1864–1956), a Capuchin friar particularly well known in Granada and eastern Andalusia and probably the most popular nonconsecrated saint today in all of Spain. In tracing the emergence of a group of contemporary legends about this holy figure, I discuss both stories that I heard in the city's streets and plazas and the formal biography, or Life, authored by a member of his order.[1] My analysis underscores the essential pluralism of the Fray Leopoldo tales, their undercurrent of resistance to institutional authority, and their deep concern for the relationship between past and present. I argue that the stories point to the existence of an at once uniquely Spanish and yet universal tradition in which individual and institutional beliefs have long been in dialogue and, often, contention. At the same time, the stories effectively illustrate the inadequacies of either-or divisions between "official" and "popular," "secular" and "sacred," and "oral" and "written" expression, as well as the complex and protean nature of what we call "the past."

The reader may well wonder at the outset why I undertook a study of saints' tales in a country that has undergone such rapid and widespread transformations in the past few decades. In reality, much of the interest of the Fray Leopoldo tales lies precisely in the highly traditional genre of the saint's legend.[2] Rooted in the past, the stories succeed in expressing a long-standing and yet at the same time peculiarly modern anti-

1. The formal biography is Fray Angel de León, *Mendigo por Dios: vida de fray Leopoldo de Alpandeire.*
2. This highly traditional character has made saints' legends extremely unpopular with a number of modern literary critics. Alexandra Hennessey Olsen notes that literary critics have tended to dismiss the Lives as "for the most part, hopelessly uninteresting." (" 'De

1

institutionalism. As such, they highlight the potential subtlety and re-silience of even the most apparently conservative folk-literary forms. Then, too, their concern for the jumble of processes customarily sub-sumed under the rubric of "modernization" attests to the compelling, even obsessive, debate that finds expression not only through the figure of Fray Leopoldo but also in countless different areas of daily life in contemporary Spain. The tales confirm beyond all doubt the fundamen-tal if fluid and extremely complex ties between narrative and social forms.

Accounts of the friar offer particularly rewarding material for inves-tigation because of their subject's close association with a very particular moment in recent Spanish history and his ability to stimulate discussion among an increasingly heterogeneous population. Fray Leopoldo's con-temporaneity, his unquestionably urban identity, and his broad appeal help to distinguish him from a multitude of other Spanish holy figures. Only one of many saints or assumed saints whose names are familiar to many residents of Granada, Fray Leopoldo is nonetheless unusual in having generated a large and diverse store of tales about his life. Fur-thermore, stories about holy figures can be found throughout Spain, but legends about the friar are still very much in the process of formation. In them, one witnesses firsthand the struggle to define and thus appro-priate a common symbol. The title *City Steeple, City Streets* under-scores the elemental pull between ecclesiastical institution and lay population. But, as we will see, the stress lines suggested by the tales are constantly shifting, with each side revealing not just diverse, but sometimes competing factions.

Currently a candidate for canonization, Fray Leopoldo, a peasant, was thirty-six years old when he took his vows as a lay brother. His activi-ties as the Granada monastery's official alms collector (*limosnero*) during much of the succeeding half-century made him a familiar figure throughout the city and surrounding countryside.[3] Reports of his mirac-

Historiis Sanctorum': A Generic Study of Hagiography," p. 47.) Although she is speaking primarily of written saints' legends, many scholars would appear to find oral accounts of holy figures equally dull and, often, reactionary.

3. Although I will follow the Capuchins themselves in using the term "monastery" (*convento*) throughout this study, mendicant brothers like Fray Leopoldo technically reside in a friary. Monks, unlike friars, are housed in the same religious residence for their entire life, sing the Divine Office, and do not go out into the streets to preach and minister. Both the Franciscans (of which the Capuchins are a branch) and the Dominicans are mendicant orders that emerged in the late medieval period precisely for the purpose of moving the religious life beyond the monastery walls into the growing cities of Europe. Although all Franciscans were originally lay brothers with no canonical standing (as was Fray Leopoldo), a good number today are also priests.

ulous powers, which began circulating during his lifetime, increased steadily in the period following his death. Today, his crypt, which lies in the basement of the sleek new Capuchin church in the center of Granada, draws tens of thousands of people each year from in and around the city, as well as visitors from other parts of Andalusia and the nation.

Despite this ample following, the devotion is almost totally devoid of those "audiovisual aids of faith" often associated with Christian as well as non-Christian popular cults.[4] Because it involves none of the colorful processions or distinctive folkways that characterize many rural pilgrimages, the phenomenon may go unnoticed by outsiders. ("Are you *sure* such a thing exists?" a distinguished Madrid-based colleague asked me. "I once spent two months in Granada and never heard a word about this Fray Leopoldo.") Some visitors come to pay their respects to the memory of the friar or to seek solutions for pressing personal problems; others simply want to satisfy their curiosity about a name they may have heard from friends or neighbors. Often, they will go on to other distinctly nonreligious landmarks and activities when they have completed their obligations to Fray Leopoldo.

Even though visits to the crypt constitute the most immediate sign of interest in the friar, they are only one manifestation of a wider and more varied concern that finds expression in numerous stories about his lifetime and the tales regarding his posthumous intercession on behalf of those in need. The people who recount these tales represent a range of ages and socioeconomic backgrounds, and they diverge, sometimes dramatically, in their opinions of the friar. Some affirm reports of his powers, while others dismiss the whole idea of saints and miracles as fraudulent or silly. "Fray Leopoldo means nothing at all to me," says one young man (Fray Leopoldo no me dice nada en absoluto).[5] Still others see the friar as an exemplary individual but express doubts about his reportedly extraordinary actions. As a result, some stories or story fragments at first glance corroborate the Life, while others explicitly challenge it.

4. Ernest Gellner (*Muslim Society*, p. 48) finds these aids of faith, "whether in the form of music, dance, intoxication or possession," to be regularly associated with Islamic saints in the city as much as in the countryside.

5. Man, age eighteen, born Barcelona, high school. Single, part-time laundromat clerk, "absolutely never" attends mass.

All of the speakers in this study are identified in terms of sex, age, birthplace, and level of formal schooling. Marital status, occupation, and self-designated degree of participation in formal religious activities are also indicated. Full-fledged narratives are offered in English in the body of the text; the Spanish is given in Appendix B, with a corresponding number. In the case of short quotations, the Spanish appears in parentheses whenever translation is difficult or clearly loses the peculiar flavor of the original. All English transcriptions and translations are my own.

This study is the outgrowth of an earlier project on narratives surrounding Padre Cícero Romão Batista (1844–1934), a holy figure of great importance in northeast Brazil.[6] I first learned of Fray Leopoldo from William A. Christian, Jr., in a conversation following his presentation on Spanish popular religious traditions at the University of Pennsylvania in 1983.[7] The friar was of particular interest to me as an approximate contemporary of the Brazilian priest. I found myself wondering about the relationship between the stories regarding these unofficial holy figures. To what degree and in what ways would the many obvious (and not so obvious) social and historical differences between Spain and Brazil affect these descendants of a common European and Iberian spiritual and literary tradition?

Although I fully expected to find divergences between the Spanish and the Brazilian stories, I was not prepared for the immense differences that my research slowly uncovered. Nor had I anticipated the degree to which an apparently marginal and even backward-looking narrative genre would encapsulate many of the themes most central to contemporary Spaniards. In rethinking my own assumptions about the saint's legend, I also found myself confronting far larger questions about modernization.

My objective at the outset was not a full-fledged study of the Fray Leopoldo stories, but, rather, was a far less ambitious overview of two sets of saints' legends. I found that although a number of the tales proved all but identical, the larger narrative constellations in which they figured revealed dissimilarities so profound and fundamental as to make any one-to-one comparison necessarily misleading. And thus, to my own surprise, the article I had envisioned gradually grew into a book that deals exclusively with the Fray Leopoldo stories. Only at the very end of this discussion do I refer back to the accounts I heard in the Brazilian backlands in an attempt to underscore the distinguishing features of the Spanish tales.

The following discussion focuses on issues of the religious imagination, narrative, and folklore that have received very little scholarly attention to date in Europe and, above all, the Iberian Peninsula.[8] Al-

6. See Slater, *Trail of Miracles*.
7. Christian mentions Fray Leopoldo in "Secular and Religious Responses." His various and important works on Spanish popular religion include *Apparitions in Late Medieval and Renaissance Spain*, *Local Religion in Sixteenth-Century Spain*, and *Person and God in a Spanish Valley*. See also his "Tapping and Defining New Power."
8. Scholarship on popular religious expression has been particularly sparse in Spain, perhaps in part because of a long-standing antipathy among many intellectuals toward religion and religious institutions as major obstacles to progress. A broader interest in popular culture, however, can be documented in various parts of the nation and especially in

though not initially conceived as an ethnography, the study offers one of very few ethnographic descriptions of a modern Spanish city.[9] In analyzing the Fray Leopoldo tales, I have looked with particular interest to the work of William A. Christian, Jr., on the historical uses of saints, of Joan Prat i Carós on problems of defining popular culture, of Ruth Behar on issues of continuity and change, and of Joan Frigolé Reixach on the relationship between religious and political traditions.[10] In addition, I have relied on the efforts both of specialists in Andalusian folk and popular culture and of various scholars who have written about other parts of Spain.[11]

The study also draws on scholarship on saints' cults and on the legend as a genre. Because of their close connections to formal literary texts and official religious institutions, accounts of holy figures have often remained the narrow province of hagiographers and literary historians. I have followed the lead of scholars such as Jean-Claude Schmitt, Stephen Wilson, and the various contributors to a number of recent collections about popular religious manifestations in attempting to see the tales as an expression of a particular group of people in a specific time and place.[12] I have also consulted the writings of legend theorists in seeking

---

Andalusia, which saw the publication of numerous studies of folk and popular culture in the nineteenth and early twentieth centuries. By far the most important figure in this movement was Antonio Machado y Alvarez (1812–1893), who edited the journal *El folklore andaluz*. For a historical overview of folklore research in the region see Aguilar Criado, "Los primeros estudios sobre la cultura popular andaluza."

9. There are very few descriptive studies of urban life in contemporary Spain. One of these works is Irwin Press, *The City as Context*, which includes a very brief account (pp. 180–88) of urban religious manifestations.

10. See Christian, *Apparitions in Late Medieval and Renaissance Spain*, *Local Religion*, and *Person and God*; Prat i Carós, " 'Religió popular' o experiencia religiosa ordinaria?"; Behar, *Santa María del Monte*; and Frigolé Reixach, "Religión y política en un pueblo murciano."

11. See Aguilar Criado, *Las hermandades de Castilleja de la Cuesta*; Aguilera, *Santa Eulalia's People*; Castón Boyer et al., *La religión en Andalucia*; Driessen, "Religious Brotherhoods"; Freeman, "Faith and Fashion in Spanish Religion"; García de la Torre, *Estudio histórico-artístico*"; Luque, "La crisis de las expresiones populares del culto religioso"; Luque Requerey, *Antropología cultural andaluza*; Maddox, "Religion, Honor and Patronage"; Moreno, *La semana santa de Sevilla*, *Las hermandades andaluzas*, and *Propiedad, clases sociales y hermandades en la baja Andalucía*; and Rodriguez Becerra and Soto, *Exvotos de Andalucía*.

See also, for example, Brandes, *Metaphors of Masculinity*; Bilinkoff, "The Avila of St. Teresa"; Lisón Tolosana, *Belmonte de los Caballeros*; Mitchell, *Violence and Piety in Spanish Folklore*; and a number of the excellent essays in Fernandez, *Persuasions and Performances*.

12. See Schmitt, *The Holy Greyhound*, and Wilson, "Cults of Saints." Another good example of recent work in the broad new interdisciplinary field of popular religion (though not saints' lore in particular) is Ginzburg, *The Night Battles* and *The Cheese and the Worms*.

to situate the Fray Leopoldo stories via-à-vis saints' tales as well as other, apparently dissimilar contemporary legends.[13]

The book is divided into six chapters. The first chapter discusses the Fray Leopoldo phenomenon in the context of Granada and modern Spain. It briefly summarizes the relationship between the Spanish church and state with emphasis on the twentieth century, provides biographical information on the friar, describes the present-day devotion to him, and offers a number of possible motives for his widespread appeal.

Chapter 2 examines the attitudes of different segments of the local Roman Catholic church toward Fray Leopoldo and suggests the politics of the canonization process. After a brief look at the official Articles of Canonization, I examine the formal biography of the friar in light of the narrative techniques through which its author seeks to affirm the enduring value of the Franciscan and, more specifically, Capuchin experience.[14] I suggest that the Life resembles a long series of hagiographical models in its presentation of a series of largely interchangeable challenges that Fray Leopoldo successfully meets.

In chapters 3 through 5 I deal with orally transmitted accounts of deeds said to have been performed by the friar during his lifetime. (Although from time to time I refer to accounts of posthumous favors, they are considerably less central to this study than individual interpretations of the historical Fray Leopoldo.) After introducing the storytellers, chapter 3 analyzes a group of narratives that I term "Legends." These accounts resemble the Life in their presentation of a series of challenges to which Fray Leopoldo inevitably rises as well as in their repetition of a number of key incidents. They nonetheless stand apart from the formal biography in their frequent shifts in focus from the friar to various members of the lay population, their heavy reliance on detail to personalize the incident, and their varying attitudes toward both the miraculous and the events described in the body of the narrative. Despite their overwhelmingly positive presentation of Fray Leopoldo, a number of the tales in this first group reveal a diffuse, but for this reason no less potent, anticlericalism.

Chapter 4 presents a second category of storytellers, whose tales I call "Counterlegends." Unlike both Legends and the Life, some of the Coun-

Among these collections are Gajano and Sebastiani, eds., *Culto dei santi;* Trinkhaus and Oberman, eds., *The Pursuit of Holiness;* and Badone, ed., *Religious Orthodoxy and Folk Belief.*

13. The contributions of scholars such as Linda Dégh and Andrew Vázsonyi, Dan Ben-Amos, Robert A. Georges, Jan van Brunvand, and Alan Dundes are noted in chapter 6.

14. *Granatensis causa de beatificación y canonización del siervo de Dios Fray Leopoldo de Alpandeire hermano capuchino de la provincia bética: artículos.*

terlegends portray Fray Leopoldo as failing to respond to challenges. Others show him forced to confront would-be opponents in the process of helping those in need. (This confrontation often becomes the real subject of the tale.) Like Legends, however, Counterlegends as a whole are strongly anecdotal and reveal a wide range of attitudes toward the miraculous. Although the stories in this second group are more explicit in their attacks on authority (and, above all, on the religious establishment), both sorts of oral narrative have a similarly anti-institutional bent.

Intense interest in the relationship between past and present constitutes a final, crucial link between the two types of tales. The fifth chapter shows how very different storytellers may use Fray Leopoldo as a springboard to discuss the rapid, often sweeping changes that Granada and Spain as a whole have undergone over the last few decades. Ongoing evocations and evaluations of an era experienced firsthand by a sizable percentage of storytellers, such accounts tend to reveal strong, often contradictory, feelings. Thus, although many tales grapple with questions of sanctity and the possibility of miracles, many are first and foremost about Generalissimo Francisco Franco and the first two bitter decades of the Franco era.

The final chapter argues that the Fray Leopoldo tales are interesting not only as particularly vivid reflections of contemporary Spain but also as effective illustrations of some of the major pitfalls inherent in any scholarly attempt to divorce the popular from the official, the oral from the written, the sacred from the secular. After summarizing some of the specific reasons why these dichotomies are inaccurate in regard to the Fray Leopoldo stories, I reflect on key differences between these stories and other saints' tales. I conclude by suggesting that in their open-endedness, intense engagement with a recent and historically specific past, and profound relativity, these seemingly traditional stories recall a number of other, often at first glance wholly unrelated, contemporary legends. This broad resemblance does not, however, negate the specifically Spanish and Andalusian character of the stories or of the social processes on which they implicitly, and sometimes explicitly, comment.

Two appendixes follow the study proper. The first compares extraordinary actions included in the Life to others that appear in the Articles of Canonization. It also indicates the number of times these same incidents appear in my collection of oral narratives. The second appendix contains the Spanish originals of stories cited in (my) English translation in the body of the text. The narratives have been numbered to facilitate comparison.

Because this book relies in large part on material I collected in Granada, a brief description of my field procedures during two stays totaling just under a year may be useful to the reader. After arriving in the city, I began talking with visitors to the Franciscan Church of the Divine Shepherdess, in which Fray Leopoldo is interred. Although the majority of these individuals come from in and around Granada, others are from neighboring Málaga as well as much more distant points such as Barcelona and Madrid, the Canary Islands, Melilla, and Ceuta. The crowds are biggest on the ninth of every month (the commemoration of the friar's death, which occurred on 9 February 1956). The crypt nonetheless daily attracts a steady trickle of visitors.[15]

My conversations with visitors dispelled a number of *a priori* assumptions about Fray Leopoldo's followers. Based in part on a photograph in one of the pamphlets on the friar that the Capuchins had sent me and in part on my own experiences in other parts of the Iberian Peninsula, I had imagined a group composed primarily of older women of limited means with strong ties to the countryside. Instead, as already suggested, I found a notably varied, if decidedly urban, population. The relatively large number of male visitors impressed me. So did the preponderance of the middle aged and of the middle, upper-middle, and lower classes. And yet, though my attendance at the crypt taught me much about the semiofficial devotion to the friar, the setting did not favor discussions about him. Visitors often had to wait in long lines for up to an hour outside the church to enter. One would think it easy to strike up conversations about the friar under such circumstances, but the noise and distraction created by peddlers and beggars impeded attempts to communicate. Those inside the hot and crowded basement were involved in prayer and meditation. Even though the municipal guards stationed there repeatedly assured me that it would be all right to take pictures, I could never bring myself to photograph, let alone address, the worshipers.

In addition, after the devotees had paid their respects to Fray Leopoldo, they were usually eager to move on. Pilgrims from outside Granada had often planned many other activities such as a tour of the palaces of the Alhambra, a swim in the big new Neptune Swimming Pool on the outskirts of the city, a shopping expedition, or a picnic in the park across from the church. Residents were also apt to be in a

15. Newspaper estimates put the February 9, 1984, crowd at more than 60,000. Fray Angel de León, author of the formal Life and vice-postulator of Fray Leopoldo's process, calculated a minimum of 700,000 visitors ("and probably many more") to the crypt each year (tape-recorded interview, 12 June 1984).

hurry, having stopped off at the crypt on their way to or from work or school.

Even when people had the time and inclination to talk, they usually had little to say about the historical figure who was my chief concern. A good number of the visitors were willing to recount instances of Fray Leopoldo's posthumous intercession on their behalf or on that of a friend, acquaintance, or family member.[16] Very few, however, went beyond their own experience to talk about his life. Moreover, those incidents they did recount often seemed directly drawn from the formal biography. Many of the people whom I questioned counseled me to buy the Life or handed me one of the official pamphlets that the Capuchins mail out to subscribers and distribute at the crypt. "Here, take this," they would say. "It explains everything much better than I ever could." Or "If you're interested in Fray Leopoldo, just ask one of the friars. After all, they are the ones who really know these things."

In an attempt to augment the range and number of stories I was collecting, I began visiting persons suggested by the Capuchins and by other contacts I was making through the University of Granada. These introductions opened the doors to carefully restored Moorish-style homes with enclosed gardens (the city's celebrated *cármenes*), to cinderblock apartments in the working-class outskirts, and to once-proud mansions with crumbling roofs propped up by variegated marble pillars.

Even though these interviews afforded me invaluable glimpses of day-to-day existence in Granada, the stories themselves revealed disturbingly little sense of urgency. Admittedly more detailed than the narrative fragments I had managed to collect at the crypt, most were still extremely close to, and indeed often seemed lifted from, the Life. Not infrequently I came away with the distinct impression that the teller had dutifully studied the biography the night before my visit. The great majority of my hosts were convinced followers of the friar and supporters of the ongoing canonization effort, which probably reinforced the sameness of their accounts. Then, too, the understandable desire to say the "right" thing about Fray Leopoldo to a foreign researcher whom they were encountering for the first time made them more reticent than they might have been under other circumstances.

My first important breakthrough occurred in the home of a mother of an acquaintance several weeks after my arrival in Granada. After re-

16. Printed accounts of posthumous intervention appear in the Articles of Canonization, pp. 51–54 and *Mendigo por Dios*, pp. 303–27. Between 1961 and 1976, 47,079 reports of similar favors were received by the vice-postulator of the process. New accounts regularly appear in the bimonthly Fray Leopoldo bulletin published by the Capuchin monastery in Granada.

lating a number of more or less conventional anecdotes about Fray Leopoldo, Doña Estrella began reminiscing in general terms about that period in which she first became acquainted with the friar. "But you didn't come all this way to hear me talk about such things," she said, cutting short an account of a young soldier whom her grandmother had hidden among the sheets in her linen closet for a few, seemingly endless hours during the civil war (1936–1939). "Oh, but I did!" I assured her with such energy that she looked surprised. "But why does she want to hear such trifles?" I later heard her whisper to her son as she prepared coffee for us in the kitchen. "These are the sorts of things that everybody knows!"

Doña Estrella did more than share a still-vivid past, knowledge of which many residents of Granada take for granted. In one of my subsequent visits to her home, she introduced me to a friend of hers, a cleaning woman named Carmela who, as a child, had often observed Fray Leopoldo in the city streets. Carmela began by repeating a number of the stories I had already heard about the friar. Suddenly, however, in the middle of recounting how Fray Leopoldo made a deaf girl hear again, she threw up her hands. "You know," she exclaimed, embarrassed but defiant:

> I really don't believe a word of this. People tell the story
> all the time, but I for one don't think it's true. To my mind,
> he was a good man, a saint, yes, in his goodness. But it's
> those friars who've made a regular business of this talk of
> miracles. "The mouth of a friar only opens to ask for
> something" (Boca de fraile sólo se abre a pedir), just like
> the saying goes.

Carmela's outburst impressed me partly because of the sentiments expressed, but even more because of the scant impression these appeared to have made on Doña Estrella. ("People have their own opinions," she later observed with a shrug.) Her nonchalance made me think both that it could not be the first time she had heard such attacks on the Capuchins' portrayal of Fray Leopoldo and that there must be other tales with little or nothing to do with the formal Life. Aware that this sort of narrative material would probably not be forthcoming in a more structured setting and feeling increasingly at home in the city, I began relying more on casual conversations that covered a broader range of topics and thus afforded a more holistic vision of life in Granada.

Andalusians are known throughout Spain for being talkative and friendly to strangers, and there is at least a measure of truth in the stereotype.[17] Although I did not expect people to bare their deepest feelings to me, it was not hard to become involved in interchanges in plazas and neighborhood restaurants, on buses, in neighborhood shops, and more than once on the corner of the street near the railroad station that bears Fray Leopoldo's name. I would, for instance, linger at the newsstand where I bought the morning paper or begin asking offhand questions of the waiter in a favorite, hole-in-the-wall café. If I went to a drugstore or bakery, a hardware shop or flower stand, I would make an effort to start talking to the salesperson or the other customers. Janitors, bus drivers, people on park benches, ticket vendors, street peddlers, students in the cafeteria at the university where I was auditing history classes, my neighbors at lectures or concerts, gardeners, cleaning women, and traffic guards thus became my sources. Although only a very few of these persons considered themselves followers of Fray Leopoldo, many were disposed to reminisce about him, and some told full-fledged stories of his life.

In the beginning I would often pick out a commercial establishment with a small statue of the friar in a window or a picture of him on the wall. "Isn't that Fray Leopoldo on the cover of that calendar?" I might ask the owner. With any luck, this individual or one or more bystanders would then begin talking about the friar. But these visual cues, while useful, were really not essential. Because Granada is home to one of southern Spain's largest universities, its residents are used to foreign students, and many simply assumed I had come to the city to study. People also assumed I was young and unattached partly because most Spanish women wear their wedding rings on the right, not the left hand, and partly because I dressed more informally than many persons my age. In addition, the apartment I had rented was next door to the Church of the Divine Shepherdess, known familiarly as the Church of Fray Leopoldo, or, more simply, "Fray Leopoldo," so questions about my place of residence often led to conversations about the friar. "So you live next to Fray Leopoldo?" the speaker might say. "Ah well, I still remember the time. . . . "

I myself might take the occasion to inquire if the person had known the friar. If he or she said yes, I might ask what he was like ("¿Y cómo era él?"). This purposely open-ended question often elicited a detailed

---

17. One recent attempt at regional character analysis is Gilmore, *Aggression and Community*. See also Brandes, *Metaphors of Masculinity*. A thoughtful review of the Brandes book and an earlier enthnographic account by Gilmore (*People of the Plain*) is Fernandez, "Consciousness and Class in Southern Spain."

physical description, which might be followed by an account of his miraculous or often not-so-miraculous deeds.

It would be misleading to imply that the residents of Granada spend hours conversing about Fray Leopoldo. During the course of my two stays in the city, I was rarely party to spontaneous discussions of the friar. Although there may indeed be people who talk regularly among themselves about him, the stories I collected were almost always a response to an offhand comment or question on my part. Bystanders often became listeners and participants in the resulting narrative performance, but it was not they who were normally its initiators. Moreover, even though some individuals went on for hours about Fray Leopoldo, others offered no more than a desultory sentence or two. Not infrequently, the arrival of a bus, the speaker's sudden recollection of other obligations, or the wailing of a hungry child cut short a promising exchange.

The wide range of attitudes about the friar demands further emphasis. Along with people who firmly believed Fray Leopoldo to be a miracle worker, I found others who recounted incidents that they were quick to label fictions. Some claimed to have no knowledge of the friar ("I may have heard the name, but . . . "). Others expressed neutrality or actual disinterest, remarking: "Ni pincho ni corto" (I'm neither for nor against). Still others expressed indignation about what they saw as the Capuchins' eagerness to commercialize the friar's extraordinary powers or irritation with the general populace's superstitious nature ("pure fanaticism this business of Fray Leopoldo!").

Throughout these informal conversations, I tried to emphasize that I did not subscribe to any particular image of the friar but, as an outsider, was eager to hear what the inhabitants of his adopted city thought. Should an exchange develop, I would explain I was an American university professor who had come to Spain to study varying conceptions of Fray Leopoldo. I almost never began with a statement to this effect, however, because it would have nipped the conversation in the bud. The minute that most people learned I was conducting research, they started apologizing for potential errors and indiscretions, often modifying earlier opinions so as to screen out anything remotely controversial. "I know almost nothing," "I'm really not very religious," or "You should talk to someone who was closer to the friar," they would exclaim despite my protests.

I always sought permission to record an individual's stories. Once he or she had launched into an account of Fray Leopoldo, I would ask if I might tape the narrative for a future book. Most people laughed or shrugged their shoulders, indicating no objection; others became serious and made an obvious effort to speak clearly into the small machine I then produced. If someone said that he or she did not want to record the story, I put away the recorder and simply listened to what they had to say. I did not ask the tellers' names but customarily inquired about their age, occupation, marital status, education, birthplace, and frequency of church attendance.

Sometimes taping proved unfeasible either because it would have been awkward to introduce the machine at that particular moment or because the story simply took me by surprise. In this event, I reconstructed the narrative from notes as soon as possible. This study is based on almost fifty hours of recording and just under six hundred pages of field notes. I quote verbatim only those tales I actually recorded.

Although extremely valuable, my conversations in the public spaces of Granada were necessarily limited. Even in the case of particularly lengthy discussions, I usually acquired a limited knowledge of the speaker as a person. Quite often, I never saw him or her again. For this reason, I was particularly grateful for the counterbalance provided by the small number of people whom I visited on a regular basis, all of whom make an appearance in the body of this study. These individuals—a cleaning woman, an unemployed young man, a retired schoolteacher from a wealthy family, a shoemaker, a middle-aged woman who sells jewelry on installment, a banker in his twenties—gave me a sense of the friar's place within their own lives. In addition, the seemingly contradictory comments they made on different occasions brought home to me both the danger of taking any remark at face value and the underlying complexity of the Fray Leopoldo phenomenon.

The people I saw most frequently of all were the sixty-nine-year-old owner of a tiny shoe repair shop, his slightly younger sister-in-law, and his adult son. Esteban, Mari, and Manolo (not their real names) welcomed me each time I appeared, invited me to their homes on occasion, and introduced me to family and friends. They took me on walking tours of the neighborhoods in which they had lived as children, fed me first-rate gazpacho, and served as a prime source of information and counsel.

They also provided me with an almost ideal research setting.[18] The men, women, and children who picked up and delivered packages or who

18. For a discussion of some of the occupational peculiarities of shoemakers that help to explain why these individuals should have been such first-rate informants see Hobsbawm with Scott, "Political Shoemakers."

dropped in to have their shoes shined represented a wide range of ages and social classes. Although many of these individuals were longtime residents of the primarily middle-class neighborhood in which the shop is located, others were students, household help, and tradespeople from other parts of the city, as well as employees of and visitors to the nearby San Juan de Dios Hospital.[19] In addition, the shoemakers themselves made the long walk to their small shop every morning from the sprawling blue-collar district known as the Cartuja.

Many of the people whom I met were longtime customers who stopped to chat while Manolo tapped the last nail into a heel or Mari ran a set of stitches through the strap on a timeworn handbag. I remember among others an eighty-year-old woman who had worked as a cook in a series of neighborhood cafés since the age of thirteen, a young dentist's assistant, a part-time electrician who had been jailed twice under Franco, and a former mayor of Granada.

Those who dropped by to retrieve shoes might or might not linger. The men who came to have their boots polished always settled into a special armchair with iron stirrups. Intrigued by the rambling conversations that accompanied the various stages of the shoe shine, I began visiting the shop toward the end of every day. Perched on one of the two rickety chairs reserved for friends and clients, I might join in a discussion. Often, however, I just listened to people talk while Mari snipped the heads off the chamomile flowers she had picked on the way to work that morning for future use in a medicinal tea, or whacked at the scraps of leather on the floor with an ancient broom. Looking back, I realize how much my understanding of the larger context of the Fray Leopoldo tales owes to these apparently aimless exchanges in which all present normally joined. The people who told jokes, talked politics, bragged or worried aloud about their jobs or families, and complained about the price of veal or taxis provided an invaluable context for more specific discussions of the friar. From time to time, I would try to bend the conversation toward Fray Leopoldo ("oh no, there she goes again!" Manolo would exclaim with a mock grimace). The stories and observations about the friar that I quite often managed to elicit in this manner, however, would have been far less meaningful had their tellers focused exclusively on Fray Leopoldo from the outset. The sorts of details about their own

19. There are actually a wide variety of neighborhoods in easy walking distance of the shoe shop and the crypt. The area behind the Elvira Arch, for instance, is primarily working class, while the Plaza del Triunfo is bordered by a number of expensive apartment houses and hotels. The hospital is surrounded by various student rooming houses as well as by middle- and lower-middle-class residences.

their own lives they shared with me provide an individual and communal context that I have tried to suggest in succeeding chapters.

The oral accounts that appear in the chapters that follow are often distinguished by their vivid imagery. "Fray Leopoldo was the last bullet I had left to fire" (Fray Leopoldo era el último cartucho que yo tenía para quemar), declares one woman, referring to a near-hopeless situation.[20]

"Between cabbage plant and cabbage plant one always finds a head of lettuce" (Entre col y col siempre hay lechuga), says another seeking to emphasize the differences between Fray Leopoldo and his fellow friars.[21]

"He had a lot of hand [influence or pull] with God" (El tenía mucha mano con Dios), asserts a second-year medical student.[22]

The artistic expression of the stories, however, owes far less to their frequent flashes of poetic language or their folk-literary motifs that predate the Middle Ages than to their ability to express multiple meanings through a common symbol. The elderly twin sisters out for their midday stroll, the teen-agers hunched over a table in an electric bingo parlor, the open-air vendor standing vigil over a plastic bathtub full of olives, and the businessman in a pinstriped suit have very different things to say about the friar. Their seemingly casual, often contradictory accounts of Fray Leopoldo point to an increasingly heterogeneous society in frank transition. At the same time, their readiness to talk about the friar and his Granada suggests the continuing expressive power of saints and saints' legends.

20. Woman, age fifty-nine, born Granada province, grade school education. Widowed, supported by husband's pension, attends mass "often, though I don't say all the time."
21. Woman, age forty-four, born Granada, some high school. Married, helps husband in drugstore, attends mass regularly.
22. Man, age twenty-four, born Granada, medical school. Married, doctor in Alpujarra region, and continuing medical student, attends mass "every once in a while."

CHAPTER ONE

Background to the Stories

Athough the narratives we will be examining deal with a local holy figure, they are often about events that have affected Spain as a whole. In this chapter I shall therefore establish the context in which the tales and the more general Fray Leopoldo phenomenon must be understood. After a necessarily brief discussion of the Spanish church as an institution, I identify the friar as a historical personage and describe the ongoing devotion at his crypt. I then offer a number of possible motives for a wider interest in him among many different sorts of people, only a portion of whom take part in the actual devotion.

Church and State in Modern Spain

In order to appreciate more fully the Fray Leopoldo stories, readers need to be aware of the church's support for Franco during the civil war and its ensuing involvement in a dictatorship that can be divided into two principal periods.[1] They should also be conscious of the close identification of church and state in Spain for many centuries as well as the existence of a deeply rooted anticlerical tradition. This anticlericalism has

---

1. I have relied heavily in the following section on Payne, *Spanish Catholicism*; Lannon, *Privilege, Persecution, and Prophecy*; and García de Cortázar's bibliographic essay, "La Nueva Historia de la Iglesia Contemporanea en España." See also Hermet, *Les catholiques dans l'Espagne de Franco*; Petschen, *La Iglesia en la España de Franco*; Gómez Pérez, *Politica y religión en el régimen de Franco*; and Ruiz Rico, *El papel político de la Iglesia católica en la España de Franco*; and the various articles in Belda et al., *Iglesia y sociedad en España*, and Gallego et al., *Estudios históricos sobre la iglesia española contemporanea*. For additional references see Payne, pp. 233–49, and García de Cortázar.

not only assumed different forms in different moments throughout Spain's history but also exhibits more than one variety today.[2]

The critical role Catholicism played in defeating the Moors in southern Spain, and Granada in particular, during the Middle Ages helps explain the church's early power.[3] The far-reaching influence of the state-controlled ecclesiastical court (known as the Spanish Inquisition), the importance of Catholic missionaries in the colonization of the New World, and the self-image of the Hapsburg emperors as defenders of the faith further enhanced the religious establishment's political force.[4]

Although the church's very preeminence tended to stifle the drive toward reform evident in other countries in the sixteenth and seventeenth centuries, criticism of religious institutions and ideas from within as well as from without is visible from early on. The Catholic humanism and moderate reformism of the Dutch scholar Erasmus greatly influenced Spanish scholars and religious leaders of the period and laid the basis for a critical tradition.[5]

Opposition to the ecclesiastical establishment assumed a new dimension during the Enlightenment, when Jansenist priests and bishops joined a number of Spanish intellectuals in attacking the ideas and practices of their more conservative counterparts. Given the church's ownership of vast tracts of some of the most desirable land, anticlerical sentiments among the populace often had as much an economic and social as an ideological basis. These feelings, to be sure, had long found expression in folk images of the greedy friar perched beside a potential donor's deathbed and the big-bellied, roving-eyed, and lazy parish priest. (We will see these stereotypes anew in some of the Fray Leopoldo tales.)

Tensions between conservatives, most of whom supported the church, and liberals, who increasingly came to see it as an obstacle to progress, intensified in the nineteenth century. When Fernando VII returned from exile at the end of the war of independence against Napoleon in 1814, he annulled the progressive constitution ratified in his absence. He also lost no time in reinstituting the Inquisition, calling back the Jesuits from exile, and driving large numbers of the more open-minded Spanish

2. For a historical overview of anticlericalism in Spain see Caro Baroja, *Introducción a una historia contemporanea del anticlericalismo*. A more psychoanalytic perspective, which addresses anticlericalism in present-day Andalusia through an analysis of the priest as father figure is Gilmore, "Andalusian Anti-Clericalism."

3. For a portrait of the distinctive society of which Granada was both a center and last bastion see Guichard, *Al-Andalus*. A good discussion of religion, nationalism, and national identity in medieval Spain and Portugal appears in Linehan, *Spanish Church and Society*.

4. These events are discussed in Elliott's now-standard overview, *Imperial Spain*.

5. See Bataillon, *Erasmo y España*.

clerics from the country. These measures helped to ensure the predominance of rightist, and often thoroughly reactionary, elements within the ecclesiastical hierarchy.[6]

The death of Fernando triggered the first of what were to be three civil wars. The support of a sizable percentage of the clergy for the monarchists helps to explain a series of increasingly angry demonstrations in the 1830s.[7] Although the church enjoyed a brief era of support following the liberal government's energetic suppression of the religious orders and policy of disamortization, the later overthrow of the Bourbon dynasty created a new crisis.

By the end of the nineteenth century Spaniards had begun to speak of "two Spains"—one rightist and Catholic, the other reformist and anticlerical, when not antireligious.[8] Although the Catholic revival of this period sought to repair the damage, the new alliance between church and state represented by the reign of Alfonso XIII aggravated already-existing tensions among poor southern peasants, urban workers, and a good portion of the lower middle classes. Many of these individuals were already suffering the effects of massive underemployment and rapid demographic growth (Spain's population had doubled during the 1800s). The nation's humiliating military defeats in Cuba, Puerto Rico, and the Philippines in the Spanish-American War in 1898 further compounded existing problems.

Opposition to the church became increasingly violent in the first decades of the twentieth century. During Barcelona's *Semana Trágica* (Tragic Week) of 1909, for example, rioters protesting a military draft vented their wrath on both church and government property.[9] Fears generated by further uprisings such as the massive Barcelona strike of 1919 helped to bring the pro-Catholic dictator, Primo de Rivera, to power four years later, thereby cementing the progressive radicalization of the Spanish left. Although the Second Republic that replaced Primo in 1931 claimed to support religious tolerance, it did little to stop mobs in vari-

6. For an introduction to the nineteenth century see Callahan, *Church, Politics, and Society in Spain*, and Cuenca Toribio, *Relaciones Iglesia-Estado en la España contemporanea*. For the history of the church in Andalusia see Cuenca Toribio, *Estudios sobre la iglesia andaluza moderna y contemporanea*.

7. The most obvious of these was the riot that broke out in Madrid in July 1934 in response to rumors (almost certainly untrue) that members of religious orders had poisoned the drinking water. See Caro Baroja, *Introducción a una historia contemporanea del anticlericalismo*, pp. 150–53, for a discussion of the event.

8. The term "two Spains" has been used to suggest this basic tension since the time of Menéndez Pelayo. Changes in its meaning over time are discussed in Whitaker, *Spain and Defense of the West*, pp. 97–100.

9. A good discussion of the *Semana Trágica* is Ullman, *The Tragic Week*.

ous regions, including Andalusia, from sacking and burning churches, monasteries, and convents a month later.

Republican proposals to terminate priests' stipends, to recognize only civil marriages, and to give the state the right to dissolve religious orders further alarmed the ecclesiastical leadership and prompted the formation of various pro-Catholic organizations. In 1933 these joined into a single political party called the Confederación Española de Derechas Autónomas (C.E.D.A.).[10] The entrance of three of the party's representatives into the Republican cabinet triggered a revolt of the Spanish left the following year. Then in 1936 the narrow victory of the exclusively Republican Popular Front resulted in a rightist military uprising that signaled the beginning of a full-scale civil war.[11] Although the war, which dragged on for three years, affected the entire nation, resistance to the Nationalist forces led by Franco was particularly bitter in the heavily Anarchist Andalusia. The much-publicized shooting of the celebrated poet Federico García Lorca by Franco's Civil Guard was only one of many similar acts of terrorism.[12]

The Nationalists' final victory in 1939 depended in good part on the church, which saw the attacks on its property and representatives as justification for a counterrevolutionary "crusade" against the left.[13] All but three prelates of the Spanish hierarchy signed a collective let-

10. Article 26 of the Republican Constitution, voted in October of the same year (1933), formally separated church and state for the first time in Spanish history and made the property of religious orders liable to nationalization. Article 27 sought to phase out education by the religious orders and declared all public religious manifestions subject to government authorization.

For a study of the tension between the church and the Second Republic see Sánchez, *Reform and Reaction.* See also Lannon, "The Church's Crusade against the Republic."

For a discussion of the C.E.D.A., see Montero, *La C.E.D.A.*

11. There is an enormous bibliography on the Spanish civil war. For an overview of the historical literature see García-Nieto, "Historiografía política de la guerra civil de España." Among works too recent to be mentioned in this review are Preston, *The Coming of the Spanish Civil War,* and Preston, ed., *Revolution and War in Spain.* See also Collier, *Socialists of Rural Andalusia;* Fraser, *Blood of Spain;* and Mintz, *The Anarchists of Casas Viejas.*

12. It is worth noting that the Spanish civil war was at once a local and a national and international event. The support of the Soviet Union and the international brigades for one side, Germany and Italy for the other, made the struggle in Spain, as various historians have suggested, a sort of dress rehearsal for World War II. For a summary of writing on international responses to the war see Viñas, "Dimensiones económicas e internacionales de la Guerra Civil."

13. Although opposition to the ecclesiastical establishment characterized the Republican period as a whole, most of the actual violence occurred during the civil war. By the end of the fighting in 1939, some seven thousand of the approximately thirty thousand members of the clergy (the majority ordinary parish priests) were dead and a large number of churches and monasteries lay in ruins. Fuller quantitative information appears in Montero Moreno, *Historia de la persecución religiosa en España.*

ter, published on 1 July 1937 that endorsed Franco's assault on the Republic.[14]

The church's moral support, as well as its military and financial assistance, was crucial not just to the winning of the war but also to the establishment of a dictatorship that would rule Spain for almost four decades.[15] In return for this aid, Franco took pains to stress his regime's "National Catholic identity," adopting numerous measures to ensure the church's presence in most areas of culture and education.[16] His regime's insistence on an individual's participation in formal religious activities as a prerequisite for social and economic advancement cemented the existing alliance between the church and the politically conservative upper sectors. Religious and class identity had long been closely associated in Spain, but under Franco they became even more so. This close relationship is obvious in the interchangeability of the terms "rich," "religious," and "Franquist" in a number of the Fray Leopoldo stories.

Ecclesiastical backing also gave the dictator a degree of respectability outside Spain both after the civil war and following World War II. He would attempt to distance himself from the defeated Fascist states, with whom he had never signed a formal agreement, and from fascism as a political system through continued insistence on the uniquely Catholic character of his regime.

Although this strategy helped Franco to retain power after World War II, the isolation of Spain within Europe exacerbated the nation's already serious financial problems. The civil war had left roughly a million Spaniards dead or in exile. Hard hit by this diminution of the workforce, the economy had been further weakened by the destruction of the transportation system, natural disasters such as drought and floods, and various misguided attempts at state-controlled industrial development. Thus, as late as the early 1950s Spain continued to be plagued by widespread shortages and hunger. The storytellers recall these difficult years time and again in their tales of Fray Leopoldo.

The specter of continuing poverty and repression had created growing dissension among some members of the clergy by the end of World War II. In an attempt to stifle this nascent discontent, Franco lobbied vigorously for a new concordat between Spain and the Vatican, which was

14. For a discussion of the letter and the church's support of Franco see Lannon, *Privilege, Persecution, and Prophecy,* pp. 198–223.

15. The immense literature on Franco and the Franco regime is summarized in Payne, *The Franco Regime,* pp. 645–54.

16. For a good introduction to National Catholicism, including further references, see Lannon, "Modern Spain."

finally signed in 1953.[17] He also ostentatiously reconsecrated the nation to the Sacred Heart of Jesus, extolling the traditional religious values ostensibly underlying his regime. While Franco was involved in these dramatic public gestures, however, he had taken deliberate first steps toward a policy of "normal" capitalist expansion in which market mechanisms would gradually replace state control. Although continuing to insist on his government's uniquely Catholic identity until his death in 1975, he would rely increasingly on material prosperity to assure his hold on power. The Franco years can therefore be divided into two broad periods, with the second half of the 1950s as a watershed. Fray Leopoldo, for his part, remains closely associated in the minds of many storytellers with the first, particularly difficult era.

The first step in opening Spain to Western capitalism occurred in 1953 when the United States agreed to make the nation a large loan in return for the establishment of four American military bases. (The Spanish electorate would vote against the continued presence of these in 1988.) Not long after, Franco launched a massive campaign to make Spain "the playground of Europe," thereby stimulating the construction industry. Beginning in 1956—the year of Fray Leopoldo's death—he also took steps to encourage Spaniards to seek employment beyond the nation's borders. The ensuing exodus of some one and a half million workers to industrial centers in northern Europe relieved unemployment at home while filling the nation's coffers.

In mapping out a combination of foreign investment, tourism, and emigration designed to inject new life into a long-moribund economy, Franco looked to the technocrats of the Catholic lay association known as Opus Dei. Founded in 1928 by an Aragonese priest, José María Escrivá de Balaguer, the small group became a formal order in 1939 and the first in a new category of "secular institutes" established by Pope Pius XII in 1947.[18]

The association, which assumed a key role in the Franquist directorate after 1957, was composed primarily of laymen under the direction of members of the clergy. By seeking success in their chosen professions, these individuals sought to extend the church's influence into places

---

17. See Fernández Catón, *El patrimonio cultural de la Iglesia en España*. Revisions to the 1953 document were signed on 29 July 1976.

18. Richard Herr points out that investigators have been unable to find any mention of Opus Dei in any publication before 1939, the date when Escrivá began to transform his small group of associates into a formal order. See his *Historical Essay on Modern Spain*, p. 226. For other discussions of Opus Dei in Spain see Artigues, *L'Opus Dei en Espagne*; Guillén, *La "elite" del poder en España*; Moncada Lorenzo, *El Opus Dei*; and Moreno, *El Opus Dei*.

where it had long been in decline. A number of Opus members privately took vows of poverty, chastity, and obedience, while others, called super-numeraries, might be married and have families. As the association never published its statutes or divulged its membership except for its highest officers, it soon acquired an air of secrecy.

The policies elaborated by Franco and his new advisors resulted in spectacular economic expansion. In a space of only ten years, the average Spaniard's income tripled. A massive shift from countryside to cities (the urban population more than doubled in a decade) also occurred. Whereas in the 1940s approximately half the nation's inhabitants had been involved in small-scale agriculture, this proportion had fallen to only about 20 percent at the time of Franco's death.[19]

Deeper cultural transformations necessarily accompanied these rapid and far-reaching economic and demographic developments.[20] Full employment and unprecedented increases in income for nearly all social classes quickly created a new de facto consumer society. Large-scale foreign tourism and mass emigration exposed much of Spanish society to new, nontraditional, and decidedly non-Catholic influences. The growing influence of the mass media helped to foment enormous shifts in values and everyday behavior. At the same time, the ever-widening gap between rhetoric and reality—the explicit ideology of the regime and the conditions necessary for continued economic expansion—heightened existing tensions at every level of society.[21]

In 1956 (again, the year of Fray Leopoldo's death), university students initiated what was to be a long series of antigovernment manifestations. That same year the Spanish archbishops made their first collective declaration in support of the working class, thereby transforming what had been scattered murmurs of protest among some members of the clergy into an official statement of discontent.[22]

The ecclesiastical establishment could not help but feel the effects of the new market-oriented economy.[23] By the beginning of the 1960s a

19. Two useful, highly readable overviews of the Spanish economy are Lieberman, *The Contemporary Spanish Economy*, and Tamames, *The Spanish Economy*.
20. See Cazorla, "Cambio social y cultura política," for an overview of some of the changes that began under Franco and have continued into the present.
21. See chapter 1, "The Internal Contradictions of Francoism, 1939–69," in Preston, *The Triumph of Democracy in Spain*, pp. 1–17.
An interesting portrait of this period is provided by the personal testimony of various artists and thinkers in Marsal, ed., *Pensar bajo el franquismo.*
22. The document, which criticizes the unequal distribution of wealth, appears in Iribarren, ed., *Documentos colectivos del Episcopado español*, p. 291.
23. The bases of this economy are confirmed in Franco's Stabilization Plan of 1959. For a discussion of the plan and its impact see Lieberman, *Contemporary Spanish Economy*, pp. 198–264.

significant number of priests and members of religious orders had publicly distanced themselves from the aging dictator. Some of the dissi-
dents were older clerics unhappy with the powerful new materialism that
threatened their own moral authority. The great majority, however, were
younger individuals troubled by obvious injustices within the political
system.[24]

The reforms of Vatican Council II, formalized in 1962–63 under Pope
John XXIII, profoundly affected local churches throughout the world.[25]
Although the council made no alterations in formal dogma, it recommended the church's dissociation from the state, enhanced the role of
the laity, reformed the liturgy, and encouraged ecumenism along with a
rethinking of practical, political questions. Its advocacy of religious autonomy made a particular impact on Spain, where more progressive
members of the religious establishment were beginning to take an increasingly militant public stand on social issues. Some of these individuals assumed a leading role in the Catholic workers' associations that
were emerging as an alternative to the ineffectual state-run syndicates.
A number of the clergy also participated in newly organized grass-roots
parish organizations called *comunidades cristianas de base* (Christian
base communities). In many cases, Vatican II not only affected local religious traditions but also changed the relationship between priest and
parish by helping to create a new style of priest less concerned with the
outward observance of religion and more concerned with inward searching for the divine in the self and in social change.[26]

Although the Spanish episcopate never formally broke with Franco,
the rift in the once apparently solid church-state alliance was unmistakable by the late 1960s. The dictator's death in 1975 ushered in a new
political era as King Juan Carlos, on whom the former had pinned his
hopes for continuity, began instead to actively campaign for reform. The
ensuing developments radically affected the status of religious institutions. Although exhorting elected officials to take into account the religious beliefs of the Spanish people and "to maintain the consequent
relations of cooperation with the Catholic church and other confessions,"

24. For a discussion of changes within the Spanish church in the 1960s see Duocastella, *Análisis sociológico del catolicismo español*, and Duocastella, ed., *Cambio social y
religioso en España*. See also Vásquez, *Realidades socio-religiosas de España*. For Andalusia
see Linz and Cazorla Pérez, "Religiosidad y estructura social en Andalucía."
25. For a summary of the council's activities see "Vatican Council II." For more information see *The Teachings of the Vatican Council; Complete Texts of the Constitutions,
Decrees, and Declarations* (Westminster, Md.: New Man Press, 1966).
26. See Behar, "The Struggle for the Church." See also Brandes, "The Priest as Agent
of Secularization."

the new constitution affirmed the state as strictly secular. As a result, the ecclesiastical establishment lost the privileged position that it had occupied for almost four decades under Franco.[27]

In surveys conducted in the early 1980s, fewer than two-fifths of adult Spaniards identified themselves as practicing Catholics.[28] The precipitate decline in the number of seminary students and in church attendance that began in the mid-1970s appears to have reached a plateau in recent years, but both figures remain low in comparison to preceding decades. Although there are exceptions to the rule, young people in particular are apt to evince a lack of interest in organized religion. At the same time, the falloff in religious observance among persons who were previously regular churchgoers reflects in part the de-emphasis on Catholicism as a requirement for economic advancement, as well as pent-up hostility over the church's role in the dictatorship.

Spanish religiosity, to be sure, cannot be equated with church attendance or with the church as an institution, and one may speak of traditions, rather than a single tradition, of anticlericalism in Spain. Although hostility toward religion as ideology has increasingly accompanied an antipathy toward the clergy, people's low opinion of the ecclesiastical hierarchy has not necessarily kept them from attending mass. (Some of the tellers of the most virulently anticlerical stories of Fray Leopoldo are regular churchgoers.) Nor has opposition to the clergy prevented at least some avowed unbelievers from showing up at other people's weddings or, on occasion, baptizing their own children.[29] By the same token, it is worth noting that the same folk forms initially dismissed as archaic by ecclesiastical authorities have on occasion been revitalized by local leftist politicians. Although this revitalization may reveal mixed, often nonreligious motives, it remains a significant fact of post-Franquist life.[30]

Anticlericalism also has not necessarily discouraged individual and communal forms of devotion—Marian pilgrimages, local saints' cults and devotions, ritual prayers and healing ceremonies—marginal to the

27. The more localized effects of these broad political changes are obvious in Frigolé Reixach's "Religión y política," a meticulous study of the conflicts surrounding a particular Marian shrine.

28. Payne cites the results of a number of recent sociological studies in his *Spanish Catholicism*, pp. 218–27. For a quantitative analysis of attendance at mass during the time of my research in Granada see "Asistencia a la Eucaristía dominical, 1983." I am grateful to Professor José Cazorla Pérez for obtaining a copy of this report for me.

29. For a discussion of "pious anticlericalism" and "political anticlericalism," see Riegelhaupt, "Popular Anti-Clericalism."

30. Luís Maldonado has commented in detail on this phenomenon. See his *Religiosidad popular* and *Génesis del catolicismo popular*.

church.[31] In fact, one might argue that it has actually encouraged these and similar practices as alternative expressions of faith as well as civic pride. The use of religious symbols to question or attack perceived abuses is obvious in the Fray Leopoldo stories' focus on a lay brother whose lack of canonical standing in no way negates his close association with the ecclesiastical establishment.

In short, then, the profound social, economic, and political transformations that have rapidly made Spain the world's tenth-largest industrial power have unquestionably affected religious institutions and ideas. And yet many of the tensions apparent in the narratives we are about to examine have a complicated history whose roots reach back far beyond Franco and the twentieth century. Both the immensity of recent changes and the persistence of long-standing conflicts and contradictions will be obvious within the Fray Leopoldo stories.

Fray Leopoldo and the Fray Leopoldo Devotion

Born in 1864, Francisco Tomás de San Juan Bautista Márquez Sánchez, the future Fray Leopoldo, grew up in the mountain hamlet of Alpandeire, southwest of Granada in the Province of Málaga.[32] The settlement was originally founded by the Arabs some ten centuries ago. Today a modern highway connects the cluster of small white houses ringed by fields to the nearby city of Ronda. But when thick mists steam up from the valleys, bringing traffic to a standstill, one can imagine how remote the world beyond its borders must once have seemed.[33]

Aside from a year of military service, the friar-to-be barely left his birthplace. He was already thirty when he attended ceremonies in Ronda marking the beatification of the Capuchin missionary Diego José de Cádiz.[34] The event affected him so deeply that he called off his impending marriage and took steps to join the order. His age and lack of formal

31. For a discussion of these and similar practices in Spain and elsewhere see Christian, "Folk Religion."
32. For a chronological summary of the main events in the friar's life see Fray Angel de León, *Mendigo por Dios*, pp. 329–30.
33. I am indebted to Fray Leopoldo's niece, Jerónima Márquez Lobato, for her hospitality during my visit to Alpandeire from 27 April to 1 May 1984.
The town of Alpandeire is well aware of the outside world's interest in Fray Leopoldo, although certainly not all of its residents appear enthusiastic about the friar. Jerónima, for her part, has had to periodically replace the door of the house in which her uncle was born and which she and her husband now inhabit because of visitors' insistence on shaving off splinters of wood to take home as mementos.
34. The name of Diego José de Cádiz is regularly linked to that of Fray Leopoldo in Capuchin publications, and the order is clearly hopeful that one cause will help the other. For a laudatory biography of the former see Juan Bautista García Sánchez, *Trotacaminos de Dios*.

education led to his initial rejection as a candidate, but he persisted and finally entered the Capuchin monastery in Seville in 1899. He took vows there as a lay brother a year later and was subsequently transferred to Granada in 1903. Aside from a few months in Antequera in 1905 and a year in Seville in 1913, he spent the next half-century of his life in his adopted city.

Fray Leopoldo initially served the monastery as its gardener. Somewhat later, he assumed the post of official alms collector (*limosnero*). Although charged with collecting food and money to support the monastery, he appears to have made liberal use of a special dispensation to aid needy members of the lay population as well. Reports by contemporaries suggest a generosity coupled with a readiness to console and counsel, which ensured his welcome among many in both city and outlying countryside.

With his long white beard, ankle-length brown robe, weatherbeaten sandals, and rough shoulder bag, or *morral*, Fray Leopoldo looked very much the part of a traditional Capuchin friar. His religious beliefs would seem to have been notably conservative as well. He was firmly convinced, for instance, of the physical existence of the devil, on whom he would blame the accident that left him bedridden for the last three years of his life. His devotion to the Virgin was particularly manifest in his practice of reciting three Hail Marys wherever the news of an accident or illness chanced to reach him. (" 'For the love of God, Fray Leopoldo,' I said to him," recalls a retired bookkeeper, " 'if you keep kneeling in the middle of the street much longer we are both sure to be run over by a car.' ")[35]

The earnestness of the friar's faith undoubtedly owes much to his upbringing in a relatively isolated rural community with no formal schooling. One should remember, however, that a great many Spaniards were still functionally illiterate at the close of the civil war. In addition, despite the existence of progressive industrial centers such as Madrid, Bilbao, and Barcelona, the nation was still, as already suggested, heavily agricultural. Although possessing greater cultural and economic resources than the small communities around it, Granada, like other Spanish cities of this period, retained strong ties to an older agrarian society.[36] The economic base of the urban elite still lay in the country-

35. Man, age seventy-four, born Granada, high school. Married, retired bookkeeper, usually attends mass.
36. In 1956, the year of Fray Leopoldo's death, 43.7 percent of Spaniards were employed in agriculture, 27 percent in industry, and 29.3 percent in the service sector. The corresponding figures for Granada were 69.7 percent, 10 percent, and 20.3 percent, reflect-

side (the well-to-do tended to divide their time between country estates and imposing townhouses), and almost all working-class rural families had ties to the city through female relatives who worked as domestics. These links were obvious in rural-urban patronage networks linking subordinates to elites.[37] Thus, even though the friar is likely to strike present-day observers as an anachronistic folk figure, his actions and beliefs were not necessarily dramatically different from those of many of his wealthier and better-educated contemporaries.

Then, too, the society in which Fray Leopoldo lived for the last two decades of his life was hardly open to new ideas. The regional newspaper on whose front page the notice of his death appears, for instance, also contains a statement of official norms for juvenile literature.[38] ("CHILDREN'S PUBLICATIONS," the headline asserts flatly, "WILL HENCEFORTH EXALT SPIRITUAL VALUES AND WILL BE BOTH BEAUTIFUL AND DIDACTIC.") Other features in this issue include an article from a series by Mussolini's son entitled "ROMMEL, A GENERAL OF WHOM NAPOLEON WOULD HAVE APPROVED," a report of the elaborate nationwide ceremonies commemorating the death of Ignatius of Loyola, and an editorial extolling the twenty years of peace following Franco's victory. The edition also gives prominence to a photograph of a decidedly boyish-looking Richard M. Nixon and a report on the inauguration of Juscelino Kubitschek, the Brazilian president who would construct Brasília.

Fray Leopoldo, to be sure, would be far less at home in today's Granada. It is extremely difficult to imagine a Capuchin in floor-length robes and homespun satchel canvassing the thirteen floors of a sleek new office complex for contributions. Indeed, the monastery has long since abolished the post of alms collector, and the handful of friars who continue to walk the streets in flowing beards and sandals in the dead of winter attract curious, even startled, looks. But the city Fray Leopoldo knew did not boast high-rise buildings. Relatively small and poor, the friar's Granada was a collection of neighborhood shops and makeshift apartment houses called *casas de vecino*, whose inhabitants were less apt to offer money than a few potatoes, a bit of cooking oil, or perhaps a choice green pear. The wealthier citizens might present the alms collector with

---

ing the province's still predominantly agricultural identity. For a discussion of changes in the second half of the twentieth century see Tezanos, "Transformaciones en la estructura social española."

37. See Maddox, "Religion, Honor, and Patronage," for a discussion of these rural-urban networks.

38. "Se murió Fray Leopoldo, Hermano Capuchino." *El Ideal,* 10 February 1956, p. 1.

more impressive portions of the produce regularly brought by mule-drawn wagon from the countryside.

As already suggested, Spain has undergone profound transformations in the past few decades. And although Granada stands apart from other Spanish cities in some respects, it has most certainly responded to these larger changes.[39] The ubiquitous posters advertising "Sexual Freedom Week," mystical awareness conferences, demonstrations for and against the North Atlantic Treaty Alliance (NATO), and an array of concerts, lectures, and political activities are only the most obvious, outward signs of a self-conscious opening toward a larger world. Rows of look-alike apartment complexes and wide streets perenially jammed with cars and buses have definitively replaced the acres of orchards. But vestiges of the past are unmistakable in the form of the Moorish palaces of the Alhambra and the Cuesta de la Lona (Canvas Hill), where the sails for the "Invincible Armada" were spun. Ultramodern laundromats, camera stores, and tourist hotels peer up at the sixteenth-century Jerónimos monastery with its halo of brown birds.[40]

The past is visible not only in monuments but also in various surviving customs. One of the areas in which it is most striking is that of the parainstitutional religious practices I describe earlier. Although at the time of my fieldwork, Granada was home to a community of Muslim converts, several Hindu ashrams, and a Hatha Yoga center, the great majority of residents remain nominally Catholic.[41] Community festivals such as striking street processions are still common here, as they are in other parts of Andalusia.[42] So are pilgrimages in honor of regional holy figures. Although only a percentage of the population actively engages in these activities, they have not only persisted but in some cases also acquired new life.

Granada, for instance, is known throughout Spain for its sumptuous Holy Week in which neighborhood parish associations vie to present

39. Among the factors that set apart Granada are its strong Moorish heritage (the city was the last to fall to Ferdinand and Isabella in 1492), its relative lack of industry, and the long-standing social and political conservatism of its upper classes. For an introduction to the city see Gallego y Burín, *Granada*. Brenan's now-classic *South from Granada* conveys a good sense of the larger region.

40. The journalistic snippets in Cuenca Toribio's *La Andalucía de la transición* give the reader a sense of some of the changes that the region has undergone.

41. The members of these communities are often from outside Granada. The ashrams tend to come and go, but the Muslim community in the Caldería Baja appears firmly rooted and invites serious study.

42. For a descriptive overview see Rodríguez Becerra, "Cultura popular y fiestas." An extensive list of feast days in the city of Granada appears in the same author's *Guía de fiestas populares de Andalucía*, pp. 352–63.

floats with the most elaborately decorated images, or *pasos*.[43] Although some residents dismiss the pageant as a tourist attraction, civic pride and esthetic pleasure have clearly reinforced the more traditional religiosity of such occasions. The reaction of a young nurse to a candle-fringed statue of the Virgin gliding through the darkened streets illustrates Granadans' often ambivalent attitudes toward Holy Week and similar religious manifestations. "I don't believe," she murmurs to her neighbor, "but in a moment like this, well, I almost do."[44] "I dress up like a Penitent each year because I was born and raised here," a middle-aged participant in a Holy Week procession explains. "I believe. But even if I didn't, I would still join my friends and family."[45]

The most famous pilgrimage in Andalusia and perhaps all of Spain is the Rocío, which draws at least a million persons to a hamlet in the Province of Huelva every year.[46] There are, in addition, many smaller devotions honoring a number of saints as well as the Virgin Mary in her various guises. (The Vírgen de la Cabeza, Vírgen del Monte, and Vírgen de las Montañas are only a few.)[47] Located in the countryside, these shrines attract large crowds from neighboring cities on feast days. In most cases, long hours of merrymaking follow the solemn visit to the holy figure.

A variety of urban-based devotions complement these rural pilgrimages. Granada, for instance, celebrates the feast day of its principal patron saint, Our Lady of Sorrows, in mid-September. In addition, despite the efforts of a number of younger, post–Vatican II parish priests to downplay their importance, long-popular spiritual intermediaries such as Saint Rita and Saint Nicholas retain a strong local following. "Our priest has taken the saints from the altar and put them in an anteroom," says one older woman. "He says, 'Why go through the branches when you can go through the trunk?' [¿Por qué ir por las ramas cuando se puede ir por el tronco?] I know that he is right, but I feel sorry for the saints, poor things, all alone now in that little room."[48]

Some Granadans also pay homage to various likenesses of Christ, most notably the Christ of the Cemetery, located near the Alhambra,

43. For a brief description of Holy Week in Granada see Briones Gómez, "La semana santa andaluza." A far more detailed, Marxist analysis of Holy Week in Seville is Moreno Navarro, *La semana santa de Sevilla.*

44. Woman, age twenty-four, born Granada province, some university. Single, nurse, "rarely" attends mass.

45. Man, age forty-three, born Granada, high-school education. Married, businessman, seldom attends mass.

46. Of the various studies of the Rocío, the best is probably Infante-Galán, *Rocío.*

47. For a discussion of the pilgrimage to the Vírgen de la Cabeza and to the Cristo del Paño see Luque, "La crisis de las expresiones populares del culto religioso."

48. Woman, age sixty-six, born Granada, some grade school. Widowed, works in souvenir shop and does embroidery, customarily attends mass.

and the Christ of the Three Favors in the Campo del Príncipe Plaza. Residents may also regularly visit the Christ of the Puerta Real, whose image occupies a niche in the outer wall of the San Juan de Dios Hospital.

Although these sites attract a steady trickle of visitors, most are associated with particular days of the week or month. The Christ of the Cemetery, for instance, attracts a small crowd every Friday, as does the Christ of the Three Favors, the latter between noon and three o'clock, the hours of the Passion. Saint Nicholas receives his guests on Monday, Saint Rita on the seventeenth of every month.

Visitors to these and numerous other local shrines are often either looking for solutions to pressing problems or expressing gratitude for past aid. They are likely to bring candles, money, and bouquets of roses and carnations, which they affix to, or lay before, these images. *Exvotos*, or votive offerings, expressing gratitude for a saint's intervention in a particular problem, take the form of handwritten messages or newspaper classifieds or photographs. Wax, metal, and plastic representations of previously afflicted parts of the body are also piled around the figure of the saint.[49]

The Fray Leopoldo phenomenon resembles these and similar local devotions in at least two principal respects. Like visitors to other shrines within Granada, many of the people who appear at the crypt are seeking divine guidance, if not overtly miraculous intervention. In addition, those who visit the friar's crypt tend to so on a set day, the ninth of every month.

Fray Leopoldo nonetheless stands apart from these other holy figures. First and most obvious, he is a recent historical personage, a candidate for canonization rather than an official saint. It is true that a number of residents of Granada honor the memory of the priest Andrés Manjón (1846–1923), founder of the Ave María schools for the poor and, like the friar, a candidate for canonization.[50] And yet, although people frequently compare Fray Leopoldo with Padre Manjón, they are far less likely to attribute miracles to the latter.[51] Other residents regularly visit the home of Conchita Barrecheguren (1905–1927), the daughter of a prominent family known for her valiant struggle against a protracted

---

49. For a study on Andalusian ex-votos that contains various intriguing illustrations see Rodríguez Becerra and Soto, *Exvotos de Andalucía*. For a list of studies on the ex-voto in various other contexts see Wilson, ed., *Saints and their Cults*, pp. 350–52.

50. For an account of Padre Manjón's life see (n.a.) *Vida de don Andrés Manjón y Manjón*, and the shorter Pino Sabio, ed., *Don Andrés Manjón*.

51. Frequent comparisons of the friar to both Padre Manjón and to the sixteenth-century San Juan de Dios merit detailed study. All three men are closely associated with Granada and with aid to the poor, although only San Juan is an official saint.

illness and yet another potential saint.[52] These individuals are more apt to credit her than Padre Manjón with supernatural actions. Neither she nor the priest, however, was part of Granada's everyday reality represented by Fray Leopoldo, whom many present-day residents of the city actually knew. As part of their everyday existence, the friar was, and remains, a familiar, spiritually accessible figure for Granadans. Thus, while some visitors to his tomb are seeking the miraculous intervention of a reputed saint with whom they have no direct connection, others are interested in paying homage to an esteemed personal acquaintance.

Then, too, the crowds that pour into the basement of the Capuchin church on the ninth of every month present a striking contrast to the far smaller numbers of persons who cluster before other, far more narrowly local shrines. Unlike these other locations, which overwhelmingly attract unaccompanied older females, almost all of whom are from the city and its immediate environs, Fray Leopoldo's selpulcher draws a number of men. In addition to the many middle-aged individuals from the lower or lower-middle classes, persons of various social classes and all ages visit the crypt. Then, too, perhaps a third of these visitors are from outside Granada proper.[53]

Finally and most important for our purposes, the visit to Fray Leopoldo's sepulcher is only one, albeit particularly obvious and important, manifestation of a broader awareness of and often personal interest in the particulars of the friar's life. Virtually no one recounts the life of Saint Rita or Saint Nicholas, and few people whom I asked could do more than identify these figures in the vaguest terms.[54] In contrast, a good number of residents tell stories about Fray Leopoldo. As we will see in considerable detail later in this discussion, these accounts, unlike those about other holy figures, often contain numerous and specific references to the era in which he lived.

In keeping with the rest of the structure that has replaced the crumbling seventeenth-century monastery that was home to Fray Leopoldo, the

52. For a laudatory biography see Pérez Ruiz, *Conchita Barrecheguren*. The Redentorist order, which the young woman's father joined after her death, actively supports her canonization and publishes a bulletin about her several times a year.

53. There are no figures available on visitors to Fray Leopoldo's crypt. My estimate is based on two one-hour spot checks, the first conducted on the afternoon of 9 March and the second on the morning of 9 June 1984. In the one case, almost two-fifths of the visitors were from outside the city of Granada; in the other, just under a quarter. By far the largest number of nonresidents in both instances were from Málaga.

54. These details are not only customarily sketchy but also often wrong. People, for instance, quite often identified Saint Rita of Cascia, a medieval Italian saint, as a seventeenth- or nineteenth-century Spaniard.

crypt located in a basement chapel of the building is streamlined, even stark. Normally, an ironwork screen with a circular opening through which visitors may slip a hand seals off the marble sepulcher containing the friar's body. On the ninth of the month, however, the screen is opened to permit full access to the chapel.

The visit to the friar is often a family affair. The chapel aisles are always full of toddlers noisily cracking sunflower seeds or talking to a stuffed toy while their parents pray. A dog sniffs at the carnation stalks littering the floor, an old man leans on his umbrella before the sepulcher, a teen-ager unwraps the foil from a garden rose and tucks it into a bright blue vase. A small boy with an iron leg, valiant in the T-shirt stamped "Athlete in Training," pats Fray Leopoldo's tomb. An older woman in rubber boots, a sack of carrots under one arm, smiles resolutely at the boy as his young mother bows her head.

A sizable number of the visitors from outside the city are from Málaga, a major industrial center with numerous tourist beaches some two and a half hours from Granada by car. Busloads of school children from parochial institutions as well as organized groups of adults visit the crypt along with other monuments such as the Alhambra and the cathedral. "It's good for them to get to know Fray Leopoldo," explains one of their teachers. "Of course, many of them have already been here with their parents."[55]

Smaller numbers of nonresidents come from small towns just outside Granada. The rest of the devotees would appear to be more or less equally divided between other parts of eastern Andalusia and more distant locations such as Valencia, Barcelona, and Madrid. Every once in a while, visitors appear from the Canary Islands or Ceuta and Melilla in what remains of Spanish Morocco. Or they have traveled from France, Australia, or Venezuela and Argentina. The majority of these individuals are Spanish citizens or their descendants and virtually all are Spanish-speaking. They have usually learned of Fray Leopoldo through friends, relatives, and various acquaintances, Capuchin missionaries, or one of the publications described in chapter 2.

From the moment shortly after dawn when the church opens on the ninth until it closes around sunset, visitors throng the sidewalk, waiting their turn to get inside. In winter they fend off a cold, fine rain with bright umbrellas before entering an interior that has been transformed into a kind of hushed greenhouse by body heat and countless flowers. When the sun beats down in July and August they may raise the same

---

55. Man, age thirty-eight, born Málaga, high-school education. Married, parochial high-school teacher, "usually" attends mass.

umbrellas to create a bit of shade. Once inside the crypt, many of the women beat the air with lace-edged paper fans at the same time as they pray.

Even in bad weather the line frequently wraps around the building, ending halfway down the adjacent block. The city routinely stations extra guards to handle the traffic snarls created by the influx of visitors. "What's that?" demands an anxious German tourist of the driver as his bus grinds to a halt before the Plaza de Triunfo. "Has there been an accident?" The driver clicks his tongue. "Oh no," he assures him. "Don't worry, sir. It's just one of our saints."

As one might expect, the crowd attracts a host of peddlers who hawk figurines of Fray Leopoldo, rosaries, calendars, and small plastic brooches with his likeness. Others offer food, cheap checkered tablecloths ("perfect for the beach, for a picnic, for the top of your refrigerator, ma'am!"), lottery tickets ("with Fray Leopoldo's blessing, how can you fail to strike it rich today?"), trinkets and toys for the children, and carnations packaged in white paper like long loaves of bread. Cripples, blind men, and beggars cradling listless infants stretch out their hands in the hope of a coin.

Once inside the crypt, many people deposit their bundles of carnations on top of Fray Leopoldo's tomb. Periodically, the heap of flowers grows so high as to threaten the lamp suspended from the ceiling. At this point someone will take it upon him or herself to remove several armfuls, thus allowing the pile to grow again.

Even those who do not bring bouquets customarily break off a flower to take with them as a token of the visit to the crypt. People often stroke a single carnation over the tomb's marble surface, then touch it to their cheeks and chin as if it were a powder puff. A few individuals wipe the length of the tomb with a handkerchief, cover it with kisses, or walk its length upon their knees. Such behavior usually prompts audible expressions of disapproval on the part of other visitors. "What fanaticism!" they may mutter. "What exaggeration!" The votive candles lit by the devotees on their way out of the chapel create a firmament of tiny flames before the image of Christ. As soon as one is extinguished, another is cemented into the still-warm stub of wax.

MOTIVES FOR THE BROADER INTEREST IN FRAY LEOPOLDO

Just as a minority of visitors to the crypt go on to attend mass in the church located above the chapel, so only a portion of the persons who tell stories about the friar have ever set foot in the crypt. Reminders of Fray Leopoldo can nonetheless be found throughout the city. They take the form of a small clay figure of the friar atop a cash register in a corner grocery store festooned with loops of sausage, a green metal key chain stamped with his image dangling from a teen-aged boy's shirt pocket, a commemorative plate on the wall of a jaunty new café. Fray Leopoldo's photograph serves a university student as a bookmark. It is taped to the corner of a beauty parlor mirror and slipped into the plastic pocket of a child's schoolbag. Both the small boy swinging at an orange with a makeshift cardboard bat and the young woman talking excitedly with a friend in Granada's only feminist tea shop wear tiny medals of the friar about their neck. Passersby take care not to step on a diaphanous chalk sketch of the friar on a downtown sidewalk, the work of a street artist hoping for a coin. Granada is full of likenesses of him in plaster, rough wood, and expensive china—tall and thin, short and chubby, cherubic and severe. Though a visitor may never notice these unobtrusive images, once one starts to look, they are everywhere.

The friar's relative ubiquity does not mean that all or most people believe in his thaumaturgic powers. "He was a good man, that's all" or "This business of Fray Leopoldo is just a story," they may say. The most highly educated persons with whom I spoke tended to alternate between enthusiasm for the friar and the spontaneous expressions of faith he has generated, and embarrassment or outright irritation at what they see as the intensely popular quality of the devotion. "If you're interested in saints, why don't you study Saint Teresa or Saint John of the Cross?" more than one demanded. Or "Why waste your time with fantasies and superstitions?"

The pervasive, if largely muted, presence of the friar in the life of the city has a number of possible explanations. I will argue in succeeding chapters that Fray Leopoldo is important because he affords people the opportunity to express competing opinions (as well as, often, their own ambivalence) about saints, the supernatural, and the church. I will also insist that his close association with a very specific historical moment is crucial to many people. By dying precisely on the eve of dramatic transformations in Spanish society, he has become a particularly effective symbol of another way of life.

Although we will leave these key points for later in our discussion, other possible reasons for Fray Leopoldo's popularity are worth mentioning at this time. Among the most noteworthy are first, the extensive personal dealings he had with many residents during his lifetime, and, second, the Capuchins' present, massive publicity campaign on his behalf. Also significant are Fray Leopoldo's close ties to the countryside, his association with Granada and Andalusia, his grandfatherly appeal, and, possibly, his Saint Joseph–like complementarity to the Virgin Mary, his membership in a religious order coupled with his lack of canonical standing, and his emotionally charged identity as the monastery's official alms collector. In addition, the relative lack of biographical details about the friar fosters projection and interpretation, reinforcing his attraction as a sort of Everyman.

The genuine warmth with which many Granadans middle aged or older remember the historical Fray Leopoldo is undoubtedly one important explanation for his persistent, if unostentatious, presence in the city. His perceived integrity and concern for others have engendered strong feelings of personal loyalty. "What I like about Fray Leopoldo is that he never stopped wearing his robes, even during the height of the Republic," a clerk in a suitcase shop explains. "My family was on the other side—my father was a hundred percent Republican—but I like people who are loyal to what they believe."[56] Even those who never knew him may speak of him with borrowed affection. "He always had a word for everyone," explains a waiter born a year after the friar's death.[57]

Although pictures of holy figures are commonplace in Granada, it is Fray Leopoldo's likeness that regularly crops up among photographs of family members in a billfold or a purse. "Fray Leopoldo," says a plumber in his late forties, "knew everything and everyone. He helped others. Why, he even helped me in a time of need."[58] This personal connection to the friar is undoubtedly what prompts many individuals to look for aid and comfort in him instead of in some other, remoter holy figure. "I go to Granada at least once a month to visit Fray Leopoldo and a married daughter who now lives there," one woman from a small town in the Alpujarra region explains.[59]

Were many people not already favorably disposed toward Fray Leopoldo, the Capuchins' efforts on his behalf would almost certainly have had a limited effect. And yet, while the order did not create and could not have created the enthusiasm for the friar from thin air, it has

56. Man, age sixty-nine, born Granada, "no formal schooling, but I learned to read at home." Widower, clerk in suitcase shop, does not normally attend mass.
57. Man, age twenty-seven, born Almería, some high school. Single, waiter, "almost never" attends mass.
58. Man, age forty-nine, born Granada, some grade school. Separated, plumber, occasionally attends mass.
59. Woman, age fifty-four, born Granada province, no formal schooling. Married, works at home, attends mass regularly.

definitely tapped, amplified, and in many cases given new direction to an existing sentiment. Capuchin missionaries have brought the friar's name to the attention of a community extending far beyond Granada. His biography and a bi-monthly devotional bulletin that reports stories of his continuing intercession on behalf of the needy have further enhanced his reputation. Statuettes, calendars, and numerous other objects bearing his image keep him in the public eye. So do radio broadcasts and articles in religious newsletters, the activities of the Fray Leopoldo Home for the Elderly, and ongoing commemorative efforts in the friar's hometown of Alpandeire.[60]

By providing individuals with a coherent framework into which they may fit their own scattered impressions, the Capuchins have effectively fostered a particular vision of the friar. Their efforts on his behalf have almost certainly encouraged some devotees to claim a supernatural dimension in their own encounters with Fray Leopoldo that they might otherwise have failed to discern, let alone assert. "I don't know," says a forty-seven-year-old housewife in describing what she sees as the friar's miraculous intervention in curing a severe childhood illness. "If it had happened just to me, I would ignore it. But there are so many people who have had experiences just like mine. One voice echoes another [una voz secunda otra] until you say, 'Wait now, there *must* be something more in this than meets the eye.' "[61]

Fray Leopoldo's prestige as a candidate for canonization leads some individuals to confer new value on their own past. People often point out a chair in which he used to sit or an object he once admired with obvious pride. "To tell you the truth," a cleaning woman in a luxury hotel asserts, "there is something very exciting about having known a saint. When I hear all these reports about his miracles, I think, 'You, Erlinda Gómez, you spend your life scrubbing other people's floors, yes, but it's you, not they, who spoke with Fray Leopoldo face to face!' "[62] Even people who express serious doubts about the friar's thaumaturgic powers often appear pleased by the prospect of his canonization. "I'll have to admit," a waiter in a small café says, "I never thought that much about

60. Among these activities is the construction of a road from the center of the hamlet to the field Fray Leopoldo worked. It is worth mentioning that the mayor of the town has identified another plot of land as that belonging to the friar so that the Capuchins will be financing a route more useful to the community than that which would lead to the real plot. ("Isn't it for saints to help the living? That's the way I look at it.")

61. Woman, age forty-seven, born Granada province, some high school. Married, works at home, attends mass regularly.

62. Woman, age sixty, born Granada, no formal education. Widowed, cleaning woman, attends mass "when I can."

him when he was alive. Still and all, I'm hoping he'll turn out to be a saint."[63]

As we shall later see in detail, the Capuchins' campaign has also had an effect on those with little interest in, or who may emphatically oppose the whole idea of, miracles or sanctity. In fact, the canonization effort has made Fray Leopoldo a particularly obvious negative example for a sizable number of individuals critical of the ecclesiastical establishment. These persons may categorically dismiss the devotion as a commercial endeavor or an attempt to capitalize on people's gullibility. And, yet, although their vision of the friar differs markedly from that actively disseminated by the order, one could argue that Fray Leopoldo's symbolic potential is as great for them as it is for persons who champion his cause.

At the same time that the friar may imbue a stream of personal memories with new value, he also possesses a strong telluric force. His rural roots imply a direct relationship to the land, which appeals to city dwellers who tend to idealize the countryside. Fray Leopoldo's initial duties as the monastery gardener reinforce this friar's connection to the earth. (The garden, which appears in various stories of the friar, was known as the Huerta de la Alegría, "garden of happiness.") In a city where the smallest sliver of balcony is home to a dozen flowerpots and where people may carry plants with them to the park so that both can enjoy the sunlight, this aspect of the friar's appeal cannot be underestimated.[64]

While Fray Leopoldo recalls the countryside, he also belongs to the city he adopted and has become a source of the civic pride local saints have long inspired. So close are the links between the friar and the city where he spent most of his adult life that some persons insist he was a native of Granada, not of Alpandeire. Their close association of Fray Leopoldo with the city suggests his identity as a de facto unofficial patron saint. "He was born in the Hospital Real," a middle-aged ice-cream vendor says. "At the time of his birth it was a maternity ward, but because of Fray Leopoldo they have since declared the building a national monument."[65]

---

63. Man, age forty-nine, born Madrid ("but my parents brought me here when I was just a baby"), some grade school. Married, waiter, seldom attends mass.

64. Particularly attractive plants excite the same sort of admiring interest among strangers that a child might. "May God give you the strength to care for that lovely cyclamen, my daughter!" an old lady once exclaimed to me.

65. Man, age forty-four, born Granada, some grade school. Married, ice-cream vendor, does not attend mass.

Others insist that the friar expressly singled out Granada as his place of residence. "They sent him to Seville," a young hotel clerk says. "But he went straight to the head of the order and said, 'Excuse me, but it is in Granada that I was meant to spend my life.'"[66]

"He couldn't take the climate in any other part of Spain," asserts a nurse in the Fray Leopoldo Home. "Only the climate of Granada agreed with him."[67]

"It is hard to ask other people for help," says a middle-aged book salesman, "but we here in Granada are known for our generosity, and so he always felt at home."[68]

The ticket vendor in a raffle intended to aid crippled children offers buyers a choice of two symbols of Granada—either a paper flag (the Spanish emblem on one side, the city's pomegranate on the other [the Spanish term for this fruit is *granada*]) or a miniature of Fray Leopoldo in a gold-colored plastic frame. Pictures of the friar regularly appear on calendars and posters distributed by local businesses and religious associations. In addition, in a number of portraits of Fray Leopoldo, the friar appears against the backdrop of the Alhambra or the old-style Moorish houses of the Albaicín. Perhaps the single most eloquent expression of the ties between the friar and the city in which he spent five decades, however, are the pictures of him edged with *taracea*. This distinctive sort of wood inlay associated with Moorish craftsmen in southern Spain, and more specifically Granada, is common in the decoration of boxes of all shapes and sizes, small tables, and chess and checkerboards. Its popularity as a frame for likenesses of Fray Leopoldo—seldom done for those of other holy figures—attests to the close relationship between him and "his" Granada.

Likewise, the stream of non-Granadan visitors to the friar's crypt (the most obvious sign of growing interest in the friar on the part of other Spaniards) is a source of satisfaction to some residents of a city who have a deep sense of Granada's distinctive history. "Of course Fray Leopoldo was a saint," says a young flower vendor. "Don't you see all these people arriving from Barcelona, from La Coruña? Why, even in Madrid people put his picture in the window. Yes, even there, where everyone looks down his nose at us Andalusians!"[69]

66. Man, age twenty-three, born Granada, some high school. Single, hotel clerk, rarely attends mass.
67. Woman, age thirty-eight, born Granada, high school. Married, nurse, regularly attends mass.
68. Man, age fifty, born Granada, high-school education. Married, book salesman, "quite often" attends mass.
69. Man, age nineteen, born Guadix, grade-school education. Single, flower vendor, does not attend mass.

As this last comment suggests, the region's long unfavorable social and economic position within the nation leads a number of persons to see in the friar a confirmation of its, and by extension their, worth.[70] Possessing some of Spain's richest farmland, Andalusia has nonetheless remained one of its poorest and least-developed regions. Recent autonomy movements connected with regional identity debates point to Andalusians' frustration with the status quo.[71] Although there are signs of an economic upturn, ownership of property is still concentrated in the hands of a few. (A little more than 1 percent of the population controls approximately half of the arable surface.)[72] The lack of adequate health services and lingering gaps in the educational system have helped to perpetuate one of the lowest standards of living in Western Europe and to foster immigration to other parts of Spain.[73]

The possibilities for economic advancement are still limited within the city. Capital of the province of the same name, Granada is home to over a third of the province's total population of 800,000. Lacking heavy industry (Puleva, Dhul, and Alhambra are all food service industries), the city depends heavily on an extensive local and regional service sector to provide employment. Three out of five residents work for one or another arm of the bureaucracy or the large public university. The overall jobless rate for Spain in 1984 was 19 percent; Granada stood a full six percentage points above the national average. This figure does not take into account the university graduates selling begonias on street corners or the many women who might work outside the home if the opportunity existed.[74]

Economic factors are not the only explanation for Fray Leopoldo's power as a symbol. The long white beard and kindly smile that are the hallmarks of so many graphic and verbal portraits of the friar suggest a grandfatherly figure and affirm the family relationships so important to an understanding of the role of Spanish, and particularly Andalusian,

70. For an introduction to the ample bibliography on the region see Iglesias de Ussel, "Materiales para el estudio de Andalucía." An overview of key themes appears in Domínguez Ortiz, *Andalucía ayer y hoy*.
71. Although these movements have not been as intense as in Catalonia and the Basque Country, they are nonetheless significant. For one statement of the cause see Acosta Sánchez, *Andalucía*.
72. For a discussion of the historical underpinnings of the agrarian question in Andalusia see Díaz del Moral, *Historia de las agitaciones campesinas andaluzas*, and Bernal, *La propiedad de la tierra*.
Figures for 1986–87 indicate a 8.3 percent growth rate for Andalusia as a whole, with 9.1 percent increase in agricultural production.
73. See Gregory, "The Andalusian Dispersion."
74. Statistical information is taken from *Estudio sobre la renta*.

saints.[75] As archetypal grandfather, he not only inspires confidence and affection but also provides a masculine counterbalance to the Virgin Mary.[76]

In line with a broader, though in no way homogeneous, Mediterranean honor code, which social scientists have described in detail, the father is expected to behave sternly toward his children.[77] Unlike the mother, who may show a certain degree of indulgence, he must insist on his unmarried daughters' chastity and his sons' readiness to actively defend the family honor. In this capacity he inspires as much fear as affection.

The grandfather, however, is a sort of father emeritus. Although titular head of the family and thus demanding of deference, he is not compelled to exhibit the same severe authority. ("You can ask things of your grandfather that you would not dare ask of your father," the twenty-three-year-old receptionist at the Fray Leopoldo Home for the Elderly explains.)[78] Both grandfathers and grandmothers are not only permitted but also are often expected to actively indulge the young.[79] Because members of the older generation frequently die before the young reach adulthood, fond associations between them and a distant, happy past are common. ("You think of your grandparents and you remember all that was good about your childhood," the young receptionist says.) The grown child is likely to remember the easily idealized grandfather as a more demonstrative, more accessible father who could be asked for favors with impunity. He or she is also likely to conveniently forget that this benign figure had himself been a stern parent and the model for his or her own father.

The caption beneath one common portrait of the friar, usually stamped on linen, reads, "Thank you, Grandfather/ for your eyes/ your gaze/ for the smile on your lips/ and the peace in your soul" (Gracias Abuelito/ por tus ojos/ tu mirada/ por la sonrisa en tus labios/ y por la

75. On the humanization of the cult of the saints in Andalusia see Moreno Navarro, *Propiedad*, and Aguilar Criado, *Las hermandades*.
For the links between family and religious symbols see Prat i Carós, "Estructura y conflicto."
76. For one psychoanalytic discussion of the dynamics of Marian devotion see Carroll, "The Cult of the Virgin Mary."
77. A now-classic collection of essays on the honor code is Peristiany, ed., *Honour and Shame.* For an update that stresses complex differences among regions as well as countries see Gilmore, ed., *Honor and Shame and the Concept of Mediterranean Unity.* An interesting discussion of father-son relationships in Andalusia is Murphy, "Emotional Confrontations between Sevillano Fathers and Sons." See also Mitchell's discussion of stern fathers and gentle mothers in his *Violence and Piety in Spanish Folklore*, pp. 182–89.
78. Woman, age twenty-three, born Granada, high-school education. Single, receptionist, customarily attends mass.
79. See Puentes, "Abuelos y nietos en la Granada de 1984."

paz en tu alma). Another very popular likeness of Fray Leopoldo shows him gazing upward with a smile at a Virgin Mary in mantilla and large gold ear hoops as she cradles the infant Jesus.

We have already noted the historical Fray Leopoldo's propensity to recite three Hail Marys in moments of need. But while the friar is fulfilling the familiar obligations of Marian devotion, he provides an important, masculine counterbalance to the Virgin. This complementarity is nowhere more obvious than in the two-photograph picture frames sold on street corners throughout the city. Portraits of Fray Leopoldo are almost always accompanied by a likeness of Mary in one of her various guises: Our Lady of Sorrows, for instance, or the Virgin of Araceli. Although various representations of the infant Jesus or the crucified Christ and a couple of male saints are also available, purchasers prefer a male-female combination. "Why did I ask for Fray Leopoldo and Our Lady?" a middle-aged woman asks. "I don't know. They just make a good pair."[80] A schoolgirl, who has also just purchased photographs of the Virgin and the friar, refers to him as "one of these very lovable grandfathers" (uno de estos abuelitos muy amorosos). "For this reason I like him better than Saint Anthony," she asserts.[81] In his humble origins, his asexuality, and relative age, Fray Leopoldo suggests an indigenous Saint Joseph.

While we are on the subject of family relationships, it is worth pointing out that Fray Leopoldo is not only an *abuelito* (grandfather) but also a *hermanico* (little brother). (The term *brother* is the same term for *friar*.) As a *hermanico*, he invites feelings of intimacy and affectionate protectiveness seldom associated with a *padre* (father or priest).[82] Although a member of a religious order, and thus of the ecclesiastical hierarchy, Fray Leopoldo's lack of canonical status makes him far more approachable than his peers who have been ordained and can thus preach and hear confession. It allows him to be used as a vehicle for criticism of institutions that the speaker would prefer not to dismiss out of hand.

Fray Leopoldo's identity as *limosnero* touches yet another deeply responsive chord. Through the figure of the friar people can express mixed feelings about giving and receiving. This ambivalence is in part a product of the tension between two apparently contradictory value systems.

---

80. Woman, age fifty-five, born Granada, some high school. Married, works at home, regularly attends mass. "The Virgin is a very motherly mother [*una madre muy madrera*] and Fray Leopoldo looks very good beside her," she goes on to explain.

81. Girl, age thirteen, born Granada, high-school student. Single, attends mass every Sunday.

82. These feelings are particularly obvious in comments on Fray Leopoldo's diminutive stature and physical frailty. ("Poor little one! So thin, so small, so poorly dressed!")

The honor code mentioned above sees debt as a form of domination and thus inadmissible subordination. The Spanish folk tradition is full of mocking proverbs about persons who voluntarily assume an inferior position in the social order by asking others for assistance. Familiar sayings such as *Quien pide a dar se obliga* (he who asks something of another commits himself to give) underscore the pressing sense of obligation engendered by even the most freely given gift.[83]

This honor code clearly conflicts with the New Testament ideal of humility. Thus, although Fray Leopoldo's activities as alms collector are ostensibly a source of admiration ("he did what many fathers would not do for their own families," says a garbage collector in his thirties), the friar is not necessarily a model for daily life.[84] On the contrary, respectful comments frequently preface an admission that the individual could or would never emulate the friar. "I believe he was a saint," a traffic policeman says, "because *only* a saint would do the sort of things he did."[85]

"I think the world of Fray Leopoldo," a janitor in a public high school comments. "But it is a man's pride that makes him truly human. It is wrong of me, perhaps, but I could never—I would *never*—go as he did from door to door."[86]

Descriptions of the friar's activities as alms collector often prompt more general comments about giving and receiving. A number of the people who see Fray Leopoldo as a spiritual intermediary feel he is repaying those who gave him alms in life. "He knew how hard it is to ask," says a farmer-turned-bus-driver, "and so he is quick to give. There are saints you ask and ask without ever getting anything. But Fray Leopoldo does not allow a person to leave his church with empty hands."[87]

---

83. Among numerous other common sayings that underscore ambivalent attitudes toward giving and receiving are *Contra el vicio de pedir, hay la virtud de no dar* (In response to the vice of asking, there is the virtue of not giving); *De quien pide, desconfia; a quien das, no te daría* (Be wary of he who asks you for something; he to whom you give wouldn't give to you); and *Quien algo te da, algo te pedirá* (He who gives you something will ask something in return).

84. Man, age thirty-eight, born Granada, "very little" grade school. Married, garbage collector, rarely attends mass.

85. Man, age forty-one, born Antequera, some high school. Married, traffic policeman, usually attends mass.

The saints, to be sure, have always been revered for their readiness to perform actions that others profess to admire but show no rush to emulate. See Brown's discussion of the holy man in his *Society and the Holy in Late Antiquity*, pp. 103–52.

86. Man, age sixty, born Granada province, no formal education ("though the priest taught us how to read a little"). Married, janitor, does not usually attend mass.

87. Man, age fifty-two, born Granada, grade-school education. Married, bus driver, attends mass from time to time.

Some individuals clearly consider the friar obligated to return favors. "My wife always regrets not having given something to Fray Leopoldo when he used to call here," says the owner of a small shoe shop in the center of the city. "She says that if she had helped him we would be rich today. Because there were those who did give and now he has to help them. Today she brings many offerings to his crypt, but she says it is not the same as giving to a saint in life."[88]

An office worker in his early thirties observes that "the saints do not have to help you. But they are a lot more likely to do so if you've expressed your belief in the past."[89] Such sentiments suggest the importance of the *limosnero* aspect of Fray Leopoldo's identity. The issues of the gift, reciprocity, what the rich owe the poor, and what the poor owe those still poorer are all central to the constructions of the differences between past and present that, I shall argue, are a key dynamic in stories of the friar.

Fray Leopoldo also exerts a different sort of attraction as a kind of Everyman who is not just approachable, but distinctly ordinary. "What stood out in him was his insignificance" (Lo que se destacaba en él era su insignificancia), says a well-known artist.[90] "He was a *periquillo el de los palotes* [a parakeet like that on every perch]," that is, a completely run-of-the-mill individual, a middle-aged seamstress remarks.[91]

"You may think this strange," a surgeon in the San Juan de Dios Hospital remarks, "but I think people have made a saint of Fray Leopoldo because he was so undistinguished. Even the simplest person can see himself in him."[92]

"He was of little account, very little account," an older woman murmurs. "He understood the poor because he had been poor himself" (era poca cosa, cosa ínfima. Entendía a los pobres por haber salido de la pobreza).[93]

Some residents of Granada find the friar's matter-of-factness uninspiring. "There are saints whose deeds would require several volumes," a supermarket cashier in her forties asserts, "but Fray Leopoldo's ninety

88. Man, age fifty-nine, born Granada, grade-school education. Married, shoe shop owner, does not usually attend mass.
89. Man, age thirty-one, born Granada, high-school education. Married, office worker, sometimes accompanies wife to mass.
90. Man, age sixty-two, born Granada, university education. Married, graphic artist, usually attends mass.
91. Woman, age forty-five, born Granada, "a little" grade school. Single, seamstress, usually attends mass.
92. Man, age thirty-four, born Granada, medical school. Married, surgeon, does not normally attend mass.
93. Woman, age seventy-four, born Granada, no formal schooling. Widowed, supported by sons and daughters, usually attends mass.

years would barely fit a pamphlet. Why, I myself have led a more adventurous life!"[94] The unprepossessing character that makes him seem dull to some renders him acceptable and appealing to many others. (Those members of Opus Dei who told me stories of him were often attracted precisely by his undramatic, workaday qualities.) Had the friar been a more colorful and therefore almost certainly more controversial figure, he would have bitter enemies as well as fervent supporters. "I don't believe in saints, and we Spaniards have had far too many priests sticking their noses where they don't belong. And yet I will admit it's hard to criticize Fray Leopoldo. I for one have nothing bad to say about him," an older salesman declares.[95]

Fray Leopoldo's outwardly unremarkable existence allows individuals to read into his life often radically different meanings. The apparent lack of personal crises in his life, the absence of stigmata or fiery sermons, encourages those who talk about him to embroider on the facts.[96] Not surprisingly, the friar who emerges in these stories corresponds in large part to needs that will become increasingly apparent in following chapters. Before turning to the narratives themselves, however, it is important to say something about both the Granada church's perspective on Fray Leopoldo and the formal Life.

94. Woman, age forty-six, born Granada, some grade school. Single, supermarket clerk, attends mass several times a week.

95. Man, age sixty, born Jaén, high-school education. Married, plumbing supply salesman, attends "funerals, baptisms, weddings, you know, this sort of thing."

96. Fray Leopoldo's unsensational character sets him apart from a number of decidedly more dramatic twentieth-century holy figures such as the Italian Padre Pio. For an interesting contrast see McKevitt's study of the latter, "Suffering and Sanctity."

CHAPTER TWO

Fray Leopoldo and the Church

The existence of a formal *vita*, or Life, of Fray Leopoldo, which was authored by a Capuchin and actively disseminated by the order, has had a profound, if often indirect, impact on the orally transmitted stories on which its author claims to have based his text.[1] The Life, however, can in no way be assumed to represent the views of the ecclesiastical establishment as a whole. The Granada religious establishment has an array of opinions about the friar, views that I shall address in the initial part of this chapter. I then turn to the narrative strategies used by the friar's biographer to bolster his conception of Fray Leopoldo as the embodiment of timeless values. As a literary construction, the Life both relies on and departs from older hagiographical models—above all, the *Fioretti* (or *Little Flowers*) of Saint Francis—but it is also the reflection of a particular individual and a specific time and place.

The Politics of Canonization: Fray Leopoldo and the Granada Church

For nearly two thousand years the Roman Catholic Church has singled out a very few of the faithful as saints.[2] It is thought that their virtuous lives imbue them with posthumous thaumaturgic or intercessory powers. In recent years Catholic theologians have argued about whether the

1. The author emphasizes his debt to the oral tradition on numerous occasions. See, for example, pp. 202–3 in Fray Angel de Léon, *Mendigo por Dios*.
2. I am grateful to both David Alvarez and Brother Ronald Isetti for a careful reading of this section, and for various bibliographical references and thoughtful observations. For a comparative discussion of the conception of sanctity see Kieckhefer and Bond, eds., *Sainthood*. The evolution of the cult of the saints in early European Catholicism is discussed by Brown in *Cult of the Saints*.

actions of holy figures, in order to qualify as miracles, must clearly transcend natural laws.[3] Despite this speculation, the church's official position is that saints have the power to aid those who seek their intervention.

Until well into the Middle Ages canonization was a largely informal process involving many local as well as regional or national constituencies. As a result, the criteria for selection varied widely. Over time, however, Rome came to assume an ever more central role in articulating and enforcing guidelines governing official declarations of sanctity.[4] The Gregorian Reforms of the first half of the thirteenth century confirmed the pontiff's supreme authority in all matters regarding canonization. The *Immensa aeterni Dei* promulgated by Sixtus V in 1588 codified the steps to be taken in the official recognition of a saint. These rules became available in printed form a half-century later under Urban VIII.[5]

The increased time, effort, and expense involved in official canonization proceedings do much to explain why a disproportionate number of saints from the late Middle Ages onward were members and often founders of religious orders.[6] But partisan backing did not always guarantee a positive outcome and might actually work against the candidate by exciting the animosity of rival interest groups.[7] Moreover, if the individual in question did not already enjoy considerable support among the lay population, his or her sponsors often had difficulty producing the requisite proofs of posthumous thaumaturgic action.

A certain degree of generalized enthusiasm for a candidate is useful and even necessary in achieving a successful outcome, but it is definitely not sufficient grounds for canonization. (John XXIII is a case in point: his candidacy for sainthood is an extremely popular cause that has garnered scant support at the highest levels.) In the canonization process,

3. For an exposition of the official position see Douillet, *What Is a Saint?* The special issue of the *Revue d'Histoire de la spiritualité* 48 (1972) entitled *La Fonction du miracle dans la spiritualité chrétienne* conveys an idea of the ongoing debate about the relationship between sanctity and the supernatural.

4. For a discussion of the canonization process in the late medieval period see Vauchez, *La Sainteté en Occident aux derniers siècles du Moyen Age.* For changing conceptions of sanctity among different groups of people see a number of the chapters in Trinkhaus, ed., *Pursuit of Holiness,* and Obelkevich, ed., *Religion and the People.*

5. An account of the legal and institutional aspects of the history of formal canonization is available in Kemp, *Canonization and Authority in the Western Church.* The latest revision of the canonization process is represented by the apostolic constitution, *Divinus Perfectionis Magister,* which simplifies and somewhat decentralizes the early stages of the process.

6. The identity of successful candidates for canonization is discussed at length in Weinstein and Bell, *Saints and Society.* See also Delooz, *Sociologie et canonisation,* and "Towards a Sociological Study of Canonized Sainthood in the Catholic Church."

7. See Geary, "Humiliation of Saints."

what matters is not what people are saying, but what the directors of the process choose to emphasize in the customarily massive collection of reports, anecdotes, and legends. Because canonizations are powerful symbols of the direction in which a pope wishes the church as an institution to move, only a handful of candidacies are chosen from the thousands proposed.[8]

The Vatican may use a cause to make an explicit political point, as in the case of Joan of Arc, whose canonization signaled the reconciliation of church and state in France's Third Republic.[9] It may also seek to reinforce a particular theological position by elevating a model of celibacy, obedience, or orthodoxy or to encourage a local church (the Philippines, Korea, and Zaire are recent illustrations). Religious orders may energetically support a cause in the hope of improving morale and enhancing recruitment, as well as to defend or define an institutional tradition.[10]

The case of Fray Leopoldo offers an excellent present-day example of an individual championed by a particular order—in this instance, the Capuchins—who is at the same time acceptable to many in the religious establishment and lay population alike. Yet if the archbishop of Granada's public support for Fray Leopoldo's cause reflects first and foremost a desire to reach out to the laity, it also underscores political realities within the local ecclesiastical community. (As the friar completed the diocesan stage of the canonization process only in 1984, the Vatican's position on his candidacy is not yet clear.)

In the preceding chapter I refer to younger members of the clergy who became active during the 1960s in both Catholic workers' groups and grass-roots parish organizations. With time, the desire for more sweeping social changes led some of these individuals to branch out beyond strictly religious associations and to ally themselves with political movements with no religious affiliation. This direct involvement in secular affairs displeased a number of generally older and more traditional members of the clergy, who looked askance at their colleagues' some-

---

8. Some popes, to be sure, are quicker to canonize than others. Pope John Paul II, for instance, has declared canonized and beatified more individuals than all of the other popes of the twentieth century combined.

9. On the canonization of Joan of Arc as political reconciliation see Hebblethwaite, *In the Vatican*, p. 114.

10. These more practical considerations are in no way a new development. For a discussion of the canonization strategies of the mendicant orders and the Franciscans in particular during the Middle Ages see Goodich, *Vita Perfecta*, pp. 159–68.

One should note, however, that the recent addition of saints to the rosters has not necessarily improved morale. This is because most of the men and women proposed for canonization lived before Vatican II, in a period when the "blind obedience" and "exacting regularity" repudiated by the council were often taken as the twin pillars of the religious life.

times blatantly Marxist rhetoric. Their opponents pointed to the church's longtime support for Franco, but traditional clergy dismissed this as an invidious comparison and declared themselves opposed on doctrinal grounds to political participation by priests and members of religious orders. [11]

In Granada, growing friction between a significant minority of socially committed priests—many of whom had specifically requested working-class parishes—and their often vocal critics had become unmistakable by the time of Franco's death. In 1977 a group of the former decided to prepare an informal report on religious practice in the City and Province of Granada for the newly appointed archbishop, Monsignor José Méndez Asensio, who they hoped might prove more sympathetic to their viewpoint than his extremely conservative predecessor. The resulting mimeographed pamphlet outlined the region's pressing socioeconomic problems, urging the church leaders to play a more active role in their solution. [12]

The report also attacked a number of popular religious practices within Granada. Singling out the devotion to Fray Leopoldo as the most egregious among a number of "pernicious superstitions," its authors accused those members of the religious establishment sympathetic to the devotion of "fomenting miracle-ism" and "atrophying the faith." [13]

The new prelate greeted the widely disseminated report with neither approval nor disapproval. A good portion of the local clergy, however, reacted angrily to the writers' specific criticisms as well as to what some saw as the report's self-righteous tone. A number went so far as to denounce the authors as political agitators masquerading as priests. One of the most active "troublemakers," Padre José Antonio Moreno Rodríguez of the San Ildefonso parish, had spent some years in Cuba. His experience there, coupled with his open support of leftist candidates for public office in Granada, led his critics to accuse him of harboring Communist sympathies. They therefore began pressuring the archbishop to remove him from the public eye. When Méndez Asensio did not actively defend Moreno Rodríguez from his attackers, the priest's supporters accused the hierarchy of political expediency.

---

11. For an overview of these tensions see Payne, *Spanish Catholicism*, pp. 192–227.

12. See "Informe sobre la diócesis para el nuevo obispo." The authors are identified as "un grupo de sacerdotes de Granada" (a group of Granada's priests). Although specifically directed to Méndez Asensio, the report was clearly conceived as a broader public opinion tool.

13. "Informe," p. 12. On the same page, the devotion to Fray Leopoldo is described as an "interesada promoción" (self-interested promotion) and "foco de desviación de la fe" (focal point of deviation from the faith).

Tensions between these opposing factions continued to mount for almost seven years. Finally, in March 1984 the forced cancelation of a scheduled public meeting by the Christian base communities prompted a bitter demonstration against the church hierarchy.[14] Moreno Rodríguez's involvement in this defiant gesture led Méndez Asensio to remove him from his post. The parishioners of San Ildefonso responded to the archbishop's decision by marching from their church toward the center of the city. When the group confronted Méndez Asensio in the cathedral, he suggested that its members meet with him next day at the episcopal residence. Unhappy with this response, the demonstrators followed the archbishop down the street until he disappeared into an acquaintance's car. The regional church-affiliated newspaper, *El Ideal*, gave the event wide publicity, and expressions of protest continued for a number of days.[15] The archbishop, however, remained adamant in his decision, giving Moreno Rodríguez no choice but to accept his new position or resign from the clergy. The priest's enemies hailed his departure as a victory for moderation. His supporters decried it as decisive proof of the church leadership's resistance to much-needed change.

This synopsis, while greatly simplified, suggests the extent to which reactions of individual clergy to Fray Leopoldo must be understood as part of a far larger debate regarding the church's role within contemporary Spanish society. Conservatives reacted with such energy to the charges of abuses, including the devotion, because they saw these as a personal assault. Their analysis was correct to the extent that those who assailed the devotion did so with an energy they would almost certainly not have mustered were it focused on a politically active figure—such as El Salvador's openly reformist Archbishop Oscar Arnulfo Romero, assassinated in 1980—and not a self-effacing member of a historically conservative religious order.[16]

"Fray Leopoldo," Moreno Rodríguez observed in a tape-recorded conversation with me several days before the announcement of his transfer, "was probably a good person who knew how to listen—a talent

14. One might surmise that this cancelation was linked to the expected celebration in the cathedral the same day of a mass in honor of Saint Joseph, conducted by the archbishop with various other priests, as well as to various other solemnities surrounding the Day of the Seminarian (18 March) and the ordination of a new deacon.

15. See "Granada: feligreses de San Ildefonso increparon al arzobispo por el traslado de su párroco," pp. 1 and 14. Further details appear in "Asamblea de vecinos de S. Ildefonso contra el traslado de su párroco," pp. 1 and 20. In both cases, the newspaper, which is linked to the ecclesiastical establishment, ran separate, adulatory articles about the mass and the archbishop.

16. I witnessed various street murals favorably depicting Romero and supporting revolutionary movements in Central America during my fieldwork in 1984 and again in 1986.

not all that common in any age."[17] He emphasized that his disapproval of the devotion had little or nothing to do with the friar's personal qualities ("Fray Leopoldo could, perhaps, have tried to make people more aware of their situation, but at least he tried to help other human beings," he affirmed). Rather, explained Moreno Rodríguez, he and his group objected to their fellow clerics' willingness to accede to, when not to actively exploit, their parishioners' propensity to seek supernatural solutions to the problems of daily life. "The church's role," he asserted, "is to teach, not to purposely misguide the faithful for its own benefit. And for this reason I feel that the Capuchins and all those who support them are doing a great disservice to those whom it is their duty to help."

Moreno Rodríguez went on to denounce the veneration of the friar as an overtly commercial operation. "You have probably seen how hundreds upon hundreds of people flock to the crypt to leave money in the hope of a miracle," he said, asking:

> What better opportunity to explain to them that all power comes from God? But, no, instead of using this occasion to insist that a person is responsible for his own life, that we all must work as well as pray to achieve the things we want for ourselves and our families, the church encourages such escapist behavior in the expectation of financial gain. And this is what I call a scandal.

The priest concluded by expressing his opposition to the canonization proceedings. "I consider them a mockery," he declared point-blank.

Although there is no formal measure of the Granada religious establishment's views on Fray Leopoldo, one would expect to find a range of beliefs and practices today, even more than in the past. It is certainly possible that some clerics actively promote the devotion to the friar. My own exchanges with priests, nuns, and members of religious orders, however, did not reveal this sort of active involvement.[18] In fact, my overriding impression was one of coolness. Various older individuals remembered the historical Fray Leopoldo with respect, but they expressed little interest, let alone belief in, reports of miraculous powers. Other

17. Interview, José Moreno Rodríguez, Granada, 14 March 1984. All quotations are from this tape-recorded conversation. English translations are my own.
18. I interviewed approximately three-dozen priests, nuns, and members of religious orders. The group included both older, sometimes extremely conservative individuals and a number of their younger, generally more liberal counterparts. Although I made a conscious effort to speak with a range of persons, there may indeed be viewpoints which I did not encounter.

generally younger and more socially active clerics, including several Capuchins, were clearly uncomfortable about the "fanaticism" surrounding the friar. None of these individuals had ever visited the crypt, and given their emphasis on this-world ethics and communal solutions to practical problems, I found it hard to imagine them encouraging their parishioners to venerate Fray Leopoldo, or indeed any official saint.

A significant percentage of the individuals with whom I spoke, including a number of the Capuchins, did evince a certain pragmatism in regard to the friar, which Moreno Rodríguez and his colleagues would probably object to as outright support. For many, the devotion was a fact of life. "Frankly," one young priest says, "I do not share my parishioners' feelings for Fray Leopoldo. But what good would it do for me to say this to them? They would lose confidence in me, not him! Furthermore, in my opinion the devotion does less harm than the arrogance of those who in the name of progress rush to tell the people what they can and cannot believe."[19]

Asked if detractors might not find his stance an example of the sort of official condonement of the "devotionalism" and paraliturgical practices criticized by Vatican II, the speaker demurs. "The same council," he asserts, "made a point of recognizing the validity of the spirit, if not necessarily the form of popular religious manifestations." It is worth noting in this connection that several of the parish priests least enthusiastic about Fray Leopoldo nonetheless underscored the church's obligation to treat such expressions with respect ("it is not every friar that people insist on seeing as a saint," one of the otherwise most critical observed).[20]

The apparent tolerance (or resignation, depending on one's perspective) manifested by a sizable and diverse segment of the Granada clergy and religious orders toward the Fray Leopoldo devotion has undoubtedly influenced the archbishop. For Méndez Asensio, as for a number of his fellows, the friar is a personal memory.[21] The archbishop spent his years as a student in Granada and recalls seeing Fray Leopoldo on numerous occasions in the city streets. In addition, Méndez Asensio's mother, who lived in the countryside, was a firm believer in Fray Leopoldo and invariably stopped by the Capuchin church to ask his blessing whenever

19. Man, age twenty-seven, born Valencia, seminary education. Single, diocesan priest, attends mass regularly.
20. Man, age sixty-one, born Granada province, seminary. Single, diocesan priest, attends mass regularly.
21. I am grateful to the archbishop for granting me an interview on 29 June 1984 in his official residence in Granada. All quotations, unless otherwise noted, are from this tape-recorded conversation. Translations into English are my own.

she came to town. So although the archbishop's opinon of Fray Leopoldo is decidedly very different from that of his mother, the recollection of her faith would make it difficult for him to ignore or dismiss the loyalty that the friar inspires among a segment of the lay population.

Méndez Asensio appears well aware of the friar's symbolic potential. The homily he delivered at the mass commemorating the close of the diocesan, or *Cognicionale,* stage of the canonization proceedings in June 1984 begins with a reference to the continuing relevance of spiritual attributes he sees embodied in the friar.[22] Fray Leopoldo's life "of simplicity, of mercy, of kindness" underscores the vitality of the Christian ideal whose ultimate guardian is the church. "The saint in modern times," asserts Méndez Asensio, "is an individual who is speaking to all men of the possibilities of achievement and of greatness which they too possess if they follow in the path of goodness." Clearly, for the archbishop, this "path of goodness" (el camino del Bien) is none other than that set of beliefs and practices that constitutes Roman Catholic dogma.

Méndez Asensio's emphasis on enduring values does not lead him to negate the friar's particular historical identity. On the contrary, he calls attention to the close association between him and the recent past. "Fray Leopoldo," he declares in the homily, "does not belong to the Middle Ages, he is not a Franciscan of that epoch or even of the last century. He is . . . of our own century, of this very Granada, of our own place and our own era." The archbishop is quick to draw attention to the friar's exemplary actions during what he delicately describes as "a time of troubles." While admitting that errors may have been committed by "even the best-intentioned" during the civil war, Méndez Asensio hails Fray Leopoldo as "a breath of fresh, young air" (un aire fresco y joven). According to him, the friar offers proof of the church's capacity for adaptation and renewal—its "unequivocal modernity."

The homily pointedly identifies the canonization effort as a joint enterprise of the Catholic hierarchy and the lay population. While reminding his listeners that it is Rome that renders final judgment on all questions regarding sanctity, the archbishop underscores the diocese's full support for the friar and thus the receptivity of the local religious establishment to the feelings and opinions of the community. "When the church calls you together to this Eucharistic celebration this morning," he says, "it does not claim that Fray Leopoldo is a saint. We do not celebrate Saint Leopoldo, but we nonetheless take pleasure in offering a

22. The text of this homily appears in *El Ideal,* 10 June 1984, p. 15. There are minor differences between it and the spoken version (which I tape-recorded), delivered in the city cathedral by Méndez Asensio the day before. I have relied on the printed version in this discussion. English translations are once again my own.

mass in Fray Leopoldo's honor. *Because testimony from this Granada will appear before the Holy Father so that he sees all that Granada thinks, says, and feels about this humble friar."* (my italics).

The archbishop's repeated stress on Fray Leopoldo's spiritual attributes contrasts with his conspicuous silence vis-à-vis the friar's reputedly miraculous powers. Méndez Asensio explains in private conversation that as the requisite authorities have not yet rendered their verdict on the testimony collected in Granada, he finds it inappropriate to express his own opinion at this point. His unwillingness to weaken the church's position by dividing the clergy almost certainly would encourage restraint in this regard. He is equally reluctant to risk alienating the friar's devotees by taking a stand on miracles, an issue the next two chapters will show to be highly controversial. His own seeming propensity to see the saints primarily as earthly models rather than as heavenly intercessors is almost certainly another likely motive for his concentration on the more concrete, didactic aspects of the Fray Leopoldo case.

Asked specifically about the charges of "miracle-ism" voiced by critics of the devotion, the archbishop replies that some visitors to the crypt "probably make the error of believing they can pay God for his favors." He insists, however, that this sort of misconception has little if any effect on Fray Leopoldo's value as a paradigm of the Christian life. Indeed, he argues, the church's role has always been "to channel" and "to purify" spontaneous outpourings of "the people's simple faith" (Es que cabe a la iglesia canalizar, purificar esta fe sencilla del pueblo cristiano).

In answer to the question of whether the friar would exert the same sort of appeal today as he did during his lifetime, Méndez Asensio observes diplomatically that "every epoch has its own expression" and that Fray Leopoldo must therefore be understood as a reflection of an earlier Granada. He adds that there is clearly more interest in the friar among older adults who knew him than among their children, who are now seeking their "own models, different models, for the present." "I find this completely normal," he continues. "Why should the young look to the past when the world is always changing, always new?"

Asked directly what he thinks about the miracles attributed to the friar by some individuals, the archbishop is equally circumspect. "These things are very complicated," he observes. "I say to you sincerely that they have no easy answer."

Fray Leopoldo and the Life
The friar's exemplary qualities occupy a similarly central role in the formal Life prepared and disseminated by the Capuchins.[23] Whereas

23. Fray Angel de León, *Mendigo por Dios*.

Méndez Asensio stresses the personal attributes and practical achievements that made the friar a fitting model for his era, the Life focuses on the unchanging spiritual qualities he embodies. Its marked concern for miracles and the miraculous and its insistence on Fray Leopoldo as representative of not just Christian, but rather specifically Franciscan, values suggest a different perspective and different purposes from those expressed in the archbishop's homily.

The Capuchins are an autonomous yet integral branch of the Order of Friars Minor ("Little Brothers") founded by Saint Francis of Assisi in 1209; they have long been known as preachers and missionaries.[24] Though one of the smaller religious communities within Spain (the Jesuits rank first with almost four thousand members; the Capuchins twelfth with only a thousand), the order as a whole has been quite effective in gaining recognition for its members.[25] The great majority of successful candidates have been from either Italy or Spain.

Like many other religious orders during the last few decades, the Capuchins have experienced both external and internal pressures to change. At the order's General Chapter in 1985 the pope explicitly charged the friars to abandon recent nontraditional practices and ideas that have ostensibly diverted some of their number from their "authentic" Franciscan heritage. Although the movement to canonize Fray Leopoldo predates this official communication, one can see the Life and related publications as the Capuchins' response to larger pressures, which the pope's directive underscores.[26]

The author of the Life and principal director (vice-postulator) of the canonization effort in Granada was Fray Angel de León (1920–1984). Undaunted by a heart attack in 1978 Fray Angel continued to treat Fray Leopoldo's cause as a full-time job. He might, for instance, talk about the friar on a local radio station in the morning, receive a visitor from Valencia wanting to report a case of miraculous intervention in the afternoon, and oversee a special program at the Fray Leopoldo Home for the Elderly before going on to work on next Sunday's sermon. An

24. For a general history of the Capuchin order in Spain see González Caballero, Los capuchinos en la Península Ibérica.

25. These statistics are from the Guía de las comunidades religiosas masculinas de España, published in 1984 by CONFER (Conferencia Española de Religiosos), as reported in the monarchist daily ABC (Madrid), 9 June 1984, p. 45.

26. The sense of generalized crisis within the religious orders is effectively conveyed in Nebreda, O renacer o morir.

For a discussion of the pope's communication see Granfield, Limits of the Papacy, p. 19. The letter insists that Franciscanism is an "established way of life" and not a "movement open to new options continually substituted by others in the insistent search for an identity, as if this identity had not been found."

unpublished poet and inveterate armchair traveler, he wore the traditional Capuchin robes over checkered shirts and comfortably scuffed shoes.

Born in a small village in the mountains of northern Spain, Fray Angel was the son of a schoolteacher who became involved in commercial ventures in Cuba and Peru.[27] When these failed, the family returned home to farm. Like Fray Leopoldo at a later age, the boy decided to join the Capuchin order after hearing the impassioned sermon of an itinerant preacher. As there were no seminaries near his home, he headed south to Antequera, now some two hours by highway from Granada.

The civil war erupted during his years as a student. In August of 1936 an anticlerical mob killed five senior members of the order on the seminary doorstep, then threatened the teen-aged seminarians who had remained inside the building. Although the attackers eventually allowed Fray Angel and his companions to leave the building unharmed, the image of the blood-stained doorway remained with him all his life. "A thing of this sort leaves a deep mark" (Una cosa de estas deja mucha huella), he once confided. "Even today I dream about it."[28]

Fray Angel first heard about Fray Leopoldo in Antequera. "The other students told many marvelous stories about him," he explained, "because even in those early days many people thought he was a saint." His personal association with the friar occurred during the two years in the early 1950s when both men lived in the Granada monastery. During this time, he was deeply impressed by Fray Leopoldo's kindness and concern for the lay population, as well as his success in the day-to-day life of the monastery, which, he noted, "is not the bed of roses an outsider might believe."[29]

In 1952 Fray Angel left the city, only to return in 1958, two years after Fray Leopoldo's death. A year later he was named vice-postulator and primary advocate of the friar's canonization process, which was formally initiated in 1961. ("Did I want the title?" he responded when I asked him. "Well, one does not request these things. But of course one

---

27. This biographical information is from one of various tape-recorded conversations with Fray Angel, all of which were conducted in the Capuchin monastery in Granada. The exchange in question occurred on 23 March 1984. English translations are my own.

28. Interview, 14 April 1984. The dead, known as "the martyrs of Antequera," have been proposed for canonization.

For the fullest account of anticlerical violence during the civil war see Montero Moreno, *Historia de la persecución religiosa en España.*

29. Both statements are from the 14 April interview.

does not accept them if one does not believe in the cause very strongly.")[30]

A former professor of rhetoric and a fiery preacher in the Capuchin tradition, Fray Angel ruefully acknowledged himself to be the product of "a very different era." Fully conscious of the order's increased emphasis on the more human aspects of sainthood, he sought to follow his superiors' injunction to write about Fray Leopoldo "as he lived and worked within the monastery and among the men surrounding him." "Miracles are not in style," he once informed me wryly.[31]

Fray Angel himself, however, was fully convinced of the friar's extraordinary powers. Although he claimed to see these first and foremost as confirmation of spiritual superiority, his own unshakable faith in divine intercession led him to express a certain irritation with skeptics, both inside and outside the religious establishment. "The Roman Catholic Church," he declared in one conversation, "has its norms by which it beatifies the saints, and the church demands miracles as one proof of sanctity. If the saints did not perform miraculous actions, if miracles were not fully possible, why then would the church demand them as a proof of sanctity?"[32] On another occasion, he emphasized his belief in progress. "But I ask you," he demanded at the end of our conversation, "has anything, could anything, ever replace the saints? Fray Leopoldo had so much love for his fellow human beings, he felt so deeply for the people who suffered, that I believe God has given him the gift of continuing, even after death, to help those in need."[33]

As part of the canonization effort, Fray Angel interviewed several hundred persons who had known Fray Leopoldo during his lifetime, plus various others who claimed to have benefited from the friar's posthumous intercession. The results of this investigation—oral testimony recorded in handwritten notes (Fray Angel was not comfortable with, and did not own, a tape recorder) as well as official typed or written communications from various witnesses—appear in the official Articles of

30. Interview, 2 April 1984. The twenty-five years that Fray Angel, at the time of this conversation, had devoted to the friar's cause must certainly have reinforced his initial sense of conviction.

31. A directive to portray Fray Leopoldo "focusing upon how he lived and worked among his brothers and the people of his community, rather than reported supernatural exploits" (my translation) appears in a letter addressed to Fray Angel by the editor of the three-volume series, Santi e santità nell'Ordine cappuccino, ed. D'Alatri. Fray Angel showed me the letter and made the comment, which I quote, in an interview on 14 April.

32. Interview, 2 April 1984.

33. Interview, 22 June 1984.

Apostolic Process.[34] (This document in turn provides the basis for the more general *vita* of Fray Leopoldo, *Mendigo por Dios* [*Beggar for God*].[35] The title is an allusion to the friar's activities as alms collector. First published in 1970, this book had gone through three editions as of 1987 for a total of more than forty thousand copies.) New accounts of alleged posthumous favors continue to appear in a bimonthly Fray Leopoldo bulletin with a circulation of approximately sixty thousand.[36] In addition, numerous summaries of various portions of the Life are available in abridged form. The book is available for a nominal fee (approximately two dollars), the pamphlets are usually free.

In line with the norms governing canonization, the Articles of Apostolic Process set out to document Fray Leopoldo's "reputation as a saint, his virtues and his miracles" (la fama de santidad, virtudes y milagros). They are intended for an ecclesiastical jury thoroughly versed in Roman Catholic dogma. In conformance with standard procedure, the two hundred and fifty propositions that make up the text are grouped in sections corresponding to the three theological virtues of faith, hope, and charity; the four moral, or "cardinal," virtues of fortitude, justice, prudence, and temperance; and the triple vow of poverty, chastity, and obedience taken by members of religious communities. Each subdivision contains from one to a dozen illustrations. The second-to-last section, "Supernatural Gifts" (Dones sobrenaturales), describes miraculous actions credited to the friar during his lifetime. Reports of seven favors attributed by those involved to his posthumous intercession follow.

Although individual sections of the articles are brief, the extremely formal and formulaic text finds reinforcement in a series of unusually long and syntactically complex sentences. As is customary, each new subdivision in this extended catalogue begins with the stock phrase *Es*

---

34. *Granatensis causa de beatificación y canonización.* Witnesses are identified by name in the concluding section devoted to the friar's posthumous intercession (pp. 51–54). Proper names also appear within the body of the text.

35. There is an enormous body on the *vita* and on various aspects of hagiographical literature. Important general studies include Aigrain, *L'Hagiographie;* Delehaye, *The Legends of the Saints,* and *Cinq leçons sur la méthode hagiographique;* Günter, *Psychologie der Legende;* Gaiffier, *Études critiques d'hagiographie et d'iconologie.* See also, in a markedly different vein, Gurevich's interesting discussion of a number of medieval Latin literary classics in *Medieval Popular Culture.*

36. The bulletin customarily offers summaries of two- to three-dozen miraculous favors credited to Fray Leopoldo by letter writers identified by name and city of residence. These narratives are followed by a list of persons who have contributed to the Fray Leopoldo Home for the Elderly and other charitable causes, and by a list of others either expressing appreciation for favors they believe they have obtained through the friar's intercession, or seeking his help. Approximately fifteen thousand copies are distributed along with the Capuchins' devotional magazine, *El Adalid Seráfico,* based in Seville and sold by subscription. The other forty-five thousand are avilable to visitors to the friar's crypt.

cierto (it is certain) or *Es verdad* (it is true) and ends with the affirmation *Esto será probado* (this will be proven). Specific actions are reduced to the bare essentials. Dialogue is rare; background information sketchy or nonexistent. As he is presenting this material to the theologically sophisticated, the author employs an elevated, studiously impersonal style.

The articles' legalistic, pared-down, and often abstract language is not characteristic of the Life, which is intended for a more heterogeneous, predominantly lay readership with little knowledge of or interest in the more technical aspects of the canonization process. Because the author of the Life includes a greater number of incidents, which he recounts in greater detail, this second version is more than four times longer than the first (330 as opposed to 54 pages). As is evident from Appendix A in the present study, an appreciable percentage of the events described are identical or similar to others in the juridical document. The biography, however, is no longer an extended catalogue of discrete elements, but, rather, a full-fledged narrative.

Its readily recognizable, largely chronological story line does not keep the Life from conveying a limited sense of evolution. The author's emphasis on the larger moral underlying individual incidents makes the anecdotes largely interchangeable. As a result, the text, like a number of other *vitae*, reveals a certain circularity that belies its apparently linear plan.[37]

This repetitive structure underscores the enduring and essentially changeless values of Christianity and the Franciscan way of life. So do a number of other factors not necessarily characteristic of either the *Fioretti* of Saint Francis, to which its author pointedly refers on various occasions, or to saints' legends as a whole.[38] The conscious juxtaposition of Fray Leopoldo with both an apparently unchanging countryside and an urban landscape representing countless centuries of cultural achieve-

---

37. On the circularity of the *vita* see Olsen, " 'De Historiis Sanctorum.' " There are, to be sure, some texts in which this quality is more pronounced than others.

38. Fray Angel's most immediate model is unquestionably the *Fioretti* of Saint Francis, a Latin compilation of which dates from the first half of the fourteenth century and which is thought to be the work of the Franciscan friar, Ugolino of Monte Giorgio. (For an English-language translation see Francis of Assisi, *The Little Flowers*.) The Life of Fray Leopoldo unquestionably resembles these stories of the founder of the Franciscan orders in its stress on the protagonist's dedication to a life of simplicity and poverty and its detailed descriptions of his activities amidst the needy of the city as well as an everyday, compassionate example to his fellow friars. The *Fioretti*, however, does not reveal the idealization of the countryside, the numerous references to well-known figures from various centuries, or the extremely cautious treatment of the supernatural, all of which characterize Fray Angel's text. (Saint Francis, for his part, engages in a number of frankly marvelous exploits such as converting to Christianity a "very fierce" wolf.) In addition, the note of defensiveness so obvious in the Life's portrayal of recent Spanish history is absent from the *Fioretti*.

ments is one of these. The establishment of a larger, more universal context for the friar through frequent references to artists, intellectuals, and holy figures from other times and places is another. A third, particularly important strategy for suggesting Fray Leopoldo's atemporality is the insistence on a large number of extraordinary deeds that stand outside the confines of space and time. Finally, the author recasts recent Spanish history as one more battle in an ongoing war between good and evil.[39]

We have already noted oral storytellers' interest in Fray Leopoldo's close association with the countryside. Following their lead while bending this theme to his own purpose, his biographer presents the friar's birthplace, Alpandeire, as a "heraldic" hamlet encrusted "like a jewel" in the rugged mountain gorges. (He will later reinforce this theme through references to its subterranean veins of gold and silver.) His description underscores not only the inherent value and nobility but also the persistence of the rural tradition. "One would think," he remarks, "that in those places inaccessible to the modern industrial movement, *time has stopped as if it remained frozen* among the thick masses of stone, age-old refuge of large bands of crows or in the depth of its valleys, cultivated with primitive tools inherited from one of the preceding civilizations which farmed them" (my italics).[40]

And yet if Fray Leopoldo is the product of a pristine rural landscape marked by fertile fields, happy children, and warbling swallows, the Life also insists on his ties to Granada. The author dwells on his subject's intimate association with a city whose "long and glorious history—and more than history, prehistory—goes back to the first generations of the New Adam." Triumphant conquest of Ferdinand and Isabella, Granada also appears here as the paradise of Moorish sovereigns. Contrast and complement to Alpandeire, which confirms age-old ties between human beings and the earth, Granada is a symbol of "historical constancy." Nature and culture thus unite in the figure of the friar.

Fray Angel cannot restrain his nostalgia for a vanished Eden on occasion. An almost audible sigh accompanies his observation that if the

---

39. This division of the world into good and evil is characteristic of much hagiographical literature. See Altman, "Two Types of Opposition."

40. "Se pensaría que en aquellos parajes, inaccesibles al movimiento industrial moderno, se ha parado el tiempo, como si permaneciera congelado entre los ingentes macizos de piedra, secular guarida de densas bandadas de cuervos, o en la profundidad de sus valles, cultivados con primitivas herramientas de trabajo heredadas de cualquiera de las civilizaciones pretéritas que los roturaron," *Mendigo de Dios*, p. 22.

It is worth noting here that the Franquist glorification of Catholicism, in which religion and power became inextricably mingled, was closely tied to the celebration of rural life and the image of rural traditionalism. See Behar, "The Struggle for the Church," pp. 15–16.

landscape is now lovely it must have been even more so in the past. He is nevertheless quick to emphasize the city's continuing hold on the imagination. According to him, Granada's beauty is "a palpable reality" whose continuing ability to inspire artists from every corner of the world is evidence of its universal and unwavering appeal.

Fray Leopoldo first appears as a product of this larger "forge of sanctity and sanctuary of mystic ecstasies."[41] He is one more page from Granada's golden legend, "the latest aureola" in its painstakingly elaborated altar screen. The author, however, almost immediately amplifies this initially limited vision of the friar by proceeding to suggest his ties to a far larger past. Apparent touristic reveries effectively emphasize the subject's membership in a community transcending a less exotic here-and-now. "But it is necessary to skip over this epoch of romance and mystery," asserts the author in a typical passage, "even though it has left an indelible mark . . . upon the city, even though we often see our Fray Leopoldo pass beneath the horseshoe-shaped arches or enter mansions which were formerly Moorish palaces."[42]

As the account progresses, the friar gradually becomes synonymous with his surroundings, his interior, spiritual qualities fusing with a familiar landscape. Recurrent images of water serve to link countryside and city as well as to suggest Fray Leopoldo's larger-than-life identity. The author describes the friar's soul as "crystalline and jubilant as the small streams of the mountain area which saw his birth."[43] His resolve proves as steadfast as the "eternal snows" that cap Granada's summits. Frequently portrayed against a backdrop of fruits and flowers, the friar speaks in a voice recalling both the mountain brooks and city fountains.[44] His life in retrospect resembles a beautiful landscape unruffled by relentless winds of change.

References to well-known writers, artists, and thinkers pepper the Life and further reinforce the notion of a larger legacy extending back over the centuries. This broader framework offers a counterbalance to the more specific bonds between the friar and "his" Granada. The author cites approximately sixty individuals, including the medieval poet Gonzalo de Berceo, the baroque painter Bartolomé Murillo, and play-

41. "Forja de santidades y santuario de místicos arrobos. . . . " (p. 75)

42. "Pero es forzoso pasar de largo por esta época de romance y misterio, aunque v◦os muchas veces a nuestro Fray Leopoldo transitar bajo sus arcos de herradura, o penetrar en mansiones que antaño fueron palacios moriscos. . . . " (p. 78)

43. "Cristalina y jubilosa, como los arroyuelos de la Serranía que le vio nacer." (p. 93)

44. The association of saints with water is common in medieval hagiographical literature and undoubtedly recalls earlier, pagan sources. For a long list of water-related miracles see Loomis, White Magic, pp. 37–43.

wright Calderón de la Barca, the nineteenth-century literary critic and writer Marcelino Menéndez y Pelayo, and the modern lyric poet Antonio Machado. Most of these individuals are from Spain, some are both saints and Spaniards. (Among the latter category are Ignatius of Loyola, Teresa of Avila, and John of the Cross.) A few others—among them the poet Al-Kattib, novelist Romain Rolland, and statesman Mahatma Gandhi—represent a larger, international community.

The author usually links these individuals to Fray Leopoldo directly by proclaiming them representatives of the same venerable tradition. But on some occasions he is content to confirm his subject's importance through association with one or another well-known figure. Noting, for instance, that the friar was a contemporary of the celebrated poet Federico García Lorca, Fray Angel conjectures that the two men's paths must have crossed on more than one occasion.[45] Although admitting that they represent opposing spiritual directions, he goes on to express certainty that Fray Leopoldo's austere appearance must have made some impression ("if only esthetic") on the poet. As García Lorca is familiar to a far wider public than is Fray Leopoldo, this coupling allows his fame to rub off on the friar. Likewise, the often lengthy quotations from a host of similarly famous figures reinforce the reader's sense of the Life's protagonist as a member of a prestigious intellectual and spiritual elite.

The Role of Miracles in the Life

The Life's repetitiveness, its association of Fray Leopoldo with a particular rural and urban landscape, and its references to a long list of famous persons from various centuries all contribute to that aura of eternity that is the author's goal. By far his single most important narrative strategy, however, is his presentation of a series of extraordinary actions. Over and over, Fray Leopoldo displays supernatural powers that place him beyond the bounds of everyday experience.[46]

45. Lorca, internationally known for his plays and poetry, was murdered by members of a Falangist "Black Squad" in Granada on 19 August 1936. Although, theoretically, it is possible that the friar and poet could have met in the years before the latter's death, it is hard to imagine two more different people. Lorca, for instance, was closely connected with the moderate left. He had publicly expressed the opinion that the conquest of Granada in 1492 by Ferdinand and Isabella had destroyed a unique civilization and created "a wasteland population by the worst bourgeoisie in Spain today." (See Preston, *Spanish Civil War*, p. 55.)
46. There is an extensive bibliography on miracles. For a definition of what constitutes a miracle and an introduction to the literature about them see the corresponding entry in *New Catholic Encyclopedia*. A more detailed discussion is Moule, ed., *Miracles*. For further bibliographical information see Wilson, *Saints and Society*, pp. 390–400.

These incidents, like all those in the Life, can be understood on a structural level wherein the friar is depicted as rising to meet a challenge. In some cases, this challenge comes directly from God, and the friar responds with exemplary humility or faith. Sometimes, as when Fray Leopoldo levitates in prayer, this response is shown to be supernatural. When the challenge originates with other human beings, Fray Leopoldo proves himself to be a model of Christian virtues and may or may not demonstrate thaumaturgic powers. Miracles are most common in situations in which an unbeliever seeks to belittle the friar or affronts God. They also occur when virtuous individuals seek his intervention in times of need.

The Life not only cites more than twice as many frankly marvelous actions as do the articles but is also far more likely to describe these deeds in detail. Moreover, incidents whose only purpose is to illustrate the friar's virtues in the juridical document tend to take on a supernatural flavor in the biography. In one story in the articles, for instance, the young Leopoldo gives away money that was needed for the purchase of cooking oil, thus confirming his innate generosity. In the account that appears in the Life, however, the focus shifts to his mysterious powers. Although he displays the same generosity in the Life, the coins inexplicably reappear in his pocket; this event now occupies the very center of the tale.[47]

This focus on the miraculous is also evident in the story of the servant girl who willfully fails to relay her mistress's message to the friar. In the articles this incident is used to exemplify Fray Leopoldo's horror of prevarication. But the Life dwells instead on his powers as a clairvoyant. Although he scolds the girl, as he does in the articles, for failing to tell the truth, his mysterious knowledge of another's mind is the true focus of the tale.

Yet in spite of the Life's considerably greater emphasis on the supernatural, its author exhibits caution in his presentation of extraordinary events. In place of the term *milagro* (miracle), for instance, he consistently prefers the less sensational term *prodigio* (prodigious or extraordinary).

The reasons for this relative circumspection are at least threefold. First, Fray Angel, like Méndez Asensio, is writing about events still not verified by the church. Second, he is, as already suggested, unquestionably responding to specific injunctions from his superiors within the Ca-

---

47. The incident corresponds to motif number V224 ("miraculous replacement of objects for saints") in Thompson, *Motif-Index of Folk Literature*, a standard reference tool for folklorists. See also Loomis, *White Magic*, pp. 86–88. The reader may also wish to consult Boggs's *Index of Spanish Folktales*, an index of Aarne-Thompson tale types.

puchin order, as well as to a more general perception of the de-emphasis of the supernatural within society as a whole. Finally and particularly important in the case of the Life, he is eager not to alienate those whom he is seeking to win over to Fray Leopoldo's cause. As a result, he tends to stress the friar's power over the human psyche instead of over natural forces and to favor improbable as opposed to frankly impossible actions. Proceeding through implication rather than direct assertion, Fray Angel relies on everyday, often humorous details in order to lighten the air of solemnity that surrounds similar accounts of holy figures.

By no coincidence, the so-called intellectual miracles of prophecy and clairvoyance performed by Fray Leopoldo account for just over half of the forty extraordinary actions in the text (twelve instances of the former, nine of the latter, appear in the course of the Life). Fray Leopoldo may allude to a future operation on an apparently healthy child, assure an anxious landlady that a tenant will indeed pay the over-due rent at exactly three o'clock the next day, or foretell the death of someone many miles away. Likewise, he may express hope for a recently conceived child whose mother has told no one of her pregnancy, answer an unspoken question, or gently chide individuals for thoughts and deeds of which only they had been aware.[48]

All of these cases invite psychological as well as supernatural inter-pretations. While some readers might proclaim them outright miracles, others will be more inclined to see merely Fray Leopoldo's powers of discernment or of the propensity of third parties to confide in him. They may similarly credit the friar's prophetic abilities to his unusually well developed, but nonetheless distinctly human, powers of deduction. In short, even though the author clearly nudges his readers to see thau-maturgy at work, his Life permits, and even encourages, a range of in-terpretations.

While only half as numerous as cases of prophecy/clairvoyance, chal-lenges to physical laws do play a role within the Life (eleven of the latter are interspersed throughout the text). The friar may heal a badly frac-tured arm or a cracked skull, shrink the tumor in a boy's knee, or inter-vene to save the victim of an inadvertent poisoning. Likewise, he may plow an entire field in a matter of minutes, manage to make an appear-ance in two places at one time, or levitate several inches above the ground on various occasions.[49]

---

48. See V223 ("saints have miraculous knowledge") and V223.3 ("saint can perceive the thoughts of another man and reveal hidden sins") in Thompson, *Motif-Index*. See also Loomis, *White Magic*, pp. 71–77, and Brewer, *Dictionary of Miracles*, pp. 256 and 466.

49. For miraculous cures see Thompson, *Motif-Index*, V221 ("miraculous healing by saints") and Loomis, *White Magic*, pp. 103–6. Bilocation is Thompson, V225 ("saint in

Although all of these events are highly improbable, the majority are not outright impossibilities. Readers are free, for instance, to take issue with the initial diagnosis of a supposedly mortal illness, or to argue that some afflictions were psychosomatic. They may also question the reliability of eyewitnesses because the author, by no coincidence, consistently invokes the testimony of others in direct challenges to natural law. The great majority of cases involving levitation and bilocation, for instance, depend on collective sources or hearsay. When there is a particular eyewitness, the report cannot be substantiated.

Fray Angel does his best to favorably dispose the reader toward the testimony in question. Thus in one instance—in which the protagonist is said to have hovered several inches above a hospital bed—he underscores the stupefaction of the young nurse's aide as well as her lack of ulterior motives in reporting the event. "But the person who heard her affirm over and over what had happened in tones of deepest sincerity had no other choice but to believe her," the author affirms, "because, among other things, there was not the slightest motive to regard her as a visionary."[50] At the same time, however, he makes clear that the young woman's fellow workers arrive too late to corroborate her testimony, and that the sole responsibility for the truth of the event therefore rests with her. As a result, the reader may dismiss the incident in question without endangering the Life's credibility.

This tendency to place the burden of proof on others is equally obvious in Fray Leopoldo's apparently miraculous extrication of a pair of frenzied mules from a deep ditch. After narrating the bulk of the incident in the present tense, the author switches to the past. An equally abrupt transition from the first person to a collective source accompanies this shift in tense. (*"They* say that . . . ," he interjects.) The effect is once again to dissociate the author from the reported action, thereby reinforcing an impression of objectivity.

These sorts of distancing techniques are particularly apparent in the small number of incidents that hinge on divine intervention. Although conspicuously absent from the articles, a half-dozen of these appear in the Life. They include two cases said to be drawn from Fray Leopoldo's childhood. In the first, previously mentioned, coins reappear in young Leopoldo's pocket. In the second, which the author credits to a group of

---

several places at once"), and Loomis, p. 131. See also Brewer, *Dictionary of Miracles*, pp. 470–71. Levitation is Thompson, D2135.0.1; Loomis, pp. 47–48; and Brewer, pp. 215–18.

50. "Pero quien la oyera afirmar una y otra vez lo sucedido con acentos de la más profunda sinceridad, no tenía más remedio que creerla, porque, entre otras cosas, no había el menor motivo para tratarla de visonaria," *Mendigo por Dios*, p. 154.

elderly informants in Alpandeire, lightning strikes a taunting peer. The Life also recounts how a mysterious soldier saves Fray Leopoldo from almost certain death and how a dove singles him out in a tumultuous crowd. In two other instances the friar encounters an angel-like figure behind the locked doors of the monastery and succeeds in finding a mysterious confessor for a remorseful man at an unlikely predawn hour.[51]

In the last, particularly noteworthy example, a man experiencing extreme guilt in the wake of a drinking binge pleads with Fray Leopoldo to find him a confessor. Because it is before dawn and all of the monastery's residents are sound asleep, the friar initially dismisses his request. The man's continued entreaties, however, finally move him to go off in search of a priest. Moments later, a Christ-like figure appears before the penitent to hear his confession.

As in the episode in which Fray Leopoldo appears to levitate above his sickbed, the biographer relies on an eyewitness whom he identifies in only the most general terms. (In the first case, she is introduced only as "Brígida"; here, he withholds his informant's name ostensibly in order to spare him embarrassment.) And once again, he fosters doubts about the individual's testimony, this time by calling attention to the man's inebriation.

Then too, the eyewitness in this case is almost as circumspect as the author. Although the man strongly implies his mysterious visitor is none other than Christ, he refrains from any sort of explicit identification. This reserve is entirely in line with the Life's more general propensity to suggest rather than to assert. The author clearly hopes to influence his readers' perception of individual events by bombarding them with case after case of "curious" (his word) examples. He himself, however, consistently avoids unequivocal statements that would oblige the reader to agree or disagree. His Fray Leopoldo is equally prone to indirect assertion. "Couldn't it happen," the friar asks his fellow Capuchins on another, similar occasion, "that the Lord might send one of his angels to our monasteries?"[52]

The Life's always cautious, sometimes frankly tentative quality owes much to its dependence on various hypothetical constructions. The author regularly employs the subjunctive, the conditional, and the future and future perfect with a subjunctive force. He also relies heavily on the

51. Retributive punishment is Thompson, Q559.5 ("punishment for opposition to saint"), Loomis, 99–100, and Brewer, 275–77. Doves single out a long list of other holy figures in Loomis, pp. 66–67, and Brewer, pp. 107–10. Mysterious strangers appear in Loomis, p. 131. See also Thompson, V232 ("angel as helper").

52. "¿No podrá suceder que el Señor enviara a alguno de sus ángeles a nuestros conventos?" (p. 192)

passive voice, on various key terms indicating uncertainty or doubt, and on parallelisms that offer the reader more than one possible interpretation of an event.

Often, the subjunctive follows close on a declarative statement as if to soften its force. An unequivocal assertion of Fray Leopoldo's joy in taking monastic vows thus introduces a hypothetical construction underscoring the bishop's unawareness of the gravity of the event. "And we can also believe," the author says, "that if the holy bishop *would have been aware* that he had just finished confirming in the faith a candidate for canonization, he *would have* evinced great joy" (my italics).[53]

Just as frequently, the friar's biographer employs the conditional to suggest what he does not care or dare to state outright: for example, "And Francis of Assisi *would smile down at him* from the sky, remembering a similar afternoon" (my italics).[54] "Jesus *would have raised him up* over the powerful and the Poor Little One of Assisi *would have smiled at him* with love," he notes on another occasion (my italics).[55]

The Life also makes heavy use of the passive voice. "There was in him a spiritual force *that could only be interpreted* as a struggle," the author observes of Fray Leopoldo.[56] Or "*it could be said* of his days that they were pages from the Rule of Saint Francis."[57]

Terms such as *casi, tal vez,* and *quizá* (all meaning "perhaps" or "maybe"), verbs such as *parecer* (to seem, or to appear), and impersonal constructions such as *es posible* (it is possible) and *no es seguro* (it is not sure) provide further distance. On a number of occasions the author introduces parallel constructions suggesting alternative interpretations of the same event. In describing Fray Leopoldo's death, for instance, he claims not to know whether the smile that lingers on the friar's face is one of hope *or* of eternal joy.[58] Likewise, he asks if the bell that announces the friar's death is simply ringing *or* ringing out glory, which would confirm his subject's sanctity.[59]

Simile and metaphor also give the author and his readers added latitude. In the story of the trapped mules, for instance, he hints that Fray

53. "Y podemos igualmente creer que si el santo obispo *hubiera tenido* revelación de que acababa de confirmar en la fe a un candidato a los altares, *hubiera confesado* lleno de gozo." (p. 39)

54. "Y Francisco de Asís *le sonreiría* del cielo, recordando una tarde similar." (p. 40)

55. "Jesús *le habrá ensalzado* sobre los poderosos, y el Pobrecillo de Asís *le habrá sonreído* con amor." (p. 17)

56. "Hubo en él una contienda espiritual *que sólo podría interpretarse* como una lucha." (p. 43)

57. "*Podría decirse* de sus días que eran páginas de la regla de San Francisco." (p. 57)

58. "No sabríamos decir si de esperanza *o* de posesión de goces eternos." (p. 13)

59. "¿Doblaba? ¿Tocaba a gloria?" (p. 15)

Leopoldo, like Saint Francis (known for his preaching to the swallow and his taming of a wolf and a pair of turtle doves), has the ability to communicate with animals.[60] He nonetheless stops short of any sort of outright claim to this effect, noting only that the beasts he addresses respond "*as if they understood* his compassionate and soothing words."[61] In the same vein, the friar succeeds in leading the first mule out of the ditch "with no more trouble *than if it had been* a level road" (my italics in both cases).[62] The earth does not close with a thunderclap, nor do the chastened creatures lie down at his feet. He does nothing more—or less—than extricate them from an apparent impasse, and it is once again left up to the reader to judge the true scope of the event.

The Life's account of Fray Leopoldo's involvement in the removal of a burdensome stone provides another excellent example of its author's reliance on metaphor.[63] A group of workers who have been trying to move the obstacle for hours finally do so when the friar appears on the scene. Suddenly the stone appears to weigh almost nothing, although no actual physical transformation occurs. "*It seemed to us* a bundle of straw," the man remarks (my italics here and below).[64] Finally, even though the eyewitness stresses his companions' openmouthed astonishment, he stops short of pronouncing the actual suspension of a natural law. ("It was *like magic*," he says.)[65]

The rhetorical question is another of the author-preacher's stock devices. "Who can say whether this is fact or fiction?" and "But how could this be?" he demands time and again.[66] Studiously refusing to draw the logical conclusion, he once again affects neutrality. "Let us restrain our flights of imagination," he interjects after presenting the testimony of the repentant sinner in the story of the mysterious confessor. "Who knows the resources these saintly men have at their disposal!" he exclaims on this and various other occasions.[67]

---

60. See Francis of Assisi, *The Little Flowers*, chaps. XVI (swallows), XXII (turtle doves), and XXI (wolf). There is, to be sure, precedent for such communication in much other hagiographical literature. The incident corresponds to Thompson, D2156.2 ("saint controls animals"), Loomis, pp. 58–70, and Brewer, pp. 360–65.
61. "*Como si comprendieran* sus frases compasivas y de aliento." (p. 276)
62. "Con no mayor dificultad *que si se tratara de camino llano*." (p. 276)
63. See Thompson, D1654.1 ("rock refuses to be moved"), Loomis, pp. 88–89, and Brewer, pp. 161–62 and 448, for other stubborn stones. In virtually all of the examples offered by Loomis and Brewer, the holy figure personally removes or transforms the obstacle.
64. "*Nos pareció* una alpaca de paja." (p. 280)
65. "Era *como de magia*." (p. 280)
66. "¿Quién puede decir si es verdad o es mentira?" and "¿Pero cómo podría ser?"
67. "Cortémosle los vuelos a la imaginación: ¡Quién sabe los recursos con que cuentan estos santos varones!" (p. 145)

Not infrequently, Fray Angel begins by dissociating himself from information that he nonetheless proceeds to share. He may note, for instance, that a self-respecting biographer cannot give credence to rumors ("even though he may appreciate their importance"). Instead of moving on to documented claims, however, he proceeds to offer a detailed example of the sort of thing which he will supposedly exclude. He then once again calls readers' attention to his reliance only on "witnesses of proven responsibility," thus encouraging them to accept as truth that information he presents.[68]

The simple language laced with colloquialisms and diminutives that Fray Leopoldo is depicted as using creates an air of intimacy absent from the articles. "But my good man [literally "man of God"], where am I supposed to find a confessor at this hour?" the friar demands of the predawn penitent.[69] "Brother, in order to get to heaven you have to swallow plenty," he informs one of his fellow friars when the subject of penance arises.[70] References to the friar's appealing provincial accent are likely designed to endear him to readers while underscoring his earthy wisdom. "Voice of the people, voice of God," he has Fray Leopoldo assert.[71]

Down-to-earth details provide a particularly effective counterbalance to intimations of the miraculous while further reinforcing the friar's popular appeal. On more than one occasion Fray Leopoldo cures an apparently fatal illness with a pat on the shoulder or a bowl of chicken soup. As in the *Fioretti*, humor may accompany these homespun touches. The author, for instance, clearly intends for the reader to chuckle over the peasant boy whose overwhelming affection for the old friar prompts him to practically knock him off his feet.

Likewise, the incident of the reappearing coins begins with a distinctly unextraordinary description of a country housewife preparing dinner. His mother's reference to the future monastic as "Frasquito Tomás" ("Frasquito" is a pet name and diminutive of "Francisco") intensifies the air of familiarity. So does the portrait of him at play among the other children of the hamlet. The exchange between mother and son, which cli-

---

68. "Un biógrafo que se precie de tal," remarks the author, "no puede dar fe a todo rumor, aunque valore su importancia. Se impone, pues, una selección de aquellos cuya autenticidad conste; no sin advertir, en este caso, que la inclusión de cuantos corren de boca en boca exigiría un volumen muy superior al presente. . . . Será necesario prescindir de muchos datos tan curiosos o más que este, no por juzgarlos infundados, sino por carecer de testimonios de probada responsabilidad." (pp. 202–3)

69. "Pero hombre de Dios, ¿dónde voy yo a estas horas por un sacerdote?" (p. 144)

70. "Hermano, para ganar el cielo hay que tragar mucha saliva." (p. 198)

71. "La voz del pueblo, voz de Dios." (p. 202)

maxes in her energetic search of the boy's pockets, is almost funny. Her discovery of the coin does not prompt her to cry out or to throw up her hands in amazement. Instead, the author notes simply that "her surprise was great."[72]

The coin incident concludes with the assurance that Fray Leopoldo's continuing acts of charity do not always have extraordinary consequences. The author suggests that the future friar must have often found himself at day's end without money, barefoot, and half-naked. Like the image of the mother searching the child's pockets, that of the small boy eagerly stripping off articles of clothing to offer to bemused passersby is intended to soften, though in no way obviate, the presence of the supernatural.

History as Ongoing Struggle between Good and Evil

A final means of emphasizing Fray Leopoldo's timelessness is the presentation of his particular historical circumstances as a variation on a recurrent theme. The Life devotes considerable space and emotional energy to the hostilities directed at the religious establishment in general, and the friar in particular, during the Spanish civil war.[73] Although its author attempts to enlist readers' sympathies through a barrage of details, he ultimately sees this era as one more battle in a much larger contest between good and evil.[74]

The view of history as a protracted struggle illustrating eternal truths is obvious very early in the Life. Fray Angel devotes much of his second chapter to contrasting Fray Leopoldo's peaceful childhood in isolated Alpandeire with the intrigue and turmoil embroiling the nation. Dismissing the liberal, urban-based revolution of 1868, known as the *Gloriosa*, as "glorious in name only," he proceeds to catalogue its negative effects on a "defenseless" countryside.

The theme of combat continues to dominate his descriptions of the twentieth century. Chapter 18, which bears the revealing title, "Blessed

---

72. "Su sorpresa fue grande. . . . " (p. 28)

73. These hostile actions included the sacking and burning of churches and convents, the wide-scale humiliation and killing of members of the religious establishment, the desecration and destruction of cultic objects, and also the exhumation and public display of long-buried corpses of the priests, nuns, and reputed holy figures. See Lincoln, "Revolutionary Exhumations," for a provocative discussion of the latter. Although one may question the author's assertions regarding the millenarian impulse underlying these manifestations, his essay elucidates the sense of persecution underlying the Life.

74. Certainly Fray Angel's perspective was, and is still to some extent, shared by other members of the ecclesiastical establishment. See, for example, the wartime pastorals of Gomá, *Por Dios y por España*. See also Bustamante's emotional *Mártires capuchinos*.

Persecution" (Bienaventuranza de la persecución), deals with the events leading up to the civil war. The author sees the Republican movement as a uniformly negative (and frightening) "eruption of Vandals," in which the cry of liberty produces only "bursts of libertinism."[75]

A full ten pages of the chapter are devoted to the sufferings of the religious establishment during what he repeatedly calls this "time of terror." Although the author dutifully acknowledges the presence of well-intentioned persons within the leftist government, he clearly cannot forgive its active opposition to the church. He describes, often in considerable detail, specific, physical attacks on property and individuals associated with religious institutions. Although striving to maintain a neutral tone in these passages, he regularly betrays a deep indignation. He refers, for instance, to the flames that destroyed many religious landmarks as "indispensable pyrotechnics," and to the left's attempts to repress its opponents as the era's "favorite sport." His description of one of various attacks on the Capuchin monastery in Granada is equally sarcastic. "Seized by iconoclastic zeal," he says, "they [the attackers] knocked over the religious images and altars, slashed the monastery's paintings, and there must have even been a music hater among them, because the harmonium was thrown down from the choir loft onto the church floor."[76]

After a prolonged description of abuses directed at the ecclesiastical establishment during this period, the author details affronts endured by Fray Leopoldo. On one occasion, a crowd pelts the friar with rocks and cobblestones. On another, a group of thugs threatens to cut off his head. In line with the challenge structure already outlined, the friar responds to threats and insults with equanimity. (Steadfastness in the face of persecution is, after all, the basis for the early martyr's tale, or *passio*.) Rather than running from the angry crowd, he kneels before the rain of stones. When the mob assures him that all members of religious orders must die, he coolly bares his throat.

The author, however, is not content to illustrate Fray Leopoldo's courage in adversity. He is even more insistent on presenting the hardships of the civil war as a spiritual test. In the eyes of his biographer, Fray Leopoldo's sufferings link him to the early martyrs and indeed to all those who have ever suffered for the Christian faith. Thus, instead of a

---

75. "Una irrupción vandálica surgió de las entrañas mismas del país," remarks the author, and "El grito de libertad produjo estallidos de libertinaje." (p. 218)

76. "Llevados de furor iconoclasta, derribaron imágenes y altares, acuchillaron los lienzos de los claustros, y hasta no faltó algún musicófobo, pues el armonio fue arrojado desde el coro contra el pavimento de la iglesia." (p. 221)

unique conjunction of social, economic, and political causes with equally specific consequences, the civil war becomes a variation on "the eternal supplication, the ceaseless mortification," which the author finds synonymous with human history.[77] For him, the recent past is, in the end, less a peculiarly Spanish tragedy than yet another cataclysmic scene from a cosmic drama of purification whose final act will only be played out on an apocalytpic judgment day.

The Concern for Timelessness

Our analysis of the Life's principal narrative strategy has documented its author's overwhelming concern for the principle of atemporality. We have seen how he suggests the enduring nature of those spiritual qualities embodied in Fray Leopoldo through the circular structure of his narrative, through emphasis on the friar's ties to a pristine countryside and a historic city, through insistence on his subject's thaumaturgic powers, and through the presentation of history as an ongoing contest between good and evil. The all-important question of motivation nevertheless remains. *Why*, one must finally ask, is the Life so intent on setting Fray Leopoldo outside the normal confines of space and time? Is the biographer simply following hagiographic convention, or are there other, more pressing personal and historical reasons for his insistence on atemporality?

The question is particularly interesting because of the contrast between the Life's insistence on the friar's timelessness and the archbishop's presentation of him as a reflection of and model for a specific and bygone era. Although the archbishop too speaks of the enduring values he sees embodied in the friar, Méndez Asensio is far more willing to see history as a series of discrete and basically nonrepeatable events ("every epoch has its own expression," he says). In addition, he displays little if any interest in the supernatural, playing down the links between the present and the past. He thus presents a stark contrast to Fray Angel, who enthusiastically assigns Fray Leopoldo near-mythic proportions ("he was like a friar out of a legend," he remarks at one point).[78]

Although the differences between the archbishop and the friar's biographer must reflect to some extent temperament and personal history, they owe in large part to Fray Angel's identity as a Capuchin, an order that has seen a marked falloff of new vocations and a decline in prestige.

---

77. "La plegaria perenne, la mortificación extenuante." (p. 231)
78. "Era como un fraile de leyenda." (p. 68)

As representative of the church as an overarching institution, the archbishop is interested in those aspects of Fray Leopoldo's cause that have meaning to the largest number of persons. The author of the Life, for his part, is far more concerned with the Capuchin order, to whose members he dedicates his book. If he speaks in its pages primarily to a larger, lay public, it is because he is seeking to win their acceptance of Fray Leopoldo, *and through him the validation of the entire Franciscan way of life.*

The Life, by no coincidence, begins with a specific reference to Saint Francis of Assisi, founder of the Franciscan order, to whom the author insists on regularly comparing Fray Leopoldo. He envisages Saint Francis, for instance, looking down in approval on the future friar when the latter offers a poor man his shoes. On another occasion Fray Leopoldo appears "as if he had become detached from the leaves of the calendar of the centuries in order to pass before our gaze like a figure from 'The Little Flowers' "[79] "Seven centuries separate us from 'The Little Flowers,' " remarks the author on yet another occasion, "But who wouldn't say that on this page their full fragrance cannot still be perceived?"[80]

In further contrast to the archbishop's homily—which concentrates on the close, ongoing relationship between the friar and the lay population—the Life depicts Fray Leopoldo as equally at home on the city streets as within the monastery walls. Its author corroborates the archbishop's remarks about the friar's outward-looking nature and activities within the larger lay community. He nevertheless devotes at least an equal amount of attention to the friar's intensely solitary struggle to uphold his vows of poverty, chastity, and obedience.

The Life stresses how hard it is, particularly in the present, for religious orders to live up to the standards they impose on themselves. Throughout the book, the friar's biographer calls attention to his psychic as well as (sometimes) physical strength, and refers to him as a "varón de Dios." Although the literal translation of this term is "man of God," the word *varón* has connotations of virility and power intended to suggest how austere and demanding the Capuchin regime is. The text dwells on the friar's pain in renouncing family life in order to assume "the

79. "Como si hubiera desprendido de las hojas del calendario de los siglos para pasar ante nuestra mirada como una figura de 'Las Florecillas.' " (p. 78)

80. "Nos separan siete siglos de 'Las Florecillas' pero ¿quién no diría que en esta página se percibe aún toda sua fragancia?" (p. 166)

Once again, although the author clearly wants the reader to make the connection between his own account of Fray Leopoldo and the *Fioretti* of Saint Francis, there are significant differences between the context in which they present the Franciscan ideal, as well as at least some of the rhetorical devices they employ.

cross of the Capuchin life."[81] "A genuinely Franciscan soul," Fray Leopoldo engages in an ongoing struggle to be faithful "not only to the Founder's Rule, but also to the other laws and praiseworthy traditions of the Order."[82]

In short, the Life both recalls and departs from older hagiographic models in its implicit rebuttal of charges or suspicions that the members of religious orders are effeminate and lazy or that the Franciscan ideal is hermetic and outmoded. The injustices he suffers attest not only to his personal strength but also to the continued resilience of the particular religious regime he represents in what Fray Angel pointedly identifies on multiple occasions as a *"supposedly* secular age" (my italics). The latter's insistence on eternal truths is from this perspective a defense against a historical moment characterized by intense questioning of traditional values by some sectors of the clergy and religious orders, as well as by the populace at large.

Fray Angel's urgency in this mission is hardly surprising given his early traumatic experiences during the civil war—the "barbarous assassination" of seven Capuchin friars in the Antequera seminary which he has Fray Leopoldo so strongly decry. He, like Méndez Asensio, sees the friar as a compelling symbol through which to address and, he hopes, to move a larger public. But while the archbishop attempts above all to reconcile the lay population with the ecclesiastical hierarchy and thus to fortify the church's image as a socially responsive, forward-looking institution, Fray Angel seeks to wash the blood from a distant doorstep and to vindicate a way—his way—of life.

81. "La cruz de la vida capuchina." (p. 58)
82. An "alma genuinamente franciscana" (p. 80), Fray Leopoldo is "fidelísimo, no sólo a la Regla, sino a las restantes leyes y laudables tradiciones de la Orden." (p. 126)

CHAPTER THREE

Legends

This chapter and the one that follows discuss orally transmitted stories that I collected in Granada's streets, shops, cafés, and plazas. I relate these stories to each other and to the formal Life. For purposes of analysis, I have divided the narratives into two broad categories according to structural criteria.[1] The accounts I call "Legends" (with a capital "L") resemble the Life in that they present Fray Leopoldo as rising to a challenge with marked success. The other tales, referred to here as "Counterlegends," depict the friar as failing to meet a challenge or show him facing opposition from others in the course of meeting a challenge. In the second instance, this opposition dominates the tale. Theoretically, the same person could relate both Legends and Counterlegends.[2] In practice, however, such crossovers are rare.[3]

Storytellers do not make structural distinctions between stories or employ the terms *Legend* and *Counterlegend*. Most, however, have a clear idea of how their perspective on Fray Leopoldo compares to that of the Capuchins. In the course of recounting stories, individuals quite often refer to the officially legitimated stance ("well, I for one don't be-

1. Structuralism as a method of analysis is closely associated with the work of Claude Lévi-Strauss. See his *Tristes Tropiques* and *Structural Anthropology*. For a bibliography of studies employing structural criteria see Hølbek, *Formal and Structural Studies of Oral Narrative*.

2. Both Legends and Counterlegends, to be sure, are legends with a small "l." *Webster's New Collegiate Dictionary* defines the legend as "a story coming down from the past; especially one popularly regarded as historical although not verifiable." Many folklorists, however, would take issue with this definition. For an understanding of some of the problems it raises see Georges, "The General Concept of Legend."

3. Just over three-fifths of the storytellers represented in my collection told Legends; the remaining two-fifths, Counterlegends. Occasionally, the tellers of Counterlegends will refer in general terms to Legends or one Legend in particular as an example of what he or she is refuting. But the reverse is rarely, if ever, true.

lieve what they [the friars] say about Fray Leopoldo" or "you've probably heard that the *Hermanico* is going to be canonized, and I say, well, he should be because . . ."). On other occasions, they responded, often in detail, to my direct questions about prevailing views of the friar. Thus, while the particular categories of analysis suggested here are my own, the relationships they suggest are in no way foreign to those who tell the stories.

It is important at the outset to emphasize that storytellers' allusions to the Life do not necessarily imply their familiarity with the actual text. Indeed, many persons give the impression of having read the biography from cover to cover, but the number who have actually done so is almost certainly very small. When storytellers alluded to the Life, I would ask them about specific incidents mentioned in the text. They often explained that they owned the book but had not yet gotten around to reading it, that they had glanced at it in someone else's home, or that they had not actually read the book because they were sure of what it would say. ("Why should I waste my time?" more than one teller of Counterlegends demanded.)

A considerably larger number of persons proved to be familiar with abridged versions of the Life (usually devotional literature distributed at the crypt or articles in various secular and religious publications). Others had heard sermons and radio broadcasts about Fray Leopoldo. Most of those with whom I spoke, however, appeared to be responding to the "official" position on the friar not only as expressed through various public channels of communication but even more as voiced by friends, relatives, and a series of acquaintances. Many of these individuals seemed to be using the term *Life* as shorthand for views that find their fullest and most explicit expression in the friar's biography, but which also extend beyond it into a broader and less clearly literary domain. For this reason, even though I will regularly refer to the biography in discussing the tape-recorded stories in my collection, I am by no means suggesting a direct, textual relationship between the two in every case. Moreover, I will argue that although the narratives recounted in the succeeding pages undoubtedly reflect their oral character, differences between them and the Life cannot be attributed solely to their mode (i.e., oral vs. written) of composition or transmission.

The sizable differences among stories in each of the two categories, as well as their ultimate similarities, merit emphasis. It should become clear as this analysis progresses that tellers of Legends and Counterlegends alike often have dramatically different beliefs about the role of the supernatural in human affairs, Fray Leopoldo, and saints in general. This essential multiplicity sets apart the oral corpus from the Life. Then, too, the tales reveal a common undercurrent of anti-institutionalism. Although this is considerably more explicit in Counterlegends, it nonetheless distinguishes all of the narratives. Finally, as I shall suggest in detail in a later chapter, both Legends and Counterlegends reveal a profound interest in the differences between past and present, which contrasts dramatically with the Life's insistence on timelessness.

In the following discussion I am less interested in identifying the total legend universe or in tracing specific variants than in suggesting primary areas of debate. Although the Fray Leopoldo stories are, on the surface, not as varied as a number of other legend corpuses, they reveal an underlying pluralism that defies any attempt at closure.

Legends and the Life

Before proceeding with examples of our first group of narratives, I should first say something about the people who recount them. Although my sample of just under five hundred tellers is too small for statistical accuracy, it nonetheless suggests a definite class (and, to a lesser extent, gender) division between the tellers of Legends and of Counterlegends.

The female Legend tellers in my collection, for instance, outnumber men roughly two to one. They therefore comprise a higher percentage of this first group than the second, which was split almost equally between men and women. Because I actively sought out tellers of both sexes in each case, the difference is considerably less accentuated than it would have been under more normal circumstances.

Then, too, even while the Legend category includes persons from a variety of socioeconomic backgrounds, its members are considerably more apt than Counterlegend tellers to be from the middle and upper-middle sectors of the population, and therefore to have more formal education and better-paying, higher-status occupations.[4] Legend tellers on the whole also reveal closer ties to organized religion.[5] All of the story-

4. Male Legend tellers are apt to have higher-status jobs than male Counterlegend tellers. (Almost a third are professionals, shopkeepers, or members of the religious establishment, as opposed to only about 5 percent of Counterlegend tellers.) Female Legend tellers are more apt to stay at home than female Counterlegend tellers. (About two-thirds of the latter work outside the home, most commonly as domestics, food-service employees, and open-air vendors.)

5. Studies show that Spanish women are more likely than men to attend mass. The greater number of females in the Legend group is therefore another factor in explaining the higher rate of church attendance. For a breakdown of participation at mass by sex, age,

tellers associated with the ecclesiastical establishment fall within this first category, and a sizable percentage of all Legend tellers regularly attend mass.[6]

If it is useful to generalize about these storytellers as a group, it would nonetheless be a mistake to underplay the differences among them. Although I encountered many who fit the stereotype of economic privilege coupled with political and religious conservatism, I met many others who did not. The people who told me the stories discussed below include both rich and poor, male and female, old and young, university graduates and illiterates, regular churchgoers and those who cannot remember the last time they went to mass, firm believers in miracles and vocal skeptics.

One of the Legend tellers with whom I had the most contact is a ninety-two-year-old retired schoolteacher from a wealthy family in the north of Spain.[7] Named after a relative reputed to be a saint ("but my name, thank goodness, is also a flower"), Doña Hortensia traveled extensively through the countryside with her engineer father.[8] Educated at Clermont-Ferrand when few women had a university education, she decided not to marry "because back then a wife and mother could not travel, and I wanted more than anything to see the world." After completing her degree, she continued to study. "I loved geography," she remembers. "I loved biology. And I loved languages and mathematics. And so when I started working as a teacher, all I earned I spent on books."

Hortensia moved with her parents to Granada when she was in her mid-twenties. The death of her father and the advent of the civil war changed her life dramatically. She has nothing good to say about those years or Franco. "I kept on teaching," she explains, "because I believed that only education would get us through that terrible time. That Franco

---

occupation, marital state, and various other categories see "Asistencia a la Eucaristía dominical, 1983."

6. Just over two-fifths of the Legend tellers said they attended mass "always" or "often"; approximately a quarter attended on occasion, and a third "infrequently" or "never." A fifth of Counterlegend tellers attended mass always or often, somewhat less than a third occasionally, and about half infrequently or never.

As already noted elsewhere, involvement in formal religious activities is closely related to a person's class identity. A number of Legend tellers appear to fit an expected pattern in which relative wealth is associated with political conservativism and participation in institutionalized religious practices.

7. Doña Hortensia died in September 1986. I have nonetheless continued to refer to her, like other storytellers, in the present tense. Although I have changed the names of the other storytellers to protect their privacy, I have followed Doña Hortensia's stated wish that I use her real name.

8. "Hortensia" is the Spanish word for "hydrangea."

was a tyrant!" It was during this period that she got to know Fray Leopoldo through her activities as secretary-treasurer of the Third Franciscan Order, a lay religious association. From the beginning she believed that he must be a saint. "He taught by his example, by his unfailing kindness," she asserts. "And I knew he could work miracles, before anybody told me."

When economic conditions finally began improving, Hortensia resumed her travels. A resident of the Fray Leopoldo Home for the Elderly for the past three years, she spends her days doing therapeutic exercises for her arthritic arms and legs ("if not, how can I hope to walk again one day?") and listening to radio broadcasts about world affairs on which she later quizzes herself ("the mind needs exercise as well"). Her room is always full of fellow residents seeking advice on personal problems or voicing complaints they know she will greet with sympathy ("so your arm is hurting, Filomena? How truly sorry I am to hear such news!"). Although she speaks in a soft voice of her fear of dying, she declares the present to be better than the past. "Human beings are not like bees, you know," she says. "They have to keep on changing."

Doña Hortensia's privileged background and essentially sanguine vision of the present make her very different from the vivacious young cleaning woman, Dori. Twenty-seven years old, Dori is married to a man who has been unemployed for almost four years ("he had a good job in Barcelona, but we missed Granada"). It is therefore she who supports her family by cleaning houses six and a half days a week. After scrubbing the floors of someone else's home early Sunday morning, she hurries home to prepare lunch and then tackle her own kitchen. "You can see that my name fits me," she declares with a rueful grin. ("Dolores," of which "Dori" is a diminutive, means "sorrows" in Spanish.)

Her difficult financial situation leads Dori to declare the past superior to the present. "Franco was bad, of course," she says matter-of-factly, "but the lack of jobs we have now is much worse. My husband says if things go on this way, there will be a revolution."

Although Dori takes a dim view of institutionalized religion and rarely goes to mass, she believes in saints and miracles. As a little girl, she learned of Fray Leopoldo from a much-loved grandmother who regularly told stories of the friar's miraculous deeds. Her aunt and uncle sell figurines of the friar in a makeshift stall just around the corner from the Capuchin church. ("Of course," Dori says, "they are there to make a living. I mean, they believe in Fray Leopoldo, but they also have to eat.")

She herself made a vow (*promesa*) to Fray Leopoldo six years ago for the safe delivery of her first child ("I haven't paid yet, but I will"). She is now thinking about taking her small daughter, who regularly gets into fights with other children, to a local healer (*curandero*) and the crypt. "If one thing doesn't work," she says, "the other almost certainly will." She has nonetheless resisted asking for divine help in her husband's job search. "It's not God. It's the bosses who keep people out of work so that they can pay those they do hire less," she asserts.

Although Hortensia and Dori are united by their belief in Fray Leopoldo and in miracles, not all Legend tellers share their faith. A young banker, Luís Antonio, who is one of Dori's employers, is an excellent example. Strikingly good-looking, he is, at the age of twenty-eight, the holder of a much-coveted management position in his company's central office and boasts both his own apartment and a shiny red sedan. He uses his vacations to go camping in other parts of Europe. "I like very old things," he explains, "and very new things too."

Luís Antonio is well aware of his good fortune. Whereas he obtained his first job shortly before unemployment became a major problem in the 1970s, it has taken his slightly younger brother several years to find a job in the computer industry. "Because my father had connections," he explained, "my brother was able to work for a friend's company for free. For free, you understand? Only in this way was he able to get the experience which finally got him the job he has today. And, look, he is working in a city with very few attractions, but there must have been hundreds of candidates for his position."

The graduate of a prestigious Catholic high school, Luís Antonio criticizes his own "very rigid" education. "One of the reasons I did not go on to the university," he explains, "is that the priests taught me to hate school." And yet, despite his assertions that the church has been a major obstacle to progress, he nonetheless attends mass on ceremonial occasions and is quick to acknowledge the primary role of Catholicism in Spain's cultural legacy.

Luís Antonio rolls his eyes when he repeats the stories he has heard of Fray Leopoldo. He nonetheless maintains a diplomatic silence in the presence of his mother, who claims to have obtained various favors from the friar. "But it is not just because she is my mother," he insists, when she is out of hearing. "I myself do not believe, but faith is a personal matter. Besides, these things—saints, miracles—help to make Spain Spanish."

Turning now to the stories proper (the individuals we have just met will reappear in the course of this and the next two chapters), we have already noted that Legends and the Life have a similar narrative structure. All of the tales that fall into this category portray Fray Leopoldo as responding positively to a test of his goodness or power, which would appear to stem from his moral superiority. In addition, many storytellers focus on incidents recounted in the formal biography or on others reminiscent of these in their general outlines. At the same time, some accounts that initially seem almost identical to those in the friar's biography (the tellers may actually acknowledge the Life as their source), closer examination reveals significant differences. For one thing, the "challenge" structure of the tales may undergo various transformations. Then, too, Legends as a group display a degree of detail as well as a diversity of opinion about the frequently supernatural events described within the body of the story in no way characteristic of the biography.

Transformations in the Challenge Structure

In the Life, Fray Leopoldo faces challenges that issue from a variety of sources. Sometimes God decides to test the friar's mettle. On other occasions, the challenge has a human source. The friar's opponents, for instance, may try to goad him with either personal insults or affronts to divine authority. In such cases, he inevitably responds in an exemplary manner, which causes the offenders to see the error of their ways.

More frequently, however, the challenge takes the form of an implicit or explicit call for help. In these instances, Fray Leopoldo gives proof of both his own concern for others and the power invested in him by aiding the needy party—often, though not always, through apparently supernatural means. The individuals whom he instructs or assists may be members of the ecclesiastical establishment—his fellow friars, for instance—who are inspired by his good example. They may also be representatives of the laity.

Although the Legends in my collection far outnumber the incidents included in the Life, the oral stories are decidedly less varied in some respects.[9] In the first place, the challenge inevitably is issued by another person. In contrast to the biography, not one of the Legends in my collection focuses exclusively on Fray Leopoldo's relationship with God. Even when he prays, the friar remains in the company of other human beings.

The actors in Legends are almost always members of the lay population. Representatives of the ecclesiastical establishment seldom make an

---

9. It is admittedly difficult to say where one story leaves off and another begins. Even so, the sheer bulk and variety of my collection leaves no doubt about the greater number of oral stories.

appearance, and the stories in which they do figure are almost always told by members of the religious hierarchy. The monastery itself often becomes a destination or a place from which the friar sets out when a particular event occurs. "He slept in the monastery," notes one young storyteller, "but he lived in the streets."[10] Unlike the Life, which frequently portrays Fray Leopoldo in the company of his fellow friars, Legends show him interacting with people who are much like the storytellers themselves. The challenge situation may involve, for instance, a mother and her young children, a baker and his customers, a clerk in a government office, a shopkeeper worried about making ends meet, a group of construction workers.

The challenges they pose are as important to the Legends as the lay identity of the characters involved. Although a few Legends (once again, their tellers tend to belong to the ecclesiastical establishment) depict Fray Leopoldo as responding to various affronts, most are about situations of need. Even though the exigencies they portray may be emotional and spiritual, they are considerably more likely to be concrete and physical.[11] As such, the stories offer a model for numerous other accounts of the friar's posthumous favors.

Similar situations of need occur quite often in the Life. The reader will recall the numerous incidents in which Fray Leopoldo cures an apparently mortal illness or removes an obstacle to progress. But the need and the needy party always play a secondary role in the Life; in at least some Legends, they assume center stage. The teller, for instance, may offer a blow-by-blow account of an epileptic seizure or outline in abundant detail the successive stages of a debilitating disease. Fray Leopoldo then steps in to assure a happy ending, but his action is no longer the focus of the tale. Fairly often indeed the problem occupies considerably more of the speaker's attention than the solution. Thus, even though Fray Leopoldo continues to cure the sick person, the real story may become X's sufferings, Y's patience in the face of various tribulations, or the anguish experienced by Z's family before his or her miraculous recovery.

This sort of shift in focus is particularly evident in stories in which the teller has a direct or, more often, indirect, personal role. A good example occurs in a story told by a woman, born and raised in the small town of Maracena, now on the outskirts of Granada. Her claim (Fray

10. Boy, age sixteen, born Granada, high-school student. Single, attends mass "when my mother says I have to."
11. This would appear to be the case in many miracle accounts. For a confirmation of the eminently practical miracles of medieval France see Sigal, *L'homme et le miracle.*

Leopoldo does nothing less than resuscitate the dead) and her perspective set the story apart from the Life.[12] Unlike the friar's biographer, who would have devoted his full attention to the extraordinary intervention, the storyteller in this instance appears more interested in recounting her resurrected niece's unhappy destiny.

The woman begins by assuring her listeners (myself, the grandson of a friend, and a half-dozen friends and neighbors) that her niece was indeed dead when the friar arrived. "Yes, yes, yes, yes," she says, as if anticipating our surprise and at least initial skepticism. "They were about to begin the wake. So then when the mother [the speaker's sister] heard that Fray Leopoldo was in Maracena she called him to the house and asked him to bring the girl back to life."

When the friar encounters the grieving mother, he first tells her the story of a woman who asks the Virgin to restore her only son to life. This tale is clearly intended as a prophetic parable. "She [the Virgin]," explains the storyteller:

1. sent her [the boy's mother] a vision in which she saw her son doing all sorts of scandalous things. But the mother paid her no attention, she still wanted her son back. Then he returns to life and causes her one suffering after another. Because of the bad things he did, you see. Then Fray Leopoldo told this story [literally, "example"] to my sister because she had no idea of what was going to happen with this daughter of hers. But she too insisted and insisted until he finally ordered the girl to get up from the bed. But right away she became involved in all sorts of bad things. [Here the speaker launches into a detailed account of her niece's ensuing misfortunes.]

> *Woman, age seventy-four, born Maracena, some grade school. Widow, retired (formerly farmed family plot), regularly attends mass.*

A similar movement away from Fray Leopoldo occurs in one account of an old couple and a mysteriously flowering tree.[13] In contrast to the Life, where the old couple would certainly be of secondary interest, here the story is really as much theirs as his. Confirming the friar's power to help others, the tale also illustrates the rewards of generosity.[14]

---

12. "Resuscitation by saint" is motif number E121.4 in Thompson, *Motif-Index*. For numerous other examples see Loomis, *White Magic*, pp. 83–84, and Brewer, *Dictionary of Miracles*, pp. 78–80.

13. See Thompson, F971.5 ("flowers bloom in winter"). Numerous examples appear in Brewer, pp. 155–56 and 163.

14. The motif is Thompson, Q45.1.3 ("hospitality to saint repaid"). See Loomis, pp. 86–88, for further examples of increase and gifts from heaven.

The narrator begins by explaining that she is from Láchar, a small town presently half an hour by bus from Granada. She claims to remember Fray Leopoldo well "because he often came to visit a nephew of his who lived there."[15] After a conventional physical description of the friar (short white beard, threadbare robe, and sandals with a single thong), she launches into the body of her account:

> 2. Once there in Láchar there was a couple who was
> extremely good, but poor—very poor. So then, when the
> *Hermanico* came to ask them for alms, they had nothing in the
> house to give him except for a few almonds. The woman
> explained that they were ashamed to offer him so little, but
> there was nothing else to eat, because there was a lot of hunger
> in that time, you see. So then he thanked them for the
> almonds and went on to another house. Moments later the
> woman opens the door and sees one of these big almond trees
> full, but I mean full of very pretty, perfumed flowers. Like a
> big pink cloud. It can still be seen there, I myself have seen it
> many times.
>
> > *Woman, age forty-four, born Láchar, sixteen
> > years in Granada, two years high school. Married, housewife, attends mass every Sunday.*

Comparable shifts in vantage point are obvious in some of the best-known stories. The narrator's attention may be less on Fray Leopoldo, for instance, than on all or one of the construction workers in the story of the stubborn stone. In these cases, unlike the Life, the friar may intervene not as a response to the men's blasphemy, but rather, out of compassion for their plight.

The same process is visible in the following account of the trapped mules. Here, the irritable blasphemer of the Life is transformed into a poor but virtuous man dependent on his animals for a livelihood. Although Fray Leopoldo succeeds, as usual, in alleviating the problem, the storyteller appears most concerned with the narrow escape from potential disaster. The virtuous individual's success in fending off misfortune in "a time of great hunger" replaces the friar's horror of profanity. It is, to be sure, Fray Leopoldo and not some other holy figure who steps in to help the driver and his family. Nonetheless, his intervention is less an illustration of his power than of God's unfailing willingness "to help the good man." The woman—Dori's aunt—says:

---

15. I could find no evidence that the friar had any relatives in Láchar.

3. This mule driver was honest but poor—very poor. He had a wife who had been sick for many years, and various little ones. He worked hauling bricks, sand, whatever—an excellent person. Then one day he was passing down one of these unpaved streets, of which there were many in that time, and the wagon turned over on him, it ended up in an enormously big rut. So he began to think about his family and how they were going to suffer [because of the money the mishap was going to cost him]. Because people were very hungry then; it wasn't like today. So in that very moment Fray Leopoldo arrives and says to him, "Friend, what's going on here?" The other says, "Ah, Brother, it's that I can't get my wagon out of here." "Don't worry," *Hermanico* Leopoldo says to him. "Because God always helps the good man." And so it was. The animals got out of there in an instant, and he didn't lose a thing.

> *Woman, age fifty-four, born Granada, some grade school. Married, sells Fray Leopoldo souvenirs and other sundries, attends mass from time to time.*

Attention to Detail

Although the shift away from Fray Leopoldo in these stories signals an important trend, it is discernible in only about a third of the tales in my collection. Virtually all of the stories I recorded, however, reveal the sort of marked attention to detail obvious in the preceding examples. Attention to particulars is a near-universal hallmark of orally transmitted narratives. But in the Legends, this is not simply a function of oral transmission. Rather, it is as much or more a reflection of the storytellers' desire to concretize and render personally meaningful even the best-known stories and to incorporate Fray Leopoldo into a larger and very specifically Spanish past.

The attention to detail found in Legends contrasts with the Life's propensity to generalize. The plot of the following account of how Fray Leopoldo gives sight to a blind girl strongly resembles an incident involving a dumb child in the friar's biography. The storyteller, a woman whose daughter lives in Luís Antonio's apartment building, claims to have read about the event in "one of those little booklets" (a devotional bulletin containing excerpts from the Life), as well as to have heard of the occurrence from various friends and relatives. Although in no way identical, the accounts which appear below reveal a number of quite obvious similarities.

In both cases, the friar makes an enigmatic prophecy regarding the girl's future ability to see or hear. Each of the two strongly suggests, without actually asserting, Fray Leopoldo's own role in the apparent miracle, which immediately follows his death. In each account the mother telephones the monastery in order to inform the friar, only to be told that he has just died.

LIFE

4. Years before [the friar's death] a woman presented her daughter to this Servant of God so that he might pray for her, because she was already seven years old and didn't speak a word, despite the fact that she could hear perfectly. Fray Leopoldo's response was a bit enigmatic: "Madam, your daughter will speak when I fall silent."
So then: that morning [following his death] she suddenly began to speak, not like one who is learning, but like one who has known how from an early age.
Her mother, in the midst of the family's rejoicing, recalled the vague prediction of the venerable Capuchin. She telephoned the monastery:
"Yes, he perished last night," was the response.

ORAL TRADITION

5. He [Fray Leopoldo] used to go from farm to farm. He used to go from farm to farm a lot, very poor, very thin because he barely ate. Those were bad times, the people endured great hunger, so he went about asking for alms and distributing all that the people gave him. So then, the first miracle he worked was on one of the farms on the road to Padul. The mother of a blind girl asked him to help her, and he felt very sorry for her—such a pretty girl who couldn't see the lovely things of this world. Dolores, the girl's name was Dolores. I met her grandmother in the house of my mother-in-law a long time ago when she [the mother-in-law] still lived on Air Street. Well, he then stroked the girl's head and told the mother, "She will see when I lose my sight." Like that. "She will see when I lose my sight." Well, the months went by. The years went by. She barely remembered anymore what he had said. Until the day, some ten years later, in which the girl begins to distinguish shapes. And soon afterward she begins to see for real. So then the mother remembers Fray Leopoldo and telephones the monastery in Granada. "Isn't there a little friar who used to travel from farm to farm a lot? Well, I want to

talk with him." Then they told her, "We are very sorry, madam, but he died a few days ago."

> *Woman, age fifty-five, born Granada, some high school. Married, works at home, attends mass regularly.*

The differences between the narratives, however, are as great as the similarities. The most obvious of all is the level of language. Spare and highly formal in the first case, language is repetitive and familiar in the second. The Life, for instance, uses the distinctly literary *algún tanto enigmático* (a bit enigmatic) as well as the more elevated *fallecer* (to die, employed exclusively for human beings) in place of *morir* (to die, used for all living creatures) in referring to the friar's death. A "Servant of God" and "venerable Capuchin" in the Life, Fray Leopoldo becomes "a little friar" in the Legend. While the author of the Life seeks to heighten the drama of the situation by keeping details to a minimum, the oral account is less focused, more diffuse. In addition, the storyteller achieves a familiar tone through the introduction of a number of colloquial-sounding diminutives ("such a pretty little girl," "her little head," and, again, "a little friar").

Another immediately apparent difference is length. Not surprisingly, the oral account of the story is twice as long as the printed version. While the friar's biographer gives no information about the girl except her age at the time of her encounter with Fray Leopoldo, the storyteller states that the child is called "Dolores" (a name that underscores her plight), that she is physically attractive, that she lives on a farm on the road to the city of Padul, and that she begins to see ten years after the friar's prophecy. The effect is both to foster the listener's sense of a particular person and to encourage sympathy for the blind child.

The Legend also makes Fray Leopoldo a physical as well as moral presence. A disembodied voice in the Life, he is shown in the Legend traveling from farm to farm distributing alms. As in the Life, the friar speaks directly to the parent, but he acknowledges the child's presence by stroking her head. Then too, at the same time that the reference in the oral account to his poverty and thinness ("he barely ate") appears to reinforce the Life's emphasis on the friar's asceticism, his physical appearance in this case also calls attention to the sufferings of the populace at large. ("Those were bad times; the people endured great hunger" the storyteller continues.)

Finally, although the account is not a personal anecdote, the speaker manages to relate the event to herself through the suggestion of an indirect acquaintance with one of the actors. That the woman's mother-in-law once met the blind girl's grandmother has no practical bearing on the event at hand. But by noting this relationship, she effectively places her own stamp on an incident familiar to many. (We have already witnessed a similar sort of personalization in the woman from Lanchal's assertion that she herself has seen the almond tree that the friar is said to have caused to spring up from the ground.)

This sense of the concrete and the resolutely individual is particularly obvious in many Legend tellers' attention to place. In line with the Life's tendency to situate events in "the center of the city" or "somewhere in the countryside" (or to omit such details altogether), the only landmark mentioned in the preceding account of the dumb child is the Capuchin monastery. The oral version, in contrast, identifies a farm on the road to Padul and a well-known street (the Calle del Aire in the Albaicín district of the city). Other storytellers may single out a café, a familiar commercial establishment, one of Granada's various plazas, or such-and-such a building in Divina Infantita ("I forget the name, but on the corner there's a rug shop"). Instead of simply stopping to aid a child seized by convulsions, Fray Leopoldo may halt "right there in front of that warehouse that used to belong to a son of the Gómez family—was it Jorge? No, Luís. Luís, I think." Many actions unfold in places associated with the city's Moorish past. Although the massive Elvira Arch, located near the Capuchin monastery, is probably the most common, the Alhambra and the Generalife also figure in a number of tales.[16]

Time is an equally important element to many storytellers. Unlike the biography, in which a hazy past usually extends into an equally undifferentiated present, the oral narratives often specify the date a particular event occurs. "It was on the twenty-seventh of July that Fray Leopoldo saved my neighbor's son from drowning," a young typist asserts. "That occurred in 1937," says a man who has just recounted how Fray Leopoldo moved the stubborn stone. Sometimes, a storyteller will even give the day and hour of a particular occurrence. Dori, for instance, recounts how Fray Leopoldo caused a lemon tree to flower on a wintry Thursday afternoon. "That's what my grandmother told me," she insists. "It made such a big impression on her that she remembered everything about it. I've forgotten a lot of details from the story because I was just a child then. But I am sure that it was a Thursday—a Thursday afternoon."

16. It is not clear to me whether the arch figures in so many tales because of its proximity to the Capuchin monastery or because of some half-forgotten magical properties associated with the Moorish past. Both factors, to be sure, may be at work.

The tendency to concretize and in the process to render the event in question both more vivid to others and more meaningful to oneself is most notable of all in relation to the actors in a given event. Sometimes the storytellers themselves appear within the narrative. Thus in relating to me and two of her coresidents how Fray Leopoldo aided a childless neighbor to conceive, Doña Hortensia reminisces about her own acquaintance with Fray Leopoldo during the years she served as secretary-treasurer of the Third Franciscan Order. She recalls both his enormous kindness ("People would come for miles so that they could talk with him about a problem") and his unfailing honesty. ("Once," she says, "he came to see me around midnight because he had found some coins among the onions at the bottom of his sack. I could see he had been torn between his worry about waking me and his discomfort with keeping money intended for the poor in his possession. Even in those times, you know, people thought he was a saint.")

Doña Hortensia then goes on to affirm her faith in miracles, and to recount an instance of divine intervention she says she witnessed as a teen-ager at Lourdes. Although she eventually reverts to her original theme and, with it, to the third person, the story below is clearly anecdotal. [17]

> 6. It's that I, yes, believe a great deal in miracles. Because it so
> happens that when I was fourteen, we went to Lourdes. And
> there we saw a woman all twisted. She couldn't walk at all;
> her leg was totally swollen, you know? So then she entered the
> water [a curative pool] and right away began to shout,
> "Thanks to the most holy Virgin! Thanks to the most holy
> Virgin!" In this way. And she was crying; everybody cried.
> And I, well, I began to cry too. [Here Doña Hortensia's eyes
> begin to tear at the memory.] So then, I believe that the saints
> work great miracles. And Fray Leopoldo was a very saintly
> man, everybody knows it.

Doña Hortensia is by no means alone in her penchant for personal reminiscence. In some stories, the teller is a principal actor. One woman, for instance, recounts how Fray Leopoldo places his hand on the head of her husband, who has been sick for months but who then hurries home, healed, and changes into work clothes. [18] A man now in his fifties tells

---

17. For a comprehensive introduction to oral personal experience narratives and scholarship about these see Stahl, *Literary Folkloristics*.

18. Woman, age fifty-five, born Granada, some grade school. Married, sells ice cream, does not attend mass.

how the friar mysteriously appears to comfort him following the loss of his mother. "I was asleep," he explains, "and when I opened my eyes I saw him standing over me, as if he were wrapped in light."[19] Still another man describes how Fray Leopoldo arrives unbidden to kiss the forehead of his apparently healthy little brother who dies unexpectedly in his sleep that night.[20]

Actors or eyewitnesses in a story may be friends, relatives, acquaintances, or friends of friends of the teller. Often, the speakers supply proper names or refer to the occupation, residence, or family background of individuals in the narrative. They may refer to a man, for instance, not simply as "Manuel" but as "Manuel López, the cousin of Pepe. The one who used to own the newsstand in the Mariana Pineda Plaza." Or they may explain how a favorite uncle just so happened to be having coffee in the café across the street from where Fray Leopoldo aids a man trampled by a stampeding horse. "He [the uncle] was sitting right there in the old Victoria when it happened," a middle-aged man says. "They've torn it down, but it was famous. And from where he was sitting he could see absolutely everything."[21] The teller of the following tale spends as much time identifying the supporting actors in the story and their surroundings as she does in describing the mysterious appearance of the oil. In so doing she manages to recreate a landscape that no longer exists.

> 7. There was a very rich woman who lived around here in a house in a cross street of Gran Capitán Avenue. A very pretty, three-story house, it had a really lovely inner courtyard full of all sorts of plants. So then he [Fray Leopoldo] always used to go there to ask alms for the poor. So then, one day he went in search of a little oil. Because today this monastery is rich, but in that time it was poor, very poor—the friars had a vegetable garden on which they depended for food. Well then, when he

---

The cure in question is one of those associated with the Elvira Arch. Because the sick man cannot sleep, the couple is taking a predawn stroll when they encounter Fray Leopoldo beneath the arch. He blesses the man, who is immediately healed at the friar's touch.

19. Man, age fifty-seven, born Granada, grade-school education. Married, supermarket guard, attends mass "from time to time."

The incident is motif V222.1 in Thomas ("marvelous light accompanying saint"). For a list of other holy figures from whose head light emanates see Loomis, *White Magic*, p. 36.

20. Man, age fifty-one, born Almería, some high school. Married, businessman, attends mass "from time to time."

The friar's kiss is not perceived as causing the child's death, but rather as foretelling an unavoidable occurrence.

21. Man, age fifty-six, born Málaga province, some grade school. Married, taxi driver, does not attend mass.

asked for the oil, the maid—her name was Emilia, she's still alive, her mistress, no, but she, Emilia, yes—then she went to look for the oil in the jug where it was kept. But there was nothing, the jug was totally empty. Then the woman said for him to come back later, that she would send for oil from the farm. But he said no, that there was already oil in the jug and that it wasn't worth the trouble to send for more. So then the maid, very puzzled, went to see again. And the jug was full, completely full.

> *Woman, age sixty-four, born Granada province, no formal education. Widowed, newspaper vendor, occasionally attends mass.*

Although personalization most often takes the form of attention to particulars, it is also obvious in the introduction of more or less lengthy tangents within the body of the story or personal reminiscence or oral history in a preface or conclusion. Thus Doña Hortensia prefaces her account of how Fray Leopoldo answered her neighbor's prayers with a long explanation of how she first met the woman ("I used to spend summers in the mountains, you see, and my house was near her cottage . . .). We have already seen that she later interrupts the action to reminisce about the friar and to affirm her own faith in miracles. Although she then resumes her account of her childless neighbor, she concludes with a long description of each of the five sons and daughters subsequently born to the couple.

Particularly in stories employing the sorts of readily recognizable folk motifs I have identified in this and other chapters, it is tempting to regard this sort of information as extraneous and to simply exclude it from analysis.[22] Storytellers themselves, however, clearly consider it integral to their accounts. Because their listeners almost never demand that they get on with the "real" story, one often encounters narratives that go on for half an hour; in the Life one might find a paragraph. The tale of Hortensia's childless neighbor, for instance, took her almost an hour to recount. And though many narratives are shorter, others are far longer.

Once again, it would be easy to attribute the abundance of detail in Legends to the special characteristics of oral creation.[23] It is quite true

22. Dégh and Vászonyi caution that the legend must be treated as a narrative entity and stress the importance of apparently extraneous aspects such as introductory remarks, interjected comments, closing remarks, and explanatory, supplementary, or contrasting stories. For a fuller explanation see their "Legend and Belief," p. 101.

23. The differences between oral transmission and written composition have generated an ample bibliography. For examples of two very different approaches see Finnegan, *Oral Poetry*, and Ong, *Orality and Literacy*.

that storytellers do not have the same space constraints faced by the friar's biographer. Their narration is limited only by the time at their disposal and their success in holding their listeners' attention. But the Legend teller also has different motives, which favor the inclusion of a wealth of detail.

We have seen that Fray Angel, like a long line of hagiographers before him, sets out to illustrate the moral qualities he finds embodied in his subject. In order to achieve this overriding didactic purpose, he strings together a long list of similar examples whose force resides in their cumulative effect. Particulars are kept to a minimum in these incidents in order not to obscure the larger points they are intended to illumine. This insistence on the general fosters a resemblance between individual incidents within the Life and a variety of medieval and Golden Age exempla.[24]

Few Legend tellers share this compelling sense of purpose. This is not to say at least some do not see Fray Leopoldo as an exemplar or that their stories do not have a discernible moral. The woman who recounts how the friar causes an almond tree to appear before a poor couple's doorstep clearly believes that generosity will be rewarded. Doña Hortensia asserts that the story of her neighbor proves that even the humblest human being can exercise miraculous powers. "A Fray Leopoldo le sobran los milagros" (Fray Leopoldo has a multitude of miracles), she declares triumphantly. But few storytellers are exclusively or even primarily interested in the larger vision so important to the friar's biographer. Most set out to make the story meaningful to themselves and others, and often, to relive a specifically Spanish past that they or others known to them experienced firsthand. Fray Angel consistently pares away anything that might deflect attention from the friar. Legend tellers enthusiastically incorporate detail.

Varying Visions of the Supernatural

Legends are also distinguished from the Life by their wide range of attitudes toward the supernatural. Some storytellers portray Fray Leopoldo

---

The conception of folk narrative as a performance rather than a text has influenced much recent folklore scholarship. For an overview see Fine, *The Folklore Text*. An excellent recent example of the "performance approach" is Bauman, *Story, Performance, and Event*.

24. The exemplum exerted a particularly strong influence in the Iberian Peninsula, where it remained in vogue into the Golden Age. For an introduction to the genre see Bremond, Le Goff, and Schmitt, *L'Exemplum*.

engaging in highly improbable, though not necessarily impossible, actions much like those we have examined in the biography. Others, however, focus on extraordinary occurrences of a sort largely foreign to the Life. Still others omit any mention of miracles or explicitly deny their possibility while continuing to portray Fray Leopoldo responding to need.

Many of the storytellers who attribute miraculous powers to Fray Leopoldo display a circumspection reminiscent of the Life. These individuals, like the friar's biographer, may utilize distancing techniques that allow them merely to suggest the extraordinary quality of the deeds in question. And although these persons make up the majority of those who relate supernatural actions, others do not shy away from, and may even call attention to, stories about the friar's suspension of natural laws. Not infrequently the storyteller will insist that Fray Leopoldo is simply following in the footsteps of other local wonder workers, most notably San Juan de Dios, the sixteenth-century founder of a number of hospitals for Granada's poor.

In contrast, for instance, to the Life's account of a startled young nurse's aide who discovers Fray Leopoldo hovering several inches above his bed, these latter storytellers may recount how he elevates high above the ground in one of the city's many churches. In the following narrative, for example, Fray Leopoldo soars upward toward the ceiling of the city cathedral in full view of the other worshippers. Although the account is unusually dramatic, it recalls a small number of other, often extremely lyrical descriptions of how the friar transforms an enormous stone into a pebble or plucks a star out of the sky to light the path of a lost child. Note that Fray Leopoldo's apparently involuntary, miraculous ascent occasions the temporary suspension, and thus takes precedence over, the formal religious celebration. (In at least one version of the story, he interrupts the particularly solemn Easter mass.)

> 8. What I know about Fray Leopoldo is this—that one day everyone was praying in the cathedral, everyone on their knees, praying, and he also, with closed eyes, on his knees. And suddenly he began to levitate, to rise upward without realizing anything was happening. Everybody saw him. He didn't notice anything until his little head had almost scraped the ceiling. But those beneath him, yes, they were astonished. "Look at the *Hermanico*," they said to one another. And the bishop had to stop the mass until he [Fray Leopoldo] returned to earth. It was my mother who told me the story, but

everybody knows it. That's to say, I didn't see it, but I know
it's true. Yes, it's true for me.

> *Man, age forty-one, some grade school. Married, janitor, attends mass "every once in a while."*

The narrator's insistence on the truth of the event is as noteworthy
as its frankly marvelous nature. Unlike the friar's biographer, who customarily places the burden of truth on either a lone eyewitness or a
vaguely defined collective source ("some say. . . . "), this man credits
the story specifically to his mother and more generally to the community at large. Moreover, he concludes by taking a personal stand on its
authenticity. The defiant tone of the last sentence suggests that he anticipates his listeners' skepticism but that the story remains true, despite
their potential objections, for him.

Not all storytellers seek to justify blatantly supernatural deeds. Indeed, some Legends are little more than extended descriptions of how
the friar catches a child who has tumbled from the window of a multistory building or how he fills an empty oven with steaming loaves of
bread.[25] If asked directly why Fray Leopoldo performs a particular extraordinary action, they may shake their head or shrug. Dori, for instance, says she does not know why the friar caused the lemon tree to
blossom in the heart of winter. "He worked many miracles, that's all,"
she asserts. For her, the attraction of the story of the stubborn stone is,
above all, its mystery. "No one can explain it!" she exclaims with obvious enthusiasm.

> 9. It's a mystery, don't you know? Because it was so cold one
> could have died, and yet there was the tree full of fruit and
> flowers. All of a sudden, with no warning. Because Fray
> Leopoldo was this way. He appeared to be one of these persons
> with no importance whatsoever but when he went down the
> street, people observed marvelous things. I can't explain it to
> you; no one can explain it. But that it happened, yes, it
> happened. Of that you can be sure.

In contrast to these individuals, for whom the miraculous action *is*
the story, others play down or omit any mention of the supernatural.
Although the underlying challenge structure remains intact, the friar
now resolves the problems with which others present him through

---

25. See Thompson, D2166 ("magic help from falling"), and D2106.1.5 ("saint multiplies food"). See also Brewer, pp. 145–49. Loomis, pp. 86–87, offers specific examples of
the multiplication of bread.

strictly this-world means. The following version of the tale of the stubborn stone, for instance, resembles others we have seen except for its conspicuous omission of all references to the supernatural. Although the efficacy of the friar's counsel is highlighted, neither the workers nor the narrator suggest the slightest challenge to natural laws.

> 10. There was a big old stone in the middle of the road near the Plaza del Triunfo. And around it five workers, one of them an acquaintance of ours by the name of Antonio—Antonio Gómez. In that time there was nothing motorized; people struggled in order to survive. So then, these workers had been battling that stone all morning. They were exhausted, on the point of quitting, when Fray Leopoldo arrived. So then, he calmed them down. "Rest a little," he told them, "because I promise you that stone is just about to budge." And that's the way it was. One of them got up and left, but the others did as he had told them. And the stone came sliding out for them without further problems.
>
> > *Man, age fifty-three, born Granada, two years high school. Married, owns open-air restaurant, mass "once every few months."*

The storyteller in this case simply skirts the issue of the supernatural. The following speaker, in contrast, clearly hesitates to compare the friar with an official saint. Although she stops short of saying that the cure was *not* miraculous, her presentation casts doubt upon its supernatural character.

> 11. I saw Fray Leopoldo a lot when I was a little girl. My father had a soda bottle warehouse on San Isidro Street, and he [Fray Leopoldo] passed through the neighborhood a lot. People had a lot of confidence in him. If a child got sick, it wasn't the doctor or priest who was called, it was Fray Leopoldo. Once I saw him spend a whole morning beside a sick child—to see if the fever wouldn't break, you know? Now I don't say he was a Saint John of God, a Saint Teresa. I don't say that he worked miracles. But all the same, the child got better. This is certain.
>
> > *Woman, age sixty-two, born Granada, forty-four years in Maracena, four years grade school. Widowed, housewife, mass every Sunday.*

This and other storytellers' cautious assessments of the friar and his actions may reflect their awareness of his as-yet unofficial status vis-à-vis the Roman Catholic Church. But their hesitation may also underscore their sense that the present is qualitatively different from the past, a point about which we will say more in a later chapter. "Such things were much more common long ago," a friend of Dori's mother notes.[26] "A man like this only appears once in a century," says a young man seeking work as a night watchman in Luís Antonio's bank. "Generosity like his does not exist today."[27] Other storytellers suggest that unassuming acts of kindness have superseded extraordinary actions as a criterion for sanctity. For them, simplicity and disinterested concern for others represent the ultimate virtues in an increasingly materialistic and self-centered world. "I am from Extremadura," a handkerchief vendor says:

> 12. I'm not from here, with the result that I never knew Saint Leopoldo. But I have many friends who have told me how he passed by here with his little burro, asking for alms and sharing everything he received with the poor.
>> *Man, age sixty-one, born Extremadura, twenty-three years in Granada, some high school. Single, handkerchief shop owner, attends mass most Sundays.*

In a small number of Legends, the friar goes so far as to explicitly eschew supernatural means. In at least one account of the unyielding stone, for instance, he informs the workers that he could singlehandedly remove the obstacle if he so chose. "But why should I do this?" he demands. "You yourselves can do the same thing if you ask God's help."[28] Buoyed by his words, the weary men renew their efforts. Minutes later they unearth a massive chunk of granite.

On other occasions it is the storyteller who affirms the friar's preference for this-world solutions. Some individuals suggest that attention-provoking miracles are at odds with Fray Leopoldo's humble, unprepossessing style. ("He was a saint," a retired telephone operator assures her listeners, "and all saints know how to work miracles, God gives them that power. But Fray Leopoldo was so modest, so ordinary [tan periquillo el de los palotes] that he did not like to call attention to himself.")[29] These individuals may contrast the friar with San Juan de

26. Woman, age fifty-eight, born Granada, grade school. Married, knits sweaters for sale in baby boutique, attends mass regularly.
27. Man, age twenty-two, born Granada, high school. Single, looking for job, attends mass from time to time.
28. Man, age twenty-nine, born Granada, some high school. Single, works as clerk in electronic goods store, does not attend mass.
29. Woman, age sixty-one, born Granada, high school. Married, retired telephone operator, attends mass "almost every Sunday." The speaker literally compares Fray Leopoldo to "a parakeet like that on every perch."

Dios, insisting that both were saints, although each had his own style. ("San Juan de Dios," one woman explains, "was a very talented professor [un catedrático de altos vuelos] and performed many great miracles. Fray Leopoldo, no, he was more simple and he taught through his own example.")[30] The implication here is that while miracles are possible, all saints are not necessarily thaumaturges.

Other persons negate any possibility of the supernatural and reject miraculous actions as a criterion of sanctity, thereby implicitly—or, from time to time, explicitly—challenging church dogma. "I believe in the saints—they are good men like Fray Leopoldo," one man says succinctly. "But I don't believe in miracles. No, ma'am. I don't believe in them a bit."[31]

Attitudes toward the Events Described

The majority of Legend tellers resemble the friar's biographer in their presentation of their stories as fact or possible fact. Although they, much like Fray Angel, may distance themselves from the events at hand through techniques such as crediting the story to a third party, the tale is still offered as a true, or at least potentially true, account.

And yet, although these persons constitute a clear majority of those who recount Legends, a significant number of others express doubt or outright disbelief about the stories they nonetheless proceed to tell. These disclaimers usually appear in a conclusion or a preface, rather than within the body of the tale. Their presence in the larger narrative performance, characteristic of legends as a genre, represents a decided departure from the Life.[32]

A good number of these accounts focus on supernatural actions much like others we have already seen. Once Fray Leopoldo has completed the action, however, the tellers proceed to place themselves at a remove from the tale in a variety of ways. They may shift the burden of proof to their sources in a manner that suggests not cautious neutrality, but rather, a decidedly un-Life-like skepticism. "This is not my story, but many people here in Granada tell it," the speaker may declare. Or "I heard this from an old woman who used to live down the street from my Aunt Rosa, but I don't know if it's true."

30. Woman, age fifty-five, born Granada, some grade school. Widow, works as cleaning woman, usually attends mass.
31. Man, age fifty-nine, born Granada, grade school. Married, watch repairman, attends mass occasionally.
32. For a discussion of belief and disbelief in the legend see Dégh and Vázsonyi, "Legend and Belief."

In addition to those who cast doubt on the action they have just described, others register outright disbelief. "I really don't believe this story," an individual may flatly assert. Some claim to find an event they have just related "hard to imagine" or "a very lovely story—but that doesn't mean that I say it really happened."

The speaker in some instances may appear to simply dismiss the incident in question. "This is just an example of the sort of tales you hear all the time in Granada," he or she may say. Luís Antonio recounts a number of Fray Leopoldo's miracles as good examples of self-deception. "I hear lots of these stories when my girlfriend's classmates are about to take an exam for which they haven't studied," he asserts with a chuckle. "Some of them need a miracle to pass the course, that's sure!" Although he admits that some of these accounts "are really not bad stories," he nonetheless dismisses them as wishful thinking. "One can believe in them only if one is willing to overlook the facts," he says.

Luís Antonio nonetheless admits that some things are harder to comprehend than others. One Sunday afternoon, for instance, when I was having tea with him and his mother in his apartment, the telephone rang. His father was calling to say that the car in which he, Luís Antonio's brother, and the brother's girlfriend had been riding had just overturned. Although no one was injured, the car was badly damaged. Luis Antonio immediately rushed off to collect the three.

When they all returned about half an hour later, the young woman recounted how she had seen Fray Leopoldo at the side of the car the moment of the accident. Luís Antonio's mother exclaimed that it must have been the friar who saved them from a potential disaster. Luís Antonio, like his brother and his father, remained silent. I later asked him what he thought about the possibility of supernatural intervention in the case. He responded with considerably greater than usual restraint. "To tell you the truth," he said:

> 13. I have more faith in my brother's reflexes than in the saint.
> But I am not going to say anything to them. What for?
> Besides, it is true that there could have been a
> disaster—something very ugly. The car was badly damaged,
> but nothing happened to them. It doesn't strike me as any sort
> of miracle, but even so, there are things in life that are not
> easily explained.

On other occasions individuals who reject the literal truth of the event in question are nonetheless quite willing to regard it as a metaphor. "I believe that a person's faith is very great," explains one woman. "Now if Fray Leopoldo actually moved mountains—well, it is *as if* he did."[33]

A denial of the literal truth of a story does not necessarily keep the tellers from professing allegiance to what they see as its underlying moral. They may, for instance, follow a description of how the friar nonchalantly moves a boulder with an assertion of the figurative truth of the event. "Of course I don't believe that a big stone can be changed into a pebble," says a friend of Luís Antonio:

> 14. It is only a way of talking. Because Fray Leopoldo had a way with people, he was able to do things which a more educated person could never have done. So when people tell you he changed stones to pebbles, they are really saying that he was an unusual person. That he was extraordinarily kind, perhaps—extraordinarily good.
>
> > *Woman, age twenty-four, born Granada, university education. Single, journalist, mass "every once in a great while."*

Other narrators identify their tales as outright fictions. This assessment, however, is not necessarily negative. Outright refutations of miracles may be accompanied by expressions of respect for the friar's ability to inspire such marvelous stories. Thus even those storytellers who dissociate themselves most emphatically from their own accounts may nonetheless pronounce the friar remarkable. "Of course Fray Leopoldo didn't spend his time catching people who fell off the top of tall buildings while he just so happened to be walking by," says a young doctor who has come to visit Doña Hortensia. "Nor did he go about causing trees to bloom in the dead of winter like he does in the story I've just told you. But for me the fact that people attribute these sorts of feats to Fray Leopoldo is indeed a miracle. What immense faith he must have inspired for people to make such claims about him!"[34]

Storytellers may also see accounts of the friar's extraordinary actions as testament to the power of the collective imagination. Artists and university professors recounted some of the most fantastic and beautiful narratives in my collection. While some of the older persons in this group were disposed to find at least a degree of truth in these stories, the majority offered them as prime examples of the esthetic worth of

33. Woman, age thirty-seven, born Granada, high school. Married, works at home, usually attends mass.
34. Man, age thirty-four, born Barcelona, medical school. Married, doctor, occasionally attends mass.

popular literary creation. One sculptor spent a whole afternoon regaling me with miracle tales he had heard from various acquaintances. He took unmistakable relish in describing how Fray Leopoldo had rescued a child who had been trapped on the top of a fifteen-story apartment building in the center of Granada and how every rosebush in an acquaintance's garden had once burst into flower on the friar's arrival. "Are these stories true?" he responded when I asked him. "They are a true reflection of the lyricism of Granada. What more could one ask?"[35]

These disclaimers, to be sure, allow the tellers to both have and eat their proverbial cake. The persons who were most skeptical of their own accounts sometimes revealed an unexpected ambivalence when pressed. Luís Antonio, for instance, regularly made a face when I mentioned Fray Leopoldo, but he looked genuinely shocked when I once jokingly declared that I was going to make a vow to the friar for success in an apparently futile situation involving a job. In keeping with the reserve he had displayed in the case of the car accident involving his own family, he counseled me to act with caution, or at least propriety ("no, no, of course I don't believe in these things, but all the same you shouldn't take them lightly"). Likewise, one man who assured me he did not believe a word of the story of a cure he had just related sported a large medal of the friar about his neck. "I wear it to please my wife," he responded with obvious embarrassment when I asked about it.[36] "People have to believe in something," storytellers often remarked. "I don't say that young people—that I—don't believe in anything," says a university student who has just finished recounting a tale of Fray Leopoldo he attributes to his grandmother:

> 15. We all probably believe a little in this business of saints in case God exists. Because if God exists, we don't want to go to hell. It's that no one knows anything about the other world, if there is one or there isn't, see?
>
> *Man, age twenty-two, born Granada, university education. Single, law student, "almost never" attends mass.*

In sum, although there are individual Legends that closely resemble the formal biography of Fray Leopoldo, the tales as a group reveal a number of important differences. Their emphasis on situations of need involving members of the lay population, their tendency toward personalization and "historicization," and their varying attitudes toward the supernatural, as well as toward the story proper on occasion, set them apart from the Life. A number of these features will reappear, albeit in different guises, as we now turn to our second group of narratives, the Counterlegends.

1. An official portrait of Fray Leopoldo taken in the
1930s. Courtesy Fray Angel de León.

2. Upper right: A representation of the friar with the Virgin Mary in the background adorns the cover of a miniature pamphlet containing information about Fray Leopoldo and various recommended prayers. Courtesy Fray Angel de León.

3. Lower right: Reproduction of a photograph of the friar distributed as a memento of the consecration of the interim crypt in the old Capuchin church, February 1959. Courtesy Fray Angel de León.

RECUERDO DE LA BENDICION SOLEMNE
DE LA CAPILLA DE LA SANTA CRUZ
Y CRIPTA DE FRAY LEOPOLDO DE ALPANDEIRE

Granada, 15-2-1959

4. The tiny tombstone in the city cemetery where Fray Leopoldo was initially buried following his death on 9 February 1956.

5. The consecration of the crypt in the new Franciscan Church of the
Divine Shepherdess on 15 February 1969.

FRAY LEOPOLDO
DE ALPANDEIRE

GRACIAS, ABUELITO
POR TUS OJOS.
TU MIRADA.
POR LA SONRISA EN TUS LABIOS
Y POR LA PAZ DE TU ALMA.

6. A popular memento of Fray Leopoldo, which pictures him against a backdrop of traditional houses and the palaces of the Alhambra. The caption reads, "Thank you, Grandfather, for your eyes, for your gaze, for the smile on your lips, and the peace in your soul."

7. Mourners waiting to view Fray Leopoldo's body. In the background one can see the narrow door of the old Capuchin church. Built in 1613, it was demolished in the latter part of the 1960s to allow for the construction of a modern building. Courtesy Romero Fotocolor.

8. Vendors outside the Church of the Divine Shepherdess in whose basement Fray Leopoldo's crypt is situated. Although they specialize in mementos of the friar, they also sell school notebooks, socks, aspirin, and hair barrettes.

9. A young beggar and her child outside the Church of the Divine Shepherdess. She is one of many such individuals who regularly seek the aid of visitors to Fray Leopoldo's crypt on the ninth of the month.

10. A storyteller and his cart in Fuentenueva Street, not far from the Plaza de Triunfo. "Do I believe Fray Leopoldo worked miracles?" he asks. "Well, I don't *disbelieve* it."

11. A woman, now in her fifties, describes the "Garden of Happiness" that Fray Leopoldo helped to tend. She and her husband used the implement that hangs above her head for weighing meat when they ran a butcher shop behind their house in the Chana district of the city. The weight and similar tools of the trade now serve as wall decorations.

12. Penitents in traditional costume pause to chat in Puentezuelas Street during one of the many neighborhood processions that take place during Holy Week.

13. A vendor and his young customer in a makeshift stall on the Plaza del Triunfo between the Capuchin monastery and the Elvira Arch, or Gate, mentioned by Arab chroniclers of the ninth century.

14. An old flower vendor in Bib-Rambla Plaza offers the cherry blossoms of early spring to passersby. A portrait of Pope John Paul II and a calendar with a picture of Fray Leopoldo hang above her head.

15. Teen-agers painting an antiautomobile mural on a wall in the Calle Elvira, once Granada's principal thoroughfare. They are mounting a campaign to reserve the street for the exclusive use of pedestrians.

16. An older woman in widow's black speaks with a Capuchin friar in sandals and flowing beard.

17. "WE WOMEN ARE THE ONES WHO GIVE BIRTH, WE SHOULD DECIDE THE RIGHT TO AN ABORTION," says the writing on the wall of a crooked street just around the corner from the archbishop's palace.

18. A girl in a parochial school uniform holds flowers for Fray
Leopoldo. In the background of the Plaza del Triunfo one can
distinguish the sixteenth-century Hospital Real, now the administrative
headquarters for the University of Granada.

19. Another child swings upside down outside an open-air café deserted in the aftermath of a late spring rain.

20. A student outside the law school of the University of Granada. A female law student dressed in pants would have been somewhat unusual during the time of Fray Leopoldo.

21. An old man in an overcoat and plaid bedroom slippers soaks up a bit of sun in a doorway in the Albaicín, the old Moorish quarter of the city.

22. A group of women converse in the middle of one of Granada's chic main arteries, the Gran Vía de Colón, not far from the Church of the Divine Shepherdess.

23. The Alhambra looms above the city, a constant reminder of Granada's Moorish past. This view is from the Albaicín.

CHAPTER FOUR

Counterlegends

All of the narratives we have seen up to this point portray Fray Leopoldo responding positively to a challenge. Although the particulars of this challenge vary, the friar's exemplary response does not. Counterlegends present a striking contrast to this by now familiar pattern. Some of the tales we will examine here revolve around an unmistakably negative response. Others, which do portray the friar in a favorable manner, center on the opposition he encounters in the course of a positive response. Although it is true that Fray Leopoldo is shown to resolve a given problem in this second instance, the true focus of the tale has shifted.

Both the structure and the often explicit anticlericalism distinguish Counterlegends from Legends. And yet the former, like the latter, reveals a wide range of attitudes toward Fray Leopoldo and the supernatural that sets them apart from the formal Life.

In the first part of this chapter, I discuss the primary characteristics of Counterlegends. I then argue that the diversity of viewpoints so evident in both Legend and Counterlegend does more than confirm their insistent pluralism; it also indicates a rejection of all manner of institutions. Even though Legends rarely, if ever, reveal the virulent anticlericalism evident in Counterlegends, they, too, often champion the individual and the local in the face of institutional authority.

Counterlegends and the Life

Before embarking on an examination of representative narratives, the reader once again may profit from a brief description of the storytellers.

127

As already noted, tellers of Counterlegends are on the whole less apt than Legend tellers to have had access to schooling and they therefore tend to hold lower-paying, lower-status jobs. They are also considerably less apt to engage in formal religious activities.

As in the case of Legend tellers, however, one can find exceptions to this pattern. Many of those who told extremely anticlerical stories, for instance, turned out to attend mass every Sunday. Likewise, some of the severest critics of the Fray Leopoldo devotion had made various successful vows (*promesas*) to the friar.

One good example of a Counterlegend teller is the shoemaker, Manolo. Short and stocky in the bright blue long-sleeved coveralls worn by Spanish workmen, he loves to listen to jokes, rumors, and all manner of stories, which he promptly passes on to others. He also likes to argue for hours about politics.

Unlike the majority of his peers, Manolo has never married. Now forty-four years old, he continues to live with his parents and an invalid sister—a nun until her illness—in a subsidized housing project. ("Our house may be ugly, but it's cheap," he says with a laugh.)

Manolo grew up in the Albaicín—the old Moorish quarter of the city where Doña Hortensia once lived—during the difficult period following the civil war. A former student of one of Padre Andrés Manjón's Ave María schools, he has strong reservations about his education ("we were so busy praying," he notes, "that we barely learned to read"). He joined his father in the shoe repair trade when he was a teen-ager. In the slow summer months, the two sold watermelons on a streetcorner. ("The richest customers would always make us cut a slice, then purse their lips and say, 'Oh no, too wet, too dry, too sweet, too sour,' " he says with a grimace and a wink.)

Like Dori, Manolo believes in the evil eye, which he describes as "a scientific fact." In contrast, he refers to religion as mere superstition. Although a calendar with Fray Leopoldo's picture hangs in Manolo's shoe shop ("someone gave it to me," he says hastily), he dismisses the friar as an invention of the Capuchins. "This business of the saints is just a business," he declares loudly. When his Aunt Mari chides him ("you have no respect," she says), he gleefully agrees.

Rosi, a large, handsome woman who does not look her nearly fifty years, shares Manolo's lack of enthusiasm for Fray Leopoldo. As a child, she lived with her parents and seven siblings in an alley behind the Capuchin monastery and often played at hide-and-seek in the monastery garden. She compares the friars' privileged situation ("they had pigs, roosters, rabbits, vegetables of every sort, and the biggest, sweetest lemons") with the hunger of the populace at large ("I could never understand how Fray Leopoldo went about asking for alms," she says, "when those friars had so much to eat right in their own backyard").

Despite harsh memories of her own early years, Rosi feels an unmistakable nostalgia for a time when "everybody knew their neighbors." Certainly her own life has changed dramatically in the last few decades. Although her mother took her out of school when she was eight years old ("she said I had learned all I would ever need to know"), Rosi later taught herself to read and write. Married at an early age, she soon grew restless ("all my husband wanted to do was go drinking with his friends," she says). She therefore took a part-time job without his knowledge. After mastering the rudiments of arithmetic, she set up her own *churros* (fried doughnut) business, which she ran with the help of her two children, her older sister Chela, and a friend.

Presently separated from her husband ("I still feel bad about it, but I wouldn't take him back for anything"), she now sells jewelry and clothing on the installment plan. "Today," she explains, "even cleaning women own a pair of gold earrings, a string of pearls, a diamond ring." Because her customers can afford this type of purchase only on installment, Rosi spends a good deal of her time collecting money. When, as frequently happens, she encounters the client empty-handed, she simply schedules an hour to return. "These people do not have a lot of money," she says matter-of-factly. "If I'm patient, they will pay me and later on buy something else."

Rosi and Chela presently share an apartment in the largely working-class district of Chana on the outskirts of Granada. The poetic names of many of the streets—Pensamiento (thought), Geranio (geranium), and Rubén Darío (the Nicaraguan poet)—contrast with the humdrum, look-alike apartment houses. All but a few lone trees have been cut down to clear space for the massive concrete buildings, yet one of Rosi's windows looks out on a field of grazing cows. "Until just a few years ago," she muses, "the men used to bring the hay through the streets at harvest time."

Despite her claims to be a skeptic, Rosi attends mass every Sunday and believes in the saints' power to work miracles. She notes that she herself once received a seemingly impossible favor from the patron of her parish church, Saint Micaela. "When I told the nuns about it, they all laughed," she says, herself chuckling. "But, after all, it wasn't they Saint Micaela helped, now was it?"

Unlike Manolo and Rosi, Ernesto—tall, with dark beard and eyes, and, at twenty-eight, the same age as Luís Antonio—is too young to remember either Fray Leopoldo or the early Franco years. Although his father, an employee of the Spanish armed forces, died almost ten years ago, the family retains the right to live in a military-owned apartment complex, a dingy building with a breathtaking view of the snow-capped sierra. His mother is a cleaning woman who looks forward to the day she can retire. The little room Ernesto shares with his younger brother is decorated with a poster of Ché Guevara and a photograph of the Alhambra with the caption, "Granada—perfume of a dream." Like Doña Hortensia at his age, Ernesto's greatest wish is to travel ("my first stop would be the Inca ruins," he declares). In the meantime he turns up his records of Andean music as high as the stereo and the next-door neighbors will permit.

One of the many young people who cannot find steady jobs in Spain today, Ernesto has worked for years at a long succession of part-time and temporary jobs. The most promising position he has held so far is that of label salesman. "Everyone needs labels," he explains enthusiastically, "funeral parlors, drugstores, record shops. There is a real market for labels. It isn't like some things where people see you coming and then, quick, slam the door."

Chronically short of money, he and his friends know a variety of shortcuts under railroad bridges and through backyards of abandoned buildings that will spare them the price of a bus ride. They regularly sneak into the city's most expensive concerts during intermission and attend innumerable free lectures and cut-rate movies. Often, they go singing through the streets at midnight until a window opens and someone yells, "Hey kids, that's enough!" They will then move on to a friend's house where they sit listening to music, taking drags on a shared cigarette, and drinking wine or tea. Long after the rest of the city is asleep, they set out for home. Theirs is, in many ways, the semibohemian life of a student. In contrast to most students, however, they are approaching their thirtieth birthdays with no guarantee that the future will be any different from the past.

Like most of his friends, Ernesto claims to have no interest in organized religion. He nonetheless owns a large stack of books about Eastern mysticism and the powers of the mind. He enjoys hearing and repeating various stories about Fray Leopoldo, particularly jocular ones that allege the friar had a roving eye. For Ernesto, the protagonist of these stories is above all a symbol of an older Granada, aspects of which have changed beyond all recognition. "How surprised Fray Leopoldo would be," Ernesto comments, "if he were to return today."

The Structure of Counterlegends

A good number of Counterlegends (about a third of those in my collection) are the mirror image of Legends. Like the latter, they portray a situation of need involving members of the lay population. Here, however, Fray Leopoldo fails to meet the challenge set before him. Instead of the generosity and concern for others which we saw time and again in Legends, he now displays hypocrisy, avarice, and egotism.[1]

These negative-response tales and, indeed, Counterlegends as a body, tend to be briefer than Legends. Although some stories do include considerable detail, the tellers—not unlike the author of the Life—have a point to make. In contrast to their often lengthy descriptions of the friar's time, their presentations of Fray Leopoldo himself are usually concise. Their narratives (like the Legends) often center on specific incidents, but they may also offer considerably more general assessments of Fray Leopoldo.

Stories that focus on the friar's negative response to a challenge occasionally begin with a denial of the truth of a particular Legend or with a more general dismissal of the Capuchins' claims for the friar ("all that they say is lies"). The teller then proceeds to offer the "real," decidedly less flattering version of Fray Leopoldo's life. On other occasions, he or she simply launches into this account without a preface.

As with Legends, storytellers may purport to have witnessed the event in question or to otherwise have proof of its veracity. Rosi, for instance, recounts the following incident involving a hungry child as if she herself had seen it. Upon questioning, she admits that the incident was related to her by a neighbor "whom one can greatly trust" (de gran confianza). She notes, however, that she and her sister once knocked on the monastery door asking for something to eat and that the friar who answered turned them away ("he said to come back the next day," she says, "but we never did"). The bitterly sarcastic conclusion is typical of many of these accounts.

> 16. It was an impossibly hard life. And there was Fray
> Leopoldo, walking through the streets every day with his
> basket, asking alms for the monastery. For the friars, you
> understand, only for the friars. "In the house of the priest,

1. Stories concerning the foibles of the members of religious orders are certainly nothing new to the tradition of the saint's legend. See appropriate motifs listed under "friar" and "priest, cleric, monk" in Thompson, *Motif-Index*, vol. 6, pp. 316 and 605–7. See also Brewer, *Dictionary of Miracles*, pp. 75–76 and 117.

there's always a feast," as the proverb says. For the people in the streets, nothing. Absolutely nothing. We were dying of hunger, but they paid us no attention. Look, there was a little eight-year-old girl who asked them for food one day and they told her there was nothing to eat in the monastery. Nothing to eat! So how can one explain that all the friars went about looking so well-fed? Undoubtedly they lived on air. Air and prayers, of course.

Other stories take the form of unflattering comparisons between Fray Leopoldo and a "real" saint. As in Legends, the latter is often the sixteenth-century San Juan de Dios, or else Padre Andrés Manjón, who, as noted in chapter 1, established a series of schools in working-class sections of the city and took a special interest in the gypsy population.[2] Born twenty years before Fray Leopoldo, the priest, like the friar, is presently a candidate for canonization.

These sorts of negative comparisons generally depict either San Juan or Padre Manjón as an active champion of the poor. Fray Leopoldo, in contrast, appears as a passive member of a religious order whose welfare he systematically places above that of the lay population. In the following account, Manolo depicts Padre Manjón not only as more assertive and quick-witted than Fray Leopoldo but also as more dedicated to the poor ("and that is what a saint is, it is someone who helps the person who has nothing to his name"). In analyzing his account, however, one should keep in mind Manolo's critical comments about his own experience as a student in one of Padre Manjón's schools. The reservations he expresses on these other occasions suggest that his celebration of the priest here serves above all to highlight objections to the friar and the Capuchins.

Manolo begins by telling the story of how Padre Manjón, "a lawyer as well as a professor of professors" (abogado y también catedrático de catedráticos), decides one day to buy a plot of land on which to found a school.[3] At exactly nine o'clock, the priest appears at the appointed site. The auctioneer in charge does not want to begin at the set hour "because, of course, at nine o'clock, all the rich are still in bed." Padre Manjón, however, uses his knowledge of the law to force the man to start the bidding. As he has no competitors, he is able to buy the

2. For a laudatory biography of San Juan de Dios see Gómez-Moreno, *Primicias históricas de San Juan de Dios*. For Padre Manjón see Pino Sabio, ed., *Don Andrés Manjón,* and (n.a.) *Vida de don Andrés Manjón y Manjón.*

3. Padre Manjón was a professor of church history and of canon law. A *catedrático* is a senior professor.

land for an otherwise impossibly low price. "And so you see," Manolo concludes:

> 17. He lived to serve the most needy. Fray Leopoldo, no, he thought only about filling his own belly. He and those other friars, they didn't think of anything else. Look, today they talk about how he went through the streets barefoot in winter, but I myself fixed his sandals and they had thick soles, I assure you!

While both Manolo and Rosi focus on reports of Fray Leopoldo's lack of concern for the least fortunate in a time of widespread hunger, other storytellers accuse him of hypocrisy in his activities as alms collector. One elderly seamstress, for instance, asserts that the friar was far less interested in helping the poor than in promoting the Capuchin order. According to her, he took advantage of his access to people's homes to paint a glowing picture of the religious life for impressionable younger members of the family. "That was all he was good for," she asserts indignantly. "People talk about his generosity, but all he really wanted was to make converts for them, for the Capuchins."[4]

Allegations of Fray Leopoldo's insensitivity to those outside the immediate circle of the monastery present a dramatic contrast to Legends and certainly to the Life. They are nonetheless considerably less startling to the outsider than that small, but significant, cluster of narratives depicting him as a libertine. Although the friar eventually repents in a number of these stories, his misdeeds dominate the action. The following description of the friar's exploits in Granada's red light district is an excellent example. The storyteller's numerous disclaimers do not diminish her willingness to pass on accusations she has heard from others.

> 18. They say that he went to bed with the whole neighborhood of San Lázaro [a well-known red light section of the city], but I don't know. It might well be a lie, but they say that in his day he was a friend of those women who, who [sentence trails off]. It might well be that he repented of having gone to bed with so many women toward the end of his life and thus went on to do penance as an alms collector. That might well be. But they say that he remained in the street until four in the morning

---

4. Woman, age sixty-two, born Granada, some grade school. Married, works at home, attends mass regularly, "but that doesn't mean that I think all priests are saints."

drinking and doing all sorts of scandalous things. That is what people say.

> *Woman, age fifty-two, born Granada, grade-school education. Married, owns small bakery shop with husband, "never" attends mass.*

Even, and indeed especially, when storytellers claim to be jesting about Fray Leopoldo's promiscuity, they may create lingering doubts in the listener's mind. Thus despite Ernesto's reference to the friar's kindness to those individuals scorned by polite society (including, to be sure, the other Capuchins), his initial pleasantry casts a shadow of uncertainty over the remainder of the tale. "It's that this Fray Leopoldo went about a lot in the zone," he says with a chuckle:

19. He confessed the prostitutes; he helped them a lot. He taught them to read and write, he brought them food, and then immediately afterwards [here he winks suggestively]. No, no, I'm joking. I swear that I am joking. He really helped them. Yes, he did. Because a friend of mine told me how he went through the streets, barefoot, among the women of ill repute with whom no one wanted anything to do. Least of all the Capuchins. It was they themselves who started saying ugly things about him, you know.

Although these stories present a strikingly different and less flattering portrait of Fray Leopoldo, they are ultimately almost never personal attacks. The protagonist of these accounts is first and foremost a representative of the Capuchins and, through them, of the entire ecclesiastical establishment. Not infrequently, storytellers begin with a proverb directed specifically at the religious orders or at the church in general. "Beato y tuno, todo es uno" (Scoundrel and saint, one and the same), they may declare, or "Gente de sotana, logra lo que le da la gana" (Persons in clerics' attire get whatever they desire). Other common sayings that find their way into many of this first type of Counterlegend are "Portero de frailes, no pregunta al que llega, '¿Qué quiere?' sino '¿Qué trae?' " (The friars' doorman doesn't ask the visitor, "What do you wish?" but rather, "What have you brought?") and "Boca de fraile, sólo el pedir la abre" (A friar's mouth only opens to ask for something).

The religious establishment as a whole is often the ultimate target of these stories. The tellers, however, may be bitterly critical of the Capuchins in particular. Of course, this singling out of the Capuchins may be a result of Fray Leopoldo's association with the order. But the frequent harshness of their comments almost certainly stems from the traditional proximity of members of religious orders, and particularly the Franciscans, to the general population. By casting aside their vows of poverty and simplicity, the friars in these stories betray not only Fray Leopoldo but also the lay community that has come to trust and confide in them. "One would expect such behavior of the Jesuits," declares one middle-aged storyteller. "After all, they have always been proud and overbearing. But to see these friars [the Capuchins], once so poor, now so given to luxury [cosas de lujo], is really very irritating."[5]

In a number of these negative-response tales, Fray Leopoldo is less a villain than a victim of his considerably more culpable fellows. The Capuchins, for instance, may insist on pressing the friar into service despite his advanced age and physical infirmities. "He had to bring them a certain sum of money—let's say thirty *duros* [about $1.50]—every day," a housewife in her fifties explains with a disapproving cluck of the tongue.

> 20. Without fail. And if he didn't get it, the other friars would not let him enter. He had to sleep there in the monastery door, poor thing! For this reason, people felt sorry for him because he was one of these clean, nice-looking old men. And so they would give him a coin or two so that he could sleep in his own bed.
>
> *Woman, age fifty-seven, born Granada, grade-school education. Married, housewife, attends mass "from time to time."*

These storytellers may go on to suggest that Fray Leopoldo would have been horrified to find himself the center of a devotion that they dismiss as a *teatro* (theatrical production), a *charada* (charade), or a *tinglado* or *montaje* (both meaning farce). Although the friar may not look good in their narratives, the Capuchins who have cynically transformed him into an *hombre-tragaperras* (human coin machine) look considerably worse. "He was not a bad person," a friend of Manolo says a bit grudgingly, "but there is nothing good about those friars who are now making a business of him" ("era un hombre nada molo pero estos frailes que están haciendo comercio de él ahora no tienen nada de bueno").[6]

5. Woman, age forty-nine, born Granada, no formal schooling, "but my mother taught all of us to read." Married, part-time supermarket clerk, attends mass occasionally.
6. Man, age forty-four, born Granada, some grade school. Separated, part-time carpenter and other odd jobs, does not attend mass.

"Poor little one," says an older woman whose husband was a close friend of Ernesto's father, "In life he never had a decent robe, but now, suddenly, he has acquired hundreds which those other friars divide into tiny pieces to sell as relics."[7] Her sister, who hastens to assert her own belief in a multitude of other saints, explicitly rejects Fray Leopoldo as an invention of the Capuchins. In this case as in others, the objection is not really to the friar but rather to his fellows' willingness to exalt him for their own ends.

> 21. Me? Yes, I believe in the saints, and I believe in miracles. I do. Now then, this business of Fray Leopoldo is no more than idle chatter. The Capuchins didn't pay Fray Leopoldo the slightest attention, poor thing. In addition, there was more than one of them who made fun of him. Today? No, of course not. They have him on a throne. Because the miracles are a big business. So many candles, so many flowers, so many things!
>
> *Woman, age fifty-eight, born Granada, three years grade school. Widowed, cook for hospital, occasionally attends mass.*

A second group of Counterlegends stands in contrast to those we have seen so far in this chapter in their extremely positive assessments of the friar. Their challenge structure—that is, their depiction of needs that Fray Leopoldo steps in to alleviate—links them to Legends. Moreover, the Fray Leopoldo of these stories often displays not only human virtues but also the superhuman powers evident in Legends as well as in the Life. He may, for instance, cure an apparently fatal illness, transform one substance into another, prophesy the future, or exhibit bilocation.

But these accounts reveal a critical difference even when they deal with the most familiar incidents, such as that of the frightened mules or the stubborn stone. Counterlegends invariably use the friar's response to need as a way to set him apart from very specific would-be detractors. As a result, the narrative becomes an extended contest in which Fray Leopoldo's ultimate victory often represents less a confirmation of those principles he champions than a denunciation of particular institutions and interest groups.

As suggested by the examples in preceding pages, the most common (though certainly not the only) targets of these stories are the Capuchins and, through them, the ecclesiastical hierarchy and the larger social sys-

7. Woman, age sixty-nine, born Granada, no formal education. Married, works at home, attends mass from time to time.

tem with which it is perceived as being allied. In these "anticlerical tales" (I am using the term broadly to include the members of religious orders), Fray Leopoldo's flawless behavior is the exception that calls attention to the rule.

Even those narrators most admiring of the friar may thoroughly lambaste his fellows. Like Manolo, who emphasizes Padre Manjón's triumphs as a foil to Fray Leopoldo's failures, they may use the friar's virtues to call attention to the Capuchins' vices. The following storyteller calls attention to both Fray Leopoldo's supernatural powers and unfailing kindness. Her account nevertheless constitutes a clear attack on the other members of his order. At the same time that she emphasizes the friar's humility, she summarily rejects their explanations of why he went barefoot through the city streets.

> 22. So then, Fray Leopoldo performed many miracles, many
> good things in these parts. He cured the sick, the blind. He
> even took off his shoes in order to give them to the most
> needy. He gave away so many pairs of shoes to the poor in this
> manner that the Capuchins told him, "Look, Fray Leopoldo,
> we're not going to give you more shoes if you keep on in this
> manner." Today they say that Fray Leopoldo was accustomed
> to going barefoot even in winter because he was so humble.
> When the truth is that they didn't want to give him so much
> as a pair of *alpargatas* [rustic leather sandals]. Of course he
> went barefoot. What else could the poor thing do?
>> *Woman, age forty-nine, born Granada, some*
>> *high school. Married, housewife, irregular at-*
>> *tendance at mass.*

The tellers of Counterlegends are unusually quick to specify a variety of motives for the hostility of Fray Leopoldo's fellow Capuchins. The most common of these—the friar's poverty, his peasant background and lack of formal education—reveal the storytellers unmistakable class consciousness. "He was the poor one of the monastery, the others were rich; they had money," explains one of Rosi's great-aunts, who began washing dishes in a bar when she was nine years old:

> 23. And he was a nonordained friar [*un lego*], poor thing, so
> he had to serve them. Because these people [members of
> religious orders who are also priests] are like that, you know.
> They always want to give the orders. So then, he swept the
> courtyards, did all the kitchen chores. He had to shine the
> others' shoes every day. He washed the bed linen and scrubbed
> the floor. Everything the others didn't want to do. Because he

was poor, he didn't know how to read, so that they laughed at him and treated him as if he were their servant.

> *Woman, age seventy-one, born Granada, "a few months" grade school. Single (fiancé killed in civil war), cook and dishwasher in restaurant (recently retired), attends mass "when I can."*

The Capuchins' standoffish, when not frankly condescending, treatment of Fray Leopoldo in these stories suggests their own feelings of inadequacy in the face of his virtue. A kind of masculine Cinderella figure, the friar displays a generosity and concern for others that irk his small-minded fellows who cannot hope to inspire the same devotion in the population at large. "Of course they couldn't stand him," one man, a clerk in a beer-bottling factory, remarks. "He made them very angry because he had grown up without studies and yet still knew more than they. They did not like the fact he spent his days in places where not one of them, you can be sure, would ever poke his nose."[8]

In the Counterlegends, the Capuchins' knowledge or suspicion that this individual of inferior social position is morally superior to them simply compounds their hostility. Envious of the powers beyond their understanding, they mercilessly mock his rustic ways. The following preface to an otherwise unremarkable account of how the friar turns a copper coin to gold contrasts his humility with their arrogant behavior.[9]

> 24. They hated Fray Leopoldo. For this reason they sent him to ask alms of the *señoritos*, of the *pompa* of Granada. (What does *pompa* mean? *Pompa* is a millionaire, it's the person who has a bank, who has a lot of land.) So then he went to ask alms in those homes in which the lady of the house was accustomed to giving the altar flowers and this type of thing. He spent all afternoon asking for alms, barefoot in sun or rain, with great humility. And when he returned to the monastery he had to endure the others' laughter. They ate the bread he had gotten for them, but they laughed at him. Although he performed many miracles. For example, that of the gold coin.
>
> *Woman, age sixty-four, born Granada, grade school. Widowed, does "a little sewing," usually attends mass.*

---

8. Man, age forty-one, born Granada, grade-school education. Married, clerk in beer-bottling factory, rarely attends mass.

9. The transformation of objects into gold is motif D475.1 in Thompson. The real interest of the story, to be sure, is in this indignant introduction.

More often than not in these stories, the other Capuchins are relieved when Fray Leopoldo dies. "He was a tremendous nuisance," they confide to one another when they think they are alone. Seeking to create the greatest possible distance between themselves and the individual who was for so long the bane of their existence, they hurriedly bury Fray Leopoldo in the public cemetery.[10] When his followers protest, they try to justify their actions by citing the absence of that special dispensation required for interment in the monastery graveyard. Like the storyteller quoted above, the following man prefaces his account of one of the friar's extraordinary actions with a negative description of his fellows. "During his life," he explains:

> 25. Fray Leopoldo did a lot, a lot for the poor people of
> Granada. But those other friars didn't pay him any attention.
> They said that everything was a lie—fanaticism. And after he
> was dead, they stuck him in the public cemetery, very far from
> everything. The friars and the nuns all got together to bury
> him. With a sad face but happy inside. They wanted to forget
> about him. They were sick of all those miracles of his that had
> caused them so much trouble.
>
> > *Man, age fifty-one, born Granada, grade*
> > *school. Married, taxi driver, rarely attends*
> > *mass.*

Even after death, however, Fray Leopoldo stubbornly continues to perform extraordinary deeds on behalf of those who seek help in his name. In some stories the beneficiaries of the friar's posthumous intercession demand that the Capuchins move his corpse into the church to facilitate its veneration by the faithful. Unable to resist the mounting pressure from the lay population on whose support they depend for their own well being, his fellows reluctantly exhume the body. Often, as in many traditional saints' legends, they discover it to be incorrupt and exuding the "odor of sanctity."[11]

At first the other friars express indignation at visitors' insistence on treating Fray Leopoldo "as if he were a saint—imagine!" But their opposition rapidly subsides as the friar's visitors begin to fill the monas-

10. Fray Leopoldo was buried in the public cemetery located near the palaces of the Alhambra following his death on 9 February 1956. His remains were transferred to the old Capuchin church in May of 1958 and installed, permanently, in the crypt of the new church in October 1969.

11. See Thompson, V222.4.1 ("aromatic smell of saint's body"). For numerous analogues see Brewer, *Dictionary of Miracles*, pp. 510–12, and Loomis, *White Magic*, pp. 54–55.

tery's coffers. With just a portion of this money, the Capuchins are soon able to construct not only a crypt to house the body but also a whole new church. "And so the poor man is now the wealth of the monastery" (Y así que el pobre es ahora la riqueza del convento), the storyteller may conclude with more than a trace of irony. He or she may also describe how the friars cut up Fray Leopoldo's robes into tiny pieces, which they sell for an exorbitant price.[12]

In other, related narratives, the friars do an about-face after Fray Leopoldo intervenes to save the previously hostile head of the monastery from a fatal illness or natural disaster. In spite of this individual's formerly bitter opposition to Fray Leopoldo, the friar intercedes on his behalf. In heartfelt appreciation (or at least grudging recognition) of this aid, the abbot orders a lavish new edifice constructed to house his benefactor's remains. The following tale recalls a number of Legends that portray Fray Leopoldo's cure of a seemingly hopeless affliction. The identity of the sick man in this case and the pointed reference to his narrow escape from the flames of hell, however, are a dramatic departure from the standard challenge pattern.

> 26. None of the Capuchins liked *Hermanico* Leopoldo—the
> head of the monastery above all. He was always saying
> horrible things about him. Lies, all lies, you understand. Until
> one day this man took sick. He became very sick; he was on
> the verge of death. Well then, at this point he suddenly thinks
> of the *Hermanico*, he makes a vow to him so that he won't die
> and go to hell. And he is saved. He is saved, yes sir. So then,
> wishing to acknowledge such a great miracle, he orders the
> construction of a church. The Triunfo Plaza Church.
> Something very luxurious, everybody knows it.
>
> > *Man, age fifty-three, born Jaén, thirty-four*
> > *years in Granada, some high school. Married,*
> > *drugstore supplier, occasionally attends mass.*

Even though Fray Leopoldo's exemplary conduct provides a necessary contrast to others' bad behavior in these stories, a number of the tellers

---

12. In point of fact, the money to construct the new church came in large part from the sale of a part of the monastery property on which the forementioned Huerta de la Alegría stood. According to Fray Angel, offerings left by visitors to the crypt are used to finance the costly canonization effort and a portion of the expenses of the Fray Leopoldo Home for the Elderly.

Shreds of cloth said to have been part of the friar's robes are indeed affixed to prayer cards found throughout Granada. These, however, appear to be distributed free of charge. At Fray Leopoldo's funeral so many of those in attendance snipped pieces of his robe to take with them as mementos that the Capuchins found themselves obliged to replace his outer garments three times.

accord him relatively little attention. In the following tale, for instance, the narrator is so intent on denouncing the greedy landowner that he barely mentions the friar.[13] Although he concludes by pronouncing Fray Leopoldo "very miraculous," this decidedly anticlimactic declaration leaves the listener wondering exactly what the friar did to thwart the rich scoundrel's scheme.

> 27. In the past there were a lot of bad people—really very bad. And the poor were all very innocent. They didn't know how to defend themselves. Today, no, things are different. Everybody has a grandson who is a lawyer and who says, "Look, Grandad, leave this life of sacrifice and come live in the city, because things are much better here." But back in the old days, for example, there was one of those very bad, very powerful landowners who wanted to take one of his worker's land. He insisted so very much that the poor man almost handed it over to him. Because he made some terrible threats that practically caused the man to die of fear. So that this shameless individual would have robbed him for sure if Fray Leopoldo hadn't shown up in that town at exactly the right moment. He was a very miraculous friar.
>
> > *Man, age fifty-one, born Granada, four years grade school. Married, deliveryman, occasionally attends mass.*

Although very clear in their denunciations of the friar's opponents, Counterlegends are not necessarily without humor. A number, indeed, are quite funny. Although, as we have seen, some storytellers express indignation at the abuses the friar suffers, others appear less outraged than amused by the foolish behavior of his fellow friars. Rather than condemning these individuals for their hypocrisy and malice, the narrators are frequently content to poke fun at their obtuseness.[14] A number pass over Fray Leopoldo's ill treatment at the hands of his would-be superiors to concentrate instead on how he outwits them.

Humor leavens the account of a man who credits the friar with his recovery from a serious illness. When this individual first relates his experience to the Capuchins, they either assure him he is greatly mis-

13. For an understanding of the roots of this agricultural system and the popular hostility it engendered see Díaz del Moral, *Historia de las agitaciones campesinas andaluzas*, and Bernal, *La propiedad de la tierra y las luchas andaluzas*.

14. For examples of this sort of humor in a number of traditional saints' legends see Brewer, *Dictionary of Miracles*, pp. 528–30. A number of Marian miracles in particular treat the shortcomings of human beings—and often, members of religious orders—with a certain levity.

taken or accuse him of prevarication. When, however, it dawns on them that he intends to make a monetary contribution to the order as a token of his gratitude, they change their tune so fast that the would-be donor wonders if he is not witnessing a second of Fray Leopoldo's miracles. Once again, although an apparently supernatural action is fundamental to the story, the Capuchins' laughably blatant self-interest is the teller's real concern.

In another particularly appealing example of this type of humorous denunciation, Fray Leopoldo spends a long day of distributing food to the hungry in the war-ravaged countryside. Only as the sun begins to set does he suddenly remember that the other friars are counting on him to bring them dinner. Realizing he has nothing left but a few crumbs, he rushes back in desperation to the monastery. As he crosses the threshold, the empty knapsack suddenly becomes heavy with fragrant, golden loaves of bread.[15]

Fray Leopoldo's fellows, of course, do not have the foggiest notion of the miracle that has just occurred on their doorstep. In fact, they proceed to berate him for his delay. Although this portrait of them, which appears below, is ultimately no more flattering than many of our other examples, an unmistakable difference nevertheless exists between these childish friars and the blackhearted miscreants who appear in a number of other Counterlegends. Note the change in tense accompanying the bread's mysterious appearance and the storyteller's apparently unintentional lapse, whereby Fray Leopoldo's "basket" becomes a "knapsack" in the course of his account.[16]

> 28. He passed through the countryside with his basket full of grain. At harvest time, the sun in his face, the fields all gold with sun, gold with grain. Today there is a good highway, but in that time there was only a dirt road. He was accustomed to spending all day asking for food and distributing it along the way because there was a lot of hunger in those days, the people suffered a lot. So it was only when it started getting dark that he suddenly remembered the friars who were waiting for him in the monastery. Because they were too proud to beg, they

---

15. See Thompson, D2106.1.5 ("saint multiplies food"). Loomis notes that bread, being the commonest form of traditional nourishment, is subjected most often to miraculous increase (see p. 86), and Brewer offers numerous examples of saints' multiplication of food (pp. 145–50). One of the instances he cites involves Saint Theodosius's conversion of a crumb of bread into a quantity so large that by the next day it has filled the monastery larder and run out through the door "in great abundance."

16. See Schiffrin, "Tense Variation in Narrative," and Wolfson, "A Feature of Performed Narrative."

depended on him for food. So then he didn't know what to do. He ran back to the monastery very worried because he had nothing left but a few grains of wheat that wouldn't have filled the stomach of a bird. But when he opens the monastery door he feels the knapsack very heavy. Because it had filled with bread. Just like that. So then he hurries to serve the Capuchins, who were already at the table. "Finally!" they say to him. "You delayed a long time on the road. And we here dying of hunger! What selfishness!" [Here the speaker and a dozen listeners bang the table with their fists and laugh delightedly.]

> *Man, age forty-one, born Málaga, some high school. Separated, owns small bar–bingo parlor, attends mass "on occasion."*

Attitudes toward the Supernatural and Saints

The stories we have seen up to this point stand apart from Legends in their structure. Although the differences are more dramatic in some cases than others, the tales can clearly be divided into two groups. The storytellers' attitudes toward the events described are less varied than is the case with Legends. Because the tellers of Counterlegends are often consciously reacting to what they perceive to be the official version of the friar's life, they are more apt than their counterparts to insist on the truth of their stories. An individual will sometimes hedge his or her account in an attempt not to offend listeners, as in the case of the storyteller who reported how the friar went to bed with all the women in a well-known red light district of Granada ("it might well be a lie," she said, but went on to recount the tale). In general, however, tellers of Counterlegends are more uniform than Legend tellers in their attitudes toward the events they describe.

This relative consensus on the clerical establishment does not, however, imply a common stance on miracles and saints. The stories just recounted in the preceding pages reveal varied attitudes toward the supernatural—reminiscent of the diversity we encountered in Legends. Although miraculous actions, as already noted, seldom figure as prominently in Counterlegends as they do in Legends, their very presence is significant. While some storytellers attribute extraordinary powers to saints in general or to Fray Leopoldo in particular, others maintain a conspicuous silence. Then too, as in our last chapter, still others explicitly deny all possibility of miracles, and thus implicitly or explicitly demand new definitions of what makes a saint.

A negative assessment of Fray Leopoldo or of the Capuchins does not necessarily signal disbelief in the supernatural. The storyteller may contrast an acknowledged miracle worker such as San Juan de Dios or Saint Teresa with the apparently humdrum friar as proof that he was not "a real saint." ("Me? Yes, I believe in the saints," an earlier storyteller asserted, "and I believe in miracles. Now then, this business of Fray Leopoldo is no more than idle chatter.")

We have also seen how the tellers of Counterlegends present others' blindness to Fray Leopoldo's miracles as proof of their larger failings. The Capuchins' ignorance of the extraordinary event that occurs beneath their noses in the story of the empty knapsack that fills with bread, for instance, illustrates a more general insensitivity on their part.

In contrast, however, to those storytellers who stress the marvelous quality of Fray Leopoldo's actions for purposes of contrast, there are others who gloss over his exploits in their eagerness to stress his opponents' failings. We have noted that the listener never learns exactly how Fray Leopoldo keeps the rich landowner from taking over the poor worker's land. Likewise, the details of the repentant abbot's recovery are left unexplained. And the listener is not offered a single example of "all those miracles" that so annoy the friar's fellow Capuchins during his lifetime. Nonetheless, storytellers in these and similar cases continue to attribute extraordinary powers to Fray Leopoldo.

Other individuals take no explicit stand on miracles. Like a number of Legend tellers, they may stress his kindness and concern for others in their stories. If asked whether the friar worked miracles, they may skirt the issue or answer indirectly. "I consider myself very Catholic," the owner of a tiny confectionery explains, "But to believe in the sky one doesn't have to stop looking at the things of this earth. Here, have a cookie. For me, Fray Leopoldo was a good man and, in the end, isn't that what is important?"[17]

Still other storytellers redefine miracles in distinctly this-world terms. One of the most appealing redefinitions occurs in an account of Fray Leopoldo's actions at a banquet in the palaces of the Alhambra. His hosts are variously described as "the rich people of Granada," "the Fascists," "the Franquists," or "the señoricos de la tierra," the latter a pejorative term for the traditional landowning aristocracy. (Because of the already noted close association of wealthy rural property holders with the Falangist and Franco movements, a number of storytellers use the

---

17. Woman, age forty-nine, born Granada, some high school. Married, confectionery owner, attends mass "most of the time."

above terms synonymously.) Although these members of the elite are normally deaf to pleas for aid, the friar convinces them on this occasion to dip into their pockets.

In one of a half-dozen variants I collected of this story, Fray Leopoldo is a poor man ("poor and small, he was so small, poor thing!") used to waiting on potential benefactors' doorsteps while a cold winter rain pours down upon his head. The teller, who is almost certainly thinking of the Salesian high school previously located down the street from the Capuchin monastery, identifies the friar as founder and mainstay of "a nearby vocational school."[18]

When Fray Leopoldo arrives at the banquet, he finds himself surrounded by crystal goblets, fine French china, and gold-embroidered table linens, which the teller delights in describing at length. He says:

> 29. They turned on the lights, and it became a thing of enchantment with that little song of the water. There was wine of the very finest which exists in all of Spain, meat of every type. . . . [Here the storyteller describes the various dinner courses in sumptuous detail.] At the end of the banquet, they served an ice-cream cake which was so pretty that it made one sorry to eat it, it was a castle, but all of ice cream. What a marvel!
>
> > *Man, age sixty-six, born Granada, "a few years" grade school. Widower, unemployed (formerly trash collector), rarely attends mass.*

This lavish display, while clearly intended to impress the listener, fails to move the barefoot friar. He informs his hosts politely but firmly that he cannot eat with them while his students are going hungry. True to his word, he refuses to touch the champagne sparkling in his goblet and calls instead for water. As the other guests devour mountains of the finest food ("They say the bread was baked in Paris"), he calmly munches on a handful of *migas* (fried crumbs, the poor man's staple) with which he has filled his pockets in preparation for the occasion. "So then, the Franquists," says the speaker, "gave him notes of five, ten, twenty thousand. Just so they could eat in peace. Because it made them uncomfortable to have Fray Leopoldo eating crumbs and drinking water while they drank champagne and heaped their plates with meat."

When asked if Fray Leopoldo went on to perform a miracle on this occasion, the storyteller laughs. "To my mind, getting money out of

18. The storyteller is probably also confusing Fray Leopoldo with Padre Andrés Manjón, who did found a number of vocational schools for Granada's poor, and whose activities are discussed later on in this chapter.

rich people is the greatest wonder of all," he says. In response to the question of whether the friar ever broke physical laws, he simply shrugs. "I don't say Fray Leopoldo could not do these things," he says, "But I ask you, why should he? To my mind, he had no need. Miracles, indeed!"

Other storytellers who display a similar disbelief or lack of interest in the miraculous have almost certainly confused Fray Leopoldo with some other individual of his or her acquaintance. The result is a composite image that bears scant resemblance to the protagonist of the formal Life. Rather than simple cases of mistaken identity, however, these inventions suggest an affirmation of values not usually attributed to the friar or his fellow holy figures.

The following speaker, for example, describes with obvious approval the friar's almost picaresque behavior. Far from looking down on commerce as a base, materialistic activity to be avoided, her Fray Leopoldo clearly enjoys the drama of buying and selling in this account in which the monastery garden is transformed into a cattle ranch. The unmistakable pleasure with which he bargains in the following description suggests that even the saints are members of a larger community that appreciates quick wits and a sharp tongue. "Fray Leopoldo?" the woman demands:

> 30. Yes, I knew him well. It was he who always came in a van full of animal hides. We used to have a leather factory and we bought the hides from the Capuchins, who in that time had many cattle. I don't know where they kept them, but they ate the meat and sold us the hides. Well then, we would add up the bill and if the total were something like three hundred, Fray Leopoldo would always say, "No, no! Five hundred, five hundred," in jest, you know. And he would laugh and laugh because he was a saint. But he was also an Andalusian, you understand, and even our saints like to bargain.
>
> > *Woman, age fifty-seven, born Granada, some high school. Widowed, part owner of small shoe shop, attends mass every Sunday ("that is, I always try to").*

Although miracles are conspicuous only by their absence in this latter narrative, other storytellers are once again quick to deny all possibility of supernatural actions. Thus the plumber who works next door to Manolo's shoe repair shop begins his account of Fray Leopoldo's distinctly quotidian activities in the streets and plazas of Granada with a heated rejection of not just supernatural actions but also of the whole concept of the afterlife. "Now this talk of miracles is pure invention," he declares.

> 31. He [Fray Leopoldo] did nothing. That is, nothing extraordinary. Furthermore, I don't believe in miracles—in the end, what good are they? In my opinion all that exists is that which is human. The good we do, the bad we do, it all remains right here on earth. And if we were all to do good unto one another, this world would be a cup of oil [*una balsa de aceite,* meaning "something very good"].
>
> > *Man, age fifty-seven, born Granada, no formal education. Married, plumber, rarely attends mass.*

The Fray Leopoldo whom he goes on to describe spends every morning collecting alms in the central square known as Plaza Nueva. Once he has filled his knapsack with a sufficient quantity of food and money for the monastery, he retires to the Café Spain, or rather, "what used to be the Café Spain because it no longer exists." There he orders his habitual *cortado* (black coffee cut by a few drops of milk). Strumming the zither he always carries, he goes on to talk for hours with fellow customers and passersby.

This figure, who bears a notable resemblance to an itinerant musician known as "El Austríaco" or "The Austrian," who lived in Granada during this period, has exchanged the usual ragged robe and sandals for a pair of black loose-fitting trousers.[19] He also wears a jaunty hat and a black shirt with a small white button on each of the two pockets. "Campechano, pero muy campechano" (good-hearted, exceptionally good-hearted), he is also more than a bit of a bohemian. "Don't get me wrong," the speaker says. "He always did his duty. But he was not one of these holier-than-thou friars who spends his whole life cooped up in a church."

The man in question goes on to explain that in Fray Leopoldo's time the Plaza Nueva was home to many *veleros*, old men who received a few coins for accompanying, candle in hand, the funeral processions that passed through the plaza on their way to the public cemetery. "So then," he concludes:

> 32. Fray Leopoldo sat down with them, he gave them bread, he gave them sausage, whatever he might happen to have. The only thing he didn't give them was money, because that was

---

19. I am grateful to Professor José Cazorla Pérez of the University of Granada for identifying this individual.

for the monastery. Though if it had been up to him, you can
be sure, those oldsters would have had the money too!

Still other storytellers, almost all young and relatively well educated,
see Fray Leopoldo as a sort of guru. Their accounts of him are interspersed with references to reincarnation, karma, magnetic forces, astrol-
ogy, and Tarot cards. Although quite willing to pronounce the friar
remarkable, they nonetheless insist on the rational nature of his seemingly extraordinary qualities. No longer inexplicable infractions of otherwise binding natural laws, his actions now illustrate a potential in all
human beings.[20]

The Fray Leopoldo of these narratives also loses his specifically Roman Catholic and Christian identity. Despite the fact that tellers may
acknowledge his affiliation with the Capuchins, most present him first
and foremost as a member of an international community of holy men
and seers. "Fray Leopoldo," Ernesto explains, "was undoubtedly a *vi-
dente*. That is, he could look into a person's mind and say exactly what
he was thinking. People in his time thought he was working miracles,
but today we know there is a scientific reason."

The single best example I can offer of Fray Leopoldo-as-guru is not a
narrative someone recounted to me, but, rather, an experience in which I
shared. One day around noon, I happened to come upon two acquaintances in a café. They introduced me to a friend of theirs, a travel agent
in his thirties who had moved with his family from Italy to Granada
some twenty years before. Upon learning I was conducting research on
Fray Leopoldo, he assured me enthusiastically that he himself was a
great admirer of the friar as well as a number of Eastern holy men and
mystics whom he found to possess many of the same psychic capacities.
He winked good-naturedly when his friends teasingly accused him of
seeking to impress me, producing a small picture of Fray Leopoldo from
his wallet as proof of his sincerity.

Increasingly hungry, the four of us decided to have lunch in a restaurant in the mountains just outside Granada. We therefore clambered
into the travel agent's car. In an attempt to get out of the city before the
already heavy traffic increased, he drove quickly down the narrow and
crowded streets. At one intersection a bicyclist suddenly appeared from
around the corner, resulting in a near-collision. The cyclist was thrown,
his sack full of yogurt tinting the street various shades of pastel. Although unscathed, he, like us, was shaken. Our apprehension mounted

---

20. The language of Eastern spirituality has become an international idiom for religious individualists. See Bellah et al., *Habits of the Heart*, pp. 219–49.

when a police car appeared. But the officer did not appear to notice anything amiss. After examining bones and bicycle, the cyclist gingerly pedaled off, prompting the travel agent to heave a deep sigh of relief. "Who knows what would have happened if we hadn't been talking about Fray Leopoldo just moments before?" he demanded.

Eager to forget the incident, his friends laughed uneasily at the suggestion. Their discomfiture annoyed the man, who insisted he was not joking. Although he said nothing more about Fray Leopoldo, he remained very quiet through lunch. When I asked him over coffee if he believed the friar had worked a miracle, he shrugged impatiently. "Of course not," he replied. "Miracles are just a way for the church to make money. They are wholly irrational. I, for my part, believe in the powers of the mind."[21]

Legends and Counterlegends as Rejections of Institutional Authority

In this and the preceding chapter, I have shown how stories of Fray Leopoldo reveal a wide variety of attitudes toward their protagonist as well as toward the supernatural, toward sanctity, and, at times, toward the very actions they describe. I have suggested that the tales' multiplicity reflects important differences among their tellers. I will now argue that it also constitutes a coherent, if not necessarily fully conscious rejection, of all manner of institutions. The Fray Leopoldo stories are thus united not only by a readily obvious debate about saints and miracles but also by a potent, if often considerably more subtle, undercurrent of antiauthoritarianism.

We are not talking here about that more obvious sort of anticlericalism characterizing a good number of Counterlegends, but rather, a more generalized distaste for constituted authority often discernible in even those Legends that may bear the most marked resemblance to the Life.[22] This distaste may be taken as a reaffirmation and intensification of the stubborn localism that has always characterized one important subgroup of saints' legends. It also represents a confirmation of the very long and

21. Man, age thirty-seven, born Palermo (Italy), high-school education. Separated, travel agent, does not attend mass.
22. It is this same impulse, I would argue, that has found its most dramatic expression in a series of Anarchist and Socialist political movements during the last century. For two excellent discussions of twentieth-century manifestations of this antiauthoritarian spirit see Mintz, *The Anarchists of Casas Viejas,* and George A. Collier, *Socialists of Rural Andalusia.*

powerful tradition of anti-institutionalism in Spain—described in chapter 1—which finds its most immediate target in Franco's self-described "National Catholic" regime.[23]

This deeply rooted antiauthoritarian impulse shows up most notably in the stories' tendency to redefine, de-emphasize, or subjectivize the supernatural, to delimit the friar's sphere of operations, and to picture him actively seeking out needy members of the lay population. It is discernible as well in the insistence on Fray Leopoldo's identity as friend rather than arbiter and in storytellers' recurring insistence on their tales' subjective truth.

Redefinition and sometimes outright rejection of miracles characterize many of the tales, Legend and Counterlegend alike. Thus, together with accounts of how Fray Leopoldo causes a lemon tree to burst into flower in the chill of winter or finds his empty knapsack filled with bread, there are numerous instances in which he simply offers sympathy or counsel. Unlike many traditional saints' tales in which the natural and supernatural form a continuum where some things are more or less probable than others, the tales we have studied reveal a clear demarcation between the possible and the impossible.[24] Although individual storytellers may and do decide to cross this conceptual great divide, few if any fail to acknowledge its existence.

One might dismiss this generalized downplaying of the supernatural as nothing more than a response to the sort of rationalization generally associated with industrialization and the introduction of new technologies. From this standpoint, the woman who hastens to assure her listeners that Fray Leopoldo did indeed raise her dead niece ("Yes, yes, yes, yes, she was dead when he arrived") and the man who insists that the friar bumped his head on the cathedral ceiling are both proposing an exception to rules both they and the community accept.

23. As one might well expect, this sort of anti-institutionalism is considerably more visible in the local legends that have come down to us in assorted shrine books, rather than written collections of saints' lives authored by members of monastic orders. It is obvious as well in a number of those Marian miracles that present an alternative to the stern, all-powerful male patron.

24. See Keith Thomas's discussion of the relationship between medieval religion and occult forces in his *Religion and the Decline of Magic*, pp. 253–79.

Here and elsewhere in this section, I have used the term "traditional legend" very loosely. I am thinking here primarily of those stories appearing in such standard collections as Caesarius of Heisterbach, *Dialogue on Miracles*; Voragine, *The Golden Legend*; and Butler, *Lives of the Saints*, as well as a number of the local legends that have come down to us through shrine books. There are, to be sure, numerous differences among these narratives. For a study of this sort of variation over time, as well as apparent constants in a number of Spanish saints' lives, see Wyatt, "Representations of Holiness in Some Spanish Hagiographical Works."

One could, however, just as easily see storytellers' generalized de-emphasis of the miraculous (and also their reluctance or refusal to expound on supernatural actions on other occasions) as a rejection of official criteria of sanctity and, by extension, of the church's definitive control over the canonization process and religious experience in general. From this perspective, the friar's insistence that the workers do not need his miraculous intervention to move an obstinate slab of granite is neither an acknowledgment of the supremacy of reason nor an attempt to conceal his inability to help the needy. Rather, it is an endorsement of an emphatically nonhierarchical, this-world approach to human problems.

The limited scale of both Legends and Counterlegends invites a similar interpretation. Nowhere in either the Life or the wide array of oral stories we have seen does Fray Leopoldo lead an army into battle, rid Granada of an epidemic, or multiply a single loaf of bread before the eyes of a hungry multitude.[25] But (in contrast to the Life, where he does appear alone at times) the great majority of the tales we have examined portray him in the company of others. The friar inevitably appears alongside another individual or individuals—a handful of workers, a mule driver and a few curious passersby, a sick child and his anxious parents.

A few of the texts presented do involve a somewhat larger than usual number of persons. We have seen how Fray Leopoldo levitates in full view of the worshipers cramming the city cathedral and have noted his presence at a great banquet in the palaces of the Alhambra. Even in these cases, a single face often stands out among the crowd. In several versions of the cathedral story, for instance, a young boy is the first to notice the friar's ascent. In addition, we have noted the numerous references—particularly in Legends, but also in a number of Counterlegends—to proper names, distinguishing physical features, and family connections. Whereas the Life speaks of "a certain man," the oral accounts refer to "the youngest brother of the García family that used to own the barbershop on Recogidas Street" or "a fruitseller, lame from birth in the left leg, who lived for many years across the street from my Great-Aunt Elvira."

This focus on small groups of very ordinary people could be taken as an illustration of the increasing privatization of religious experience, which some scholars have observed in various complex industrial

25. For numerous examples of these sorts of occurrences consult appropriate headings in Loomis, *White Magic*, and Brewer, *Dictionary of Miracles*.

societies.[26] One could argue that the friar deals almost exclusively with small numbers of people because he—and the religious establishment with which he is associated—has largely lost the hold it once commanded over public institutions.[27]

It is equally possible, however, to see Fray Leopoldo's notably limited circle of activities as an affirmation of the individual and the near-at-hand. The woman who describes how Fray Leopoldo cures her husband beneath the Elvira Arch or the newspaper vendor who relates how an acquaintance witnesses an empty jug fill to the brim with cooking oil reveal a proximity to the events in question that stands in contrast to the distance cultivated by the friar's biographer. The absence of crowds and the highly idiosyncratic actors in both Legends and Counterlegends may constitute a further rejection of the anonymity and massification often synonymous with bureaucratic process.

A third general characteristic of the stories cited in the preceding pages is their situation of the friar in not just concrete, but familiar *and public* places such as plazas, shops, and historical landmarks. Time and again, he remains on the threshold instead of disappearing behind the doors of a private residence. Even those Counterlegends that depict the friar amidst his fellow Capuchins customarily include scenes of his activities in the countryside or city streets. Fray Leopoldo may come trudging back to Granada along a dirt road "gold with sun, gold with grain," or spend long hours helping the prostitutes in a section of the city where "no priest, you can be sure, would ever poke his nose."

Moreover, the friar is not simply situated within the public domain. Rather, he *moves* within it. Legends and Counterlegends alike show him circumnavigating Granada and its immediate environs, rather than staying in the monastery or one of the churches mentioned in the Life. In the course of his travels, he regularly happens on situations of need. Although people do sometimes seek out the friar with problems, he is far more likely to intervene of his own accord at a critical moment. Just as a scheming landowner is about to browbeat a poor farmer into sur-

---

26. Clearly, this privatization does not occur in all cases. Theories of modernization, extremely influential in the 1960s and the early 1970s, fell out of favor precisely because their globalizing predictions were emphatically belied by developments in a number of non-Western nations. In addition, one could argue that "privatization" in the Spanish case often has a quite different meaning than in other, apparently similar contexts.

27. See Berger, *Sacred Canopy*, pp. 127–53, for a discussion of the diminished power of religious institutions in modern, industrial societies. Although Berger's generalizations would not be true for some societies, there is no question but that the Spanish church occupied a privileged position during the Franco era which it no longer enjoys. For an overview of secularization as a sociological concept see Martin, *General Theory of Secularization*, and Glasner, *Sociology of Secularisation*.

rendering his tiny plot, at the very moment that a mule driver despairs of being able to feed his family, exactly when a small child who has just lost his mother feels most alone, the friar appears.

It is noteworthy that the beneficiaries of Fray Leopoldo's intervention do not necessarily call on him for help. In this respect, the tales depart from not only the Life but also from many other saints' legends in which the needy go to considerable pains to seek out the holy figure. (Recall the repentant man in chapter 2 who crosses town to implore Fray Leopoldo's aid at three o'clock in the morning.) The oral accounts are wholly devoid of these arduous pilgrimages. On the contrary, it is the friar who is the pilgrim in these stories, and he who makes the rounds of countryside and city.

Fray Leopoldo's extreme accessibility might be seen as an attempt to drum up business in a time of increasing competition among proliferating sects.[28] But this same accessibility can also be viewed as a rejection of a hierarchical model in which spiritual aid must be actively solicited, often at considerable cost to the needy party. The friar's spontaneous appearance in critical moments suggests the ready availability of such assistance. Because Fray Leopoldo knows without their having to say so when people need him, they do not have to importune him or to offer gifts (constituting a kind of advance payment) for his help. He continues to think of them even when their mind is elsewhere. Unlike official saints, he is not located physically or metaphorically in a separate sphere—that of the religious institution—but remains close at hand.

Moreover, the friar shares not only the plazas and the streets with storytellers but also a common status. Not by chance do so many storytellers insist on his diminutive stature, lack of formal education, rustic accent, and shabby clothes. While the author of the Life repeatedly refers to him as a Servant of God—a title given to candidates for canonization—and a "varón de Dios" (man of God), storytellers ignore these high-sounding appellations in favor of others that stress his supreme ordinariness and thus his proximity to them. In their eyes he is an endearing, vaguely humorous, and unequivocally intimate *frailecico* (little friar), *viejito* (little old man), and *santico* (little saint). We have seen that the very family roles he represents—*abuelito* (grandfather) and *hermanico* (little brother)—undercut, while never wholly rejecting, patriarchal authority. As "father emeritus" and lay member of a religious order, he is at once within and outside the system.

28. Berger compares the pluralistic situation to a market economy in which religious "products" must be marketed to a population of uncoerced consumers. (*Sacred Canopy*, p. 145)

The Life resembles many older hagiographical models in its portrayal of the friar as stern and demanding in all matters concerning religious thought and practice. Although Fray Leopoldo does not engage in the more spectacular displays of displeasure in which a long line of saints throughout the centuries have indulged, he regularly chides wrongdoers (who, one may note, are usually women of inferior social status). He is, for instance, quick to admonish a young servant who lies about her mistress's whereabouts and to scold a nun for thinking about forsaking her religious vows. In addition, the friar's biographer makes reference to one instance in which lightning strikes a boy who fails to follow the future friar in taking refuge from a thunderstorm.

Oral accounts, in contrast, rarely if ever show Fray Leopoldo chastising a would-be offender. Although the *Hermanico* recalls a number of traditional holy figures in his readiness to console and counsel, his reluctance to punish those who challenge his authority makes him more like a friend. It is therefore not surprising that the three versions I recorded of the story of the thunderstorm make no mention of a challenge to Fray Leopoldo, but instead portray all of the frightened children huddling behind a rock.[29] No more than half a dozen of all of the tales in my collection do so much as hint at the redress of a personal wrong. In both Legends and Counterlegends, actions that would almost certainly be taken as affronts in the Life regularly pass without notice. Whereas, for instance, hagiographic tradition dictates that the disgruntled worker who abandons the group in one version of the stubborn stone should suffer for his action, our storyteller reports his departure as a simple fact.[30]

Likewise, accounts of the blow Fray Leopoldo receives upon asking two men in a café for alms omit any reference to retribution ("that was not his way," storytellers explain if pressed). The friar is content to respond with a play on the verb *dar*, which means both "to strike" and "to give." Then too, although his hosts at the Alhambra banquet finally contribute to his school, they do so not out of remorse, but rather, to be

29. Significantly, I collected all three versions of this story in the hamlet of Alpandeire. Although the tale appears in the formal Life, no one in Granada repeated it to me, which would appear to suggest either a lack of interest or discomfort with the theme of retribution among residents of the city.

30. "Punishment for opposition to saint" is motif number Q559.5 in Thompson. For a wide array of punishments by saints see Loomis, *White Magic*, pp. 55, 84–85, 98–99, 101–2, and Brewer, *Dictionary of Miracles*, pp. 275–78. A list of studies of medieval punishment stories appears in Wilson, ed., *Saints and Their Cults*, pp. 401–2. For more general discussions of divine wrath see Halpert, "Supernatural Sanctions and the Legend," and Hand, "Deformity, Disease, and Physical Ailment as Divine Retribution."

rid of him so they can go on with their lavish meal. In striking contrast to a number of saints' tales from other times and places, none of the stories I collected includes the slightest suggestion of reform.[31]

Fray Leopoldo's pacific and even passive behavior in the great majority of stories may be taken as another, quite straightforward indication of the diminished power of religious ideology and institutions in some modern industrial states. Unable to command allegiance to a once theoretically uniform code of behavior, the friar has no other option than to coax and cajole.[32] One can also interpret the stories, however, as a considerably more subtle rejection of the saint as arbiter. From this standpoint, Fray Leopoldo does not exact moral compliance, because the tellers have rejected force on principle. Rather than a reflection of his diminished power and obvious indication of weakness, his failure to assert authority in the most varied oral accounts becomes a statement of principle and show of strength. The stories would thus appear to confirm the demise of patronage as an ideal, but not that of the holy figure as a metaphor.[33]

Finally, if the profound multiplicity we have taken pains to document can be understood as a unifying factor, so can storytellers' insistence on the subjective truth of their narratives. ("There's no arguing about faith," they say time and again. Or "Well, this story's true for me.") This insistence may in part reflect individuals' perception of an increasingly pluralistic Spain. Unanimity, however, may strike storytellers not simply as impossible but, above all, as undesirable. As such, the tales signal a long-standing and, indeed, premodern agreement to disagree.

In short then, oral accounts of Fray Leopoldo, while profoundly diverse in some respects are nonetheless united by their antiauthoritarianism. Although individual stories may recall specific narrative features of the Capuchins' biography, as well as its more general guiding vision, the tales as a body represent a debate about the friar, about sanctity, and

31. Reform routinely accompanies retribution in traditional saints' legends. Those individuals who do not die as a consequence of their insulting behavior (and there are a good number of these) customarily become staunch followers of the holy figure who has vented his or her wrath upon them.

32. Berger explains these codes as legitimating or "plausibility" structures. See *Sacred Canopy*, pp. 45–47.

33. For a discussion of the relationship between popular religious practice and the ideal of patronage see Maddox, "Religion, Honor, and Patronage." In their use of a holy figure to attack the concept of the all-powerful male patron, the stories cast doubt on the thesis put forward by some scholars in the 1970s that the decline of patronage as both ideology and socioeconomic system necessarily results in the diminution of the symbolic power of the saints. (See, for example, Boissevain, "When the Saints Go Marching Out.")

about the role or nonrole of the supernatural in everyday life—a debate that is wholly alien to the printed text. Moreover, Legends and Counterlegends alike reveal a number of narrative constants that affirm the individual and local in the face of all manner of institutions and thus provide a striking contrast to the Life.

CHAPTER FIVE

Presentations of the Past

Even when the storytellers quoted in chapters 3 and 4 focused directly on the figure of Fray Leopoldo, their accounts often included various references to an older Granada. The reader will recall the story about the friar in which the teller notes how Fray Leopoldo always took his morning coffee in the Café Spain and then pauses to explain that the place has long since gone out of business. Another remarks on the lack of the simplest labor-saving devices in the friar's time ("people had to work like burros"). Many others alluded to the extreme famine that plagued both city dwellers and those in the countryside following the civil war or to a time before modern highways had replaced winding country roads. Although this focus on the recent past appears incidental to many of the oral narratives, it constitutes a crucial part of the Legends and Counterlegends. This specificity regarding time, in addition to the tales' essential pluralism and anti-institutionalism, thus clearly distinguishes the oral narratives from the insistently timeless Life.

The chapter at hand examines how storytellers employ the friar as a springboard to a wide assortment of reflections, evaluations, and extended recollections.[1] Clearly, the amount of time storytellers devote to such material will vary, as will their perspective on the recent changes the city and the nation have undergone. Even the chronological definition of "the past" may shift somewhat depending on the age of the teller. For some older persons, "Fray Leopoldo's era" is above all the Spanish civil war, while younger people may be speaking of the 1950s. "The past" is often equated with what one has personally experienced, but storytellers may have strong opinions as well on times before their own.

---

1. A number of these reflections recall the oral histories discussed in Fraser, *Tajos*.

On the whole, Legend tellers are somewhat more likely than Counter-legend tellers to express nostalgia for the Franco years. (This nostalgia is particularly striking among older people and those born in the country-side.) There is, nonetheless, considerable diversity of opinion within each group. In both cases, some individuals find the present, on the whole, superior to the past, while others judge the past to be better than the present, and still others (the great majority) see advantages as well as disadvantages in both past and present.

We have already had a glimpse of some of these mixed perceptions of the rapid and widespread changes Spain has undergone since the mid-1950s. Doña Hortensia, for instance, declares change to be both positive and inevitable ("human beings are not like bees"), while Dori asserts that things were better under Franco "because at least there were jobs." A staunch proponent of continued technological progress, Luís Antonio nonetheless laments a weakening of local and regional traditions ("I want Spain to be modern, but I don't want it to be just like the United States"). Manolo and Rosi, who both experienced prolonged hunger as children, are highly ambivalent about the changes they have experienced in their own lives. Outspoken about the abuses of the Franco era ("the person who opened his mouth to complain was beaten like a drum," says Manolo), they nonetheless find that relations among individuals were often warmer in the past ("today we know more but we care less about one another," Rosi says). Ernesto, for his part, is sure the present is better "because in Fray Leopoldo's day children thought just like their parents and Granada was just like a country town."

References to change within the stories proper may appear in clarify-ing details and tangents of a sort we have already seen. They are also evident in extended postcripts to some tales. Although, as already noted, these often rambling reminiscences and bits and pieces of oral histories are apt to strike the outside observer as extraneous, most storytellers unquestionably find them integral to their narratives. Indeed, tales that lack these "afterthoughts" often strike listeners as less interesting or somehow less complete.

Because tales I had collected in previous research in the backlands of northeastern Brazil focused very closely on the holy figure who was their subject, the tendency of Spanish storytellers to expand and trans-form accounts of the friar into more general treatments of his era sur-prised me.[2] When they began to edge away from strict accounts of Fray Leopoldo, talking about seemingly unrelated matters, I would try to

2. See Slater, *Trail of Miracles*.

nudge them back to the original subject. They would often humor me by responding to specific questions about the friar. Minutes later, however, they would once again be describing now-archaic customs, denouncing various abuses associated with the Franco years, or reliving key events of the civil war. The length and frequency of these apparent digressions were initially perplexing. Could something be wrong, I wondered, with my way of asking questions? Or did the problem lie instead with my subject? Why did he seem to be so much less compelling to storytellers than his Brazilian counterpart?

It took me many months of fieldwork to realize that the friar was important to people *precisely because* of his power to conjure up a larger, far more diffuse past. Many of Fray Leopoldo's contemporaries might evoke similar reflections, but the friar's unusually close association with ordinary Granadans, and his death on the eve of momentous changes, makes him a particularly compelling, distinctly communal symbol of an era. To attempt to separate accounts of Fray Leopoldo from more all-encompassing descriptions of the recent past is to fail to see his importance as a gateway to a period about which many residents of Granada—and Spaniards as a whole—have strong and often contradictory feelings.

Change, to be sure, is not specifically Spanish. Sooner or later, we all experience mutability firsthand, and this essentially individual projection is only one facet of the Fray Leopoldo tales. The profound social, political, and economic transformations that have touched virtually every corner of the nation in relatively few years have intensified and made particularly poignant what might otherwise be an essentially private awareness. ("No European country," says one writer categorically, "has experienced such a rapid period of industrialization and social change as Spain.")[3]

Then too, the continuing trauma of the civil war and its long, repressive aftermath cannot be underestimated. For many Spaniards, thinking back on their own lives means reliving painful memories.[4] The collective fears and personal rancors associated with the war and the ensuing Franco dictatorship have created a lingering taboo about, and corresponding obsession with, the past that lingers on into the present.[5] Not

3. See Graham, *Spain*, p. 277.
4. Some of these sorts of memories are recorded in George A. Collier, *Socialists of Rural Andalusia*, Fraser, *Blood of Spain*, and Mintz, *The Anarchists of Casas Viejas*.
5. It is almost impossible to pick up a newspaper today in Spain without encountering one or another article relating to the civil war and early Franco years. One may read, for instance, about a soldier expelled from the Civil Guard for his supposed political views who

unlike the Japanese, Spaniards have had to deal simultaneously with swift, relentless changes linked to new technologies and bitter memories (as well as the practical consequences) of a catastrophic war.[6] Having concealed their true feelings not only from others but also, often, even from themselves, a number of storytellers find it far easier to talk about Fray Leopoldo than to speak directly of the past. Questions about the friar do not evoke that reflex of suspicion and, sometimes, actual terror as other questions with an apparent political intention may do.[7] As such queries focus on a third party rather than on personal feelings, they are also usually much easier to answer, even though the response may itself be couched in personal terms.

Comparing Past and Present

A very small percentage of the persons who tell stories about Fray Leopoldo claim to perceive no appreciable difference between the present and the recent past. A few of these individuals negate the passage of time completely, ignoring or denying all evidence to the contrary. One woman, for instance, insists that the Capuchins' ultramodern church dates back to Fray Leopoldo's arrival in Granada almost a century ago. "It has not changed a bit since the day he first set foot there," she says with obvious satisfaction.[8]

A somewhat larger number of storytellers readily acknowledge outward transformations, such as the substitution of the new church for the much older structure that was home to the friar, while downplaying their importance. For them, as for his biographer, the spiritual attributes Fray Leopoldo embodies defy the vicissitudes of time. "Generosity like his has been present from the beginning of the world and will be here until the end," a clerk in a neighborhood drugstore says firmly.[9]

---

is to receive back pay, or the return of an elderly Republican resistance fighter to the native village he has not seen for half a century.

6. While not wishing in any way to minimize the many significant differences between the Japanese and Spanish war experience, I would nonetheless suggest the existence of a number of interesting parallels. For a description of the Japanese case see Kelly, "Rationalization and Nostalgia."

7. When I did ask older people directly about the civil war, a number became obviously uncomfortable. Some asked me, or others who knew me, why I was asking them such questions. "You'll have to pardon my mother," one friend said to me later. "It's that she knows she has no cause to be afraid, and still she can't forget all those years when people feared their shadow."

8. Woman, age forty, born Granada, some high school. Married, works at home, attends mass regularly.

9. Man, age thirty-seven, born Granada, some high school. Married, drugstore clerk, occasionally attends mass.

Not everyone who minimizes the differences between past and present focuses on the friar's enduring spiritual legacy. Some argue that because human nature is impervious to change, the present cannot be very different from a decidedly imperfect past. "In Fray Leopoldo's time," one of Manolo's longtime customers says glumly, "people got drunk on cheap wine. Now they get drunk on *cuba libres*. Well, it's another drink, of course, but the result is just the same."[10]

Many of these persons would appear to be pessimists by temperament. Many are quite old. Along with them, however, one also encounters an apparently growing number of other, often younger individuals who are strongly disillusioned with the present. Many of these persons note that they originally believed in the changes promised by the Socialist government that took power in the early 1980s but have since lost faith in its proposed solutions to Spain's problems ("all politicians are the same," they often complain).

"It's that we've passed from one form of slavery to another," a university graduate in his late thirties comments:

> 33. From that of illiteracy and poverty to that of the television and these things that allow no one to think. My daughter [here he points to the eleven-year-old accompanying him on a tour of the Alhambra] can only talk about the latest gimmicks—she wants this record, those tennis shoes, that dolly. Look. I would like to believe that we are better off now than in Fray Leopoldo's era. But from my point of view, things look very much, all too much, the same. And the government? Better to say nothing [*mejor ni hablar*]! All of these politicians say one thing and do another.
>
> > *Man, age thirty-eight, born Granada, university education. Married, rare coin salesman, attends mass from time to time.*

In contrast to this small if often vocal minority that minimizes, when it does not flatly deny, change, most storytellers are quick to point out, and even exaggerate, differences between past and present. Although some clearly find their lives less than ideal, in their eyes they are far better off than they were in Fray Leopoldo's era. These persons are particularly apt to denounce the material hardships, the repressive social and political system, and the limited opportunities for self-fulfillment they associate with the Franco regime.

10. Man, age sixty-six, born Granada province, no formal education. Married, button distributor, usually attends mass.

Storytellers repeatedly refer to the difficult living conditions in the aftermath of the civil war. Persons who attribute miraculous cures to Fray Leopoldo, for instance, frequently take pains to impress on their listeners the absence of modern medical care. "This was a time," the teller may explain before launching into the story proper, "when people really suffered. Because, you see, there were almost no hospitals, no doctors, and no medicines."[11] In her account of the long-childless woman who succeeds in conceiving after the friar's miraculous intervention, Doña Hortensia takes care to point out that the event occurred "before there were any test-tube babies, before doctors, too, worked miracles."

In the same way, individuals who recount the familiar story of how the friar wrests a pair of mules from a deep trench are likely to decry the terrible condition of the roads of that time ("they weren't paved at all," an eighty-year-old man explains in an aside, "and some had potholes a foot deep").[12] References to the lack of even the most rudimentary machinery abound in this and other stories. "Today you'd just call in a crane to lift the rock and that would be that," another older man observes in a postscript to his account of how the friar steps in to help a group of workers move a stubborn stone. "But in that time totally without machines [aquella época totalmente desmotorizada] people could rely on nothing other than a pick and shovel. Today things run on electricity, but back then they ran on sweat."[13]

Often, accounts of Fray Leopoldo's activities as alms collector paint as clear or clearer a picture of a hungry, war-ravaged population as they do of him. We have seen how both storytellers who praise the friar's altruism and those who berate his self-interest may offer all-but-identical descriptions of a time of near-starvation when "heaven was a pinch of sugar, a scrap of meat, an egg." "Today they talk about how Fray Leopoldo wore sandals even in winter as if that were really special," Dori's mother says with a mixture of amusement and indignation. "But in that time, who wore shoes, I ask you? No one but the Lord's first cousin!"[14]

Those who experienced privation firsthand might insert scenes from their own past into stories of the friar. One man, now in his early fifties,

11. Man, age sixty-two, born Granada, some high school. Marital status not given, suitcase salesman, occasionally attends mass.
12. Man, age eighty, born Granada, no formal education. Widowed, retired, does not attend mass.
13. Man, age seventy-four, born Granada, grade-school education. Married, retired, usually attends mass.
14. Woman, age sixty-two, born Granada, no formal education. Widowed, cleaning woman, attends mass "when I can."

interrupts his account of how Fray Leopoldo causes a baker's empty oven
to fill with bread to recollect how he once stole a loaf from those stacked
in a basket just inside the door of a shop ("I still feel bad about it, but I
was so hungry," he recalls).[15] Manolo, for his part, remembers how he
once hoisted a neighbor boy through the locked window of his house so
the boy could wolf down a handful of the fried crumbs that were the
family's only food. "In appreciation for my help, he gave me a bit for
myself," he says. "And they were terrible—it was just like eating saw-
dust. You know, even today when I think about that time I get a bad
taste in my mouth."

Not infrequently, vivid personal recollections crowd out more specific
memories of Fray Leopoldo. Rosi recollects that she was eighteen before
she ever saw the seacoast, now an hour by bus from Granada. ("One
day," she says, "my mother rented a truck which she filled with benches
and then sold seats to the neighbors. Then we went thumping down
those terrible roads until we finally reached the water. I can tell you I
was thrilled!")

Other of Rosi's memories are less pleasant. She shudders perceptibly
as she recounts how she and her brothers and sisters used to wait with
their mother for hours in an icy train station for the daily shipment of
coal to arrive. (The mother brought her children to help carry home the
fuel she then sold to neighbors.) "You have to understand," she says:

> 34. In Fray Leopoldo's day there was a lot of hunger. We were
> eight brothers and sisters, and we had to go to the station with
> my mother to wait for the coal car that passed through
> Granada every day. It didn't have a set arrival time, so that we
> would always leave home at four in the morning, in the
> freezing cold. Sometimes the car came right away but
> sometimes we had to wait until eight or ten in the morning.
> Ah, what a hard life!

Storytellers, to be sure, are not always bitter about past hardships.
Younger persons may recount borrowed memories with obvious admiration for the courage of parents or grandparents during what has become
for many a great adventure. Not surprisingly, a number of older storytellers take pleasure in relating (and, frequently, embellishing) now-
distant tribulations. Thus Rosi smiles and at the same time shakes her
head on remembering how the formerly most irreverent men in a certain parish became devoted churchgoers once the priest began offering

15. Man, age fifty-two, born Granada, some grade school. Single, part-time carpenter,
almost never attends mass.

each communicant a plate of rice after the mass ('' 'Father,' they would
ask, 'can I take communion twice today?' '').[16] And Chela laughs outright at the thought of how their mother once spirited a side of pork into
the city. Because guards had been posted to prevent the unauthorized
importation of foodstuffs from the countryside into the city, the woman
tied slabs of meat to her body with strips of cloth, gambling that the
men would not ask her to remove her dress.[17] Chela recalls:

> 35. And so when she finally arrived home, the neighbors were
> waiting—an enormous line in front of the door. The people
> almost killed each other to buy a piece because there was no
> meat whatsoever for sale in the street, you see. But even so
> my mother forced everyone to wait. The meat smelled so
> much, so much that she had to take a bath first. What a
> demanding life that was! Good God, what a smell! [She holds
> her nose and both sisters chuckle.]

The immense contrast between past and present threatens to over-
whelm some storytellers, whose childhood experiences of want now
strike them as remote and often unreal. Manolo confides that he sometimes wonders if Fray Leopoldo and his own early years were not a
dream. He says:

> 36. Because everything, you see, was so very difficult. Look.
> Today my nephew asks my mother for a snack of bread and
> jam, and she wants to know what kind of jam he wants: peach,
> grape, orange? But in that time when Fray Leopoldo went
> about Granada begging, what child dared dream of jam? What
> an idea! Why, there was no bread!

Some storytellers' criteria for judging the merits of past vs. present
are largely or exclusively material. For them, the present is undeniably
better because, as one of Ernesto's neighbors says, "today the cafés are
full at any hour and there are more cars in the streets than jailhouse
dogs."[18] Other individuals' distaste for the past has less to do with physical hardships than with the injustice and repression they associate with
the civil war and the first half in particular of the ensuing Franco re-

16. In 1936, following a prolonged drought, heavy rains ruined much of Andalusia's
olive, and then wheat and barley crops. The economic crisis provoked by these natural
disasters was exacerbated by the war, and widespread hunger followed.

17. Several storytellers insist that Fray Leopoldo himself smuggled food into the city
during this period.

18. Woman, age sixty-three, born Granada, some grade school. Cleaning woman, usually attends mass.

gime. Although, again, a good percentage draw on firsthand memories in their judgments, even those storytellers born after the mid-fifties may have firm opinions on the subject.

Even while Dori, for instance, asserts that the Franco era held more stability for the worker, she nonetheless recounts various anecdotes about the hunger her parents and grandparents experienced. "My mother says I didn't live through the very bad times and is always trying to convince me that today is better," she remarks. Both Ernesto and Luís Antonio underscore the repressiveness of the Franco regime. "If you were caught thinking, you went to jail," Ernesto says with a grimace. "Franco worked hard at keeping Spain backward," declares Luís Antonio.

Tales of Fray Leopoldo's compassion toward the defeated following the war are often condemnations of the victors. These accounts reflect the particularly bloody events in Granada, given the activities of the Falangist "Black Squad," which the military authorities permitted to sow panic among the population by taking leftists from their homes at night to be shot in the cemetery.[19] In recalling the friar's kindness toward him as an individual, the following storyteller recreates in a compelling manner the hostility and fear of the time, explaining:

> 37. I was still very young when they assassinated my father.
> He was a Republican, so they killed him right there in the
> street. Afterward no one wanted to talk to us. They lowered
> their eyes when they saw us coming because everyone knew he
> had been a Red. No one said anything to us. Out of fear, you
> see? Only Fray Leopoldo crossed the street to greet us. The
> guards and the people in the street all watching us—a terrible,
> enormous silence. So then he ran his hand over my head and
> said to me in a loud voice, "Don't be troubled, little boy. Your
> father was a good man and is certainly with God."
>
> *Man, age sixty-one, born Granada, high school.*
> *Single, retired, attends mass "fairly regularly."*

Memories of Fray Leopoldo serve other storytellers as an introduction to more general denunciations of the era as well as Franco. Thus Doña Hortensia interrupts her account of one of the friar's miraculous cures to recall how he pleaded unsuccessfully with a group of soldiers not to arrest the young father of a large family. ("Of course, they took him off and shot him," she says with a sigh. "Those were terrible years. I have nothing, truly nothing good to say about them or that tyrant Franco.")

19. Preston notes that in the course of the war about five thousand civilians were shot in Granada. See his *Spanish Civil War*, pp. 54–55.

Another woman moves from an account of how Fray Leopoldo helps a terrified family to flee Granada to a detailed description of how Nationalist guards gun down a whole family in the Albaicín district because the mother has unthinkingly set out a red shirt on the clothesline. Although she mentions the friar's later kindness to the youngest son—who hid from the soldiers in a large empty jug used for holding quantitites of water before the advent of indoor plumbing—the massacre, and not the friar's ensuing aid, is her real interest. "I don't know," she reflects aloud at the conclusion, "Fray Leopoldo told us to forgive those who wronged us. But I have often asked myself, who could ever forgive so great an injustice?"[20]

As should be more than obvious from the examples here and in preceding chapters, stories of the friar are frequently, at heart, accounts of Franco and the Franco era. In some cases the storyteller may explicitly contrast the one's concern for the individual with the other's disregard for human life. While Fray Leopoldo is curing the sick, Franco is busy gunning down the able-bodied. "He, yes," one woman says of Franco:

> 38. He murdered many people. I say this to you because he killed two of my brothers, also a daughter-in-law, and a nephew of mine who tried to defend his mother. We saw it all without being able to do anything at all. So that's why I tell you that the world has its saints and its assassins. Both together. Because didn't Fray Leopoldo live right in the time of Franco?
>
> > *Woman, age fifty-four, born Granada, some grade school. Widowed, hairdresser, attends mass occasionally ("I'm a Catholic, but you could say I try not to overdo it").*

Franco, while the prime target of these extended narratives, is not their only villain. As we saw in the preceding chapter, tellers of Counterlegends often speak out against the ecclesiastical establishment, which they find implicated in, when not directly responsible for, the past's failings. This anticlericalism may be in the body of the story or in an addendum to the tale. "Those archbishops and cardinals talked for hours on end about charity, but they had Franco beneath a *palio* [a ceremonial canopy used to protect religious images] as if he were Our Lord," one woman complains somewhat unexpectedly toward the end of her tale.

---

20. Woman, age fifty-five, born Granada, high-school education. Single, runs beauty shop, usually attends mass.

Repression was particularly heavy in the largely working-class Albaicín, which was shelled and bombed by Nationalist forces.

She has just recounted how the friar successfully encounters a lost child for whom the police refuse to search because his father is a member of the opposition. "Fray Leopoldo did not talk at all, he only spoke through actions."[21]

Similarly, some storytellers suggest the friar's dislike for the aristocratic landowners, or *señoritos*, who were allied with Franco but as previously indicated, had existed long before the dictatorship. Others may find fault with an unthinking allegiance to tradition hostile to the slightest hint of change. One man observes bitterly:

39. In Fray Leopoldo's day parents thought that their children were going to be just like them. It never entered their head that the world could change. And so parents didn't send their children to school. What for? Weren't their lives going to be the same old thing? They had been born to work, to serve as arms for the rich [literally "the fat"].

> *Man, age forty-six, born Granada, some high school. Married, antique dealer, attends mass "every once in a while."*

Younger women are particularly likely to look askance at the sort of life led by their mothers and grandmothers.[22] "It's that they thought only about work and the family," a stylishly dressed young saleswoman in a leather shop explains with a toss of the head. "Me, I want to meet new people, to see new things, to travel."[23] At the same time that members of this younger generation express affection and respect for Fray Leopoldo (as well, sometimes, as faith in his miraculous powers), they make clear that they would not want to return to the past. "In those days," a sixteen-year-old manicurist born in France says with a disdainful flip of the hand, "one got married just to marry. If I were alive back then I'd probably be dressing saints! [Yo me habría quedado para vestir santos]."[24]

---

21. Woman, age fifty-two, born Granada, some grade school. Widowed, supported by husband's pension, usually attends mass.

22. See Jane F. Collier, "From Mary to Modern Woman." Although the changes in attitude the author describes would appear to be more total than those I encountered, the basic phenomenon she describes is very much in evidence among the younger women who told me stories.

23. Woman, age nineteen, born Granada, high school. Single, salesperson in leather shop, usually attends mass.

24. Girl, age sixteen, born Paris, some high school. Single, manicurist, attends mass from time to time.

The saints to which she refers are the wooden or plaster images in parish churches whose clothing unmarried women are entrusted with changing. The expression *quedarse para vestir santos* has the pejorative sense of remaining a spinster.

Dori echoes these sentiments when she asserts that women today have more freedom. "My husband and I had a real balcony-to-balcony romance," she says fondly. "I married him because I loved him. My mother, no. Poor thing. In her day a woman's parents would say, 'This one yes, and this one no.' So from this point of view, at least, the present, yes, is better."

From time to time, storytellers of both sexes attribute prophecies to Fray Leopoldo in which the friar pointedly assures his followers that the future will be better than the past. He may console a grieving mother, for instance, with the promise that the day will come when no one will suffer from the illness that has just claimed her infant son. Or he may guarantee a man whose brother has languished for many years in one of Franco's prisons that his grandchildren will be free to speak their mind. Although the friar may caution that the future will also have its problems, there is no question in these cases that he, like the speaker, clearly finds it an improvement.

For every individual who expresses doubts about, or outright dissatisfaction with, the past, there is another who considers it superior to the present. In contrast to the examples we have just seen, a number of the Fray Leopoldo tales express undisguised nostalgia for a bygone era and, occasionally, for Franco. The present is not devoid of redeeming features, but their preference for the past is clear.

Just as those who judged the present superior often cited many of the same reasons, so those who prefer the past tend to reiterate a few key themes. The perceived esthetic qualities of the past, its apparent simplicity and distinctive flavor, and the ostensibly greater interaction among people are unquestionably the most common. Not surprisingly, a good number of the storytellers are older individuals for whom this time holds numerous happy as well as not-so-happy memories.

The bits and pieces of an older way of life that surface in both Legends and Counterlegends may possess an apparently informational function. One woman, for instance, follows her account of how the friar predicts the birth of a baby to her long-childless sister with a description of the folkways formerly surrounding baptism. ("In Fray Leopoldo's time," she remembers, "the godmother would take the child saying, 'I take your child a Moor, to return him to you a Christian.' And the mother would respond, 'God give you health to make Christians of many Moors.' ")[25] Likewise, an eighty-two-year-old man recalls

---

25. Woman, age forty-nine, born Granada, some high school. Married, works at home, "almost always" attends mass.

his own surprise as a child on seeing the friar with a man in a navy blue suit ("in those days," he explains, "everyone wore black").[26]

"That was a different era," confirms Manolo's Aunt Mari. "On Good Friday husbands and wives slept apart. Whole families wore black and everyone avoided mirrors. 'Hush, now,' mothers would tell their children if they talked or giggled. 'Don't you know Our Lord is dying on the cross?' "[27]

In contrast to these fragments of oral history, which make no explicit judgment about the friar's era, other speakers firmly assert the past's superiority to the present. Time and again, the figure of Fray Leopoldo conjures up a verdant and unspoiled Granada whose disappearance implies larger transformations and impending losses that may be hard for older storytellers in particular to accept. Thus an artist in his eighties who begins by reminiscing about how he used to sketch in the gardens of the Generalife ends by expressing blanket skepticism about the present. For him, the physical beauty of a vanished landscape is part and parcel of a deeper harmony (and a particular set of aristocratic values) that time has severely eroded if not inalterably destroyed. He says:

40. I had, you see, very good professors. But the greatest of all has been the Generalife itself. Before becoming a state historical landmark, it was the private property of some dukes. Whoever wanted to paint there knocked on the door and a servant came to open it. Today painters work from photographs, but it isn't the same thing. Nature itself teaches you so much. It would seem that a green cypress could not have cast a violet shadow, but I've seen it, I've seen it, and, so, yes, it can be. The watered gardens, the enormous, scarlet cabbages had as much esthetic value as the *cármenes* [traditional homes]. And today they are no more, no more. They've torn down the house in which I first met Fray Leopoldo. That one and so many others.

> *Man, age eighty-four, born Granada, high school. Married, artist and art critic, "usually" attends mass.*

This storyteller is not alone in arguing that life was previously "purer" because of its greater proximity to nature. Some storytellers recollect with a trace of nostalgia or frank regret for another era how

---

26. Man, age eighty-two, born Granada, no formal education. Widowed, retired, does not usually attend mass.

27. Woman, age sixty-three, born Granada, grade-school education. Widowed, works in shoe shop, customarily attends mass.

The temporary avoidance of mirrors symbolizes a rejection of concern for one's own image in the face of Christ's death.

farmhands used to bring the harvest through the city streets. Rosi, though not actually saying the old days were better, insists that even the weather today is different because of atmospheric pollution. "In the past," she says, "it rained in winter, as it should. Today the winter may be dry and the summer cold and wet. Really, there is nothing one can count on any more."

In much the same vein, individuals may look back wistfully on a time before they had to worry about the effects on their own day-to-day existence of drug addiction, industrial and sound pollution, traffic jams, and widespread, often violent crime. Conveniently forgetting those less-than-ideal features so obvious to our preceding group of storytellers, they may dwell on the pleasures of a "more innocent" era—Christmas carolers accompanied by the rustic drum called the *zambomba*, street peddlers with their distinctive chants, bellringers whose once humble art has become the stuff of doctoral theses and concerts.[28] For at least one middle-aged man, the early seventeenth-century monastery that was home to Fray Leopoldo symbolizes a tranquility wholly alien to a frenetic present. Although he dwells on the building's physical appearance, he is clearly interested in those more spiritual qualities he associates with a bygone age. (The speaker, one might note, is an active member of Opus Dei.)

> 41. The monastery had a very simple doorway, a double line of cypresses, a statue of Christ to the left. And in front of the Christ was the principal entrance. Above, it read, "Oh, fortunate solitude; oh, sole happiness!" And at the end of the path was the entrance to the church. A very old, very simple church. It was pretty, and at heart it had a seraphic spirit. *It was like entering another world.* [my italics]
>
> > *Man, age fifty-one, born Granada, high-school education. Married, owns export agency, attends mass regularly.*

Storytellers may also argue that friendships and family ties used to be stronger and more meaningful. "In that time," one woman explains at the conclusion of an account of how Fray Leopoldo restores a young girl's paralytic shoulder, "We didn't lead one life but four [No llevamos

---

28. See "Francisco Llop: antropólogo valenciano que escribe una tesis doctoral sobre los toques de campaña." *El País*, 11 June 1984, p. 56. The article notes that bell-playing is presently 1 percent of what it was thirty years ago, and that trained bellringers have all but disappeared.

una vida sino cuatro]."[29] Rosi, for her part, remembers how all of the occupants in the old makeshift apartment house where her family lived used to place their mattresses in the courtyard on sweltering summer nights, huddling together under the staircase to pray to Saint Barbara for protection from lightning during thunderstorms. She says:

> 42. Today this is no more, but in that time the life of the heart was simpler. Great poverty, great ignorance, but in the moment in which you start thinking back, it all strikes you as so innocent, so attractive, so good. And now life is so different, so complicated. It's that we have many things, but we are more isolated from one another.

The obvious idealization of so many of these portraits of a bygone age makes it easy for the outsider to dismiss these memories as reactionary, and, indeed, some are. In the course of collecting stories about Fray Leopoldo, I encountered a handful of people who were as eager to canonize Franco as the friar. ("Two saints!" one older woman exclaims with glowing eyes.)[30] This fondness for the past may indicate an unwillingness or inability to deal with the present, but the individual who creates a resplendent image of the past is not necessarily uninterested in or hostile to the here-and-now. On the contrary, much as the friar's good deeds are used to call attention to the abuses that are the true subject of numerous Counterlegends, so exaggeration of the past's merits may highlight imperfections in a present, which is the narrator's true concern. "Who is the person today who would sacrifice himself for others like Fray Leopoldo did?" demands Ernesto's mother sadly. "Once upon a time, there were such people. But none, not one, remains."[31]

The following speaker, a young carpenter's assistant who is a friend of Manolo's, has clearly confused Fray Leopoldo with Padre Andrés Manjón in what becomes a scathing indictment of contemporary values. "This friar was very simple," he says:

> 43. He ate only what was necessary, drank only what was necessary, and that was that. He didn't want anything else for

29. Woman, age forty-five, born Granada, "very little" grade school. Married, works inside home, usually attends mass.

30. Woman, age sixty-one, born Granada, high-school education. Widowed, runs husband's bookstore, regularly attends mass.

This woman is not alone in her enthusiasm. A pro-Franco military coup was attempted on 23 February, 1981, and a relatively small but nonetheless significant number of persons regularly makes pilgrimages to the mausoleum that Franco shares with José Antonio Primo de Rivera in the Valle de los Caídos (valley of the fallen), north of Madrid. The Franquist party, however, has obtained a minimal percentage of the votes in recent elections.

31. Woman, age sixty-three, birthplace, educational level not stated. Cleaning woman, regularly attends mass.

himself. Today, no. We are in very bad shape. The world is a disaster because people don't talk to each other—they don't help each other any more. It wasn't like that in the time of Fray Leopoldo, understand? He helped the little gypsies. He founded a school for them. He gave them food, clothes, shoes. But today everyone runs after money. Everyone is afraid of others, and no one enjoys what he has.

> *Man, age twenty-two, born Granada, some high school. Single, carpenter's assistant, "almost never" attends mass.*

Glorification of the supposed simplicity and fellow feeling of the past often serves to call attention to the perceived materialism of the present. Ironically, though not surprisingly, many of the most vocal critics of the present are the sons and daughters of urban laborers or fieldhands who have worked long and hard to better their socioeconomic position, but who may nevertheless feel uncomfortable on some level with the consumer society of which they are most certainly a part. Like Rosi, who is extremely proud of the secondhand car and bright red refrigerator she has been able to buy with careful economizing, they have no desire to return to an impoverished past. Also like her, however, they feel they have lost something along the way ("it's hard to say exactly why, but things seemed better then"). One could argue they have lost nothing other than their youth. Underlying many of their comments, however, one also senses a resistance to a profit-oriented capitalistic system that has supplanted a still largely agrarian subsistence economy that placed great importance on personal honor and interpersonal obligations.

More than once, an individual who had just finished decrying the rampant consumerism of today's Granada would try to sell me something. ("Here, take my card," says one man. "Tell all your friends about me! I have the cheapest, nicest handkerchiefs in town.")[32] Likewise, the same elderly woman who laments the younger generation's supposed lack of interest in home and family wishes out loud that her own daughter were thinner and more stylish (más delgadita, más moderna).

This apparently contradictory behavior does not imply that the people in question are hypocrites or muddled thinkers. While they may sincerely admire those values they see embodied in Fray Leopoldo (and, in many cases, their own childhood), they may also feel intense pressure to

---

32. Man, age fifty-five, born Huelva, grade school. Married, handkerchief merchant, does not usually attend mass.

conduct their own lives quite differently. "He knew everything because he was above things" (El sabía de todo porque estaba por encima de las cosas), one woman explains, gazing up a bit ruefully at the profusion of roses and forget-me-nots embroidered on the towels that cover the walls of her small shop.[33] "Fray Leopoldo knew how to teach the rich," comments a clerk in a new, conspicuously high-tech laundromat:

> 44. He knew how to show them that wealth can't be the goal of life. He asked alms from the rich to give to the poor. He knew that the rich should be poorer and the poor richer. He knew that the world would be better if we were a little more equal. But, of course, he was a saint. And me—well, I have to think of money.
>
> *Man, age twenty-five, born Baeza, high school.*
> *Single, clerk, attends mass "from time to time."*

Then too, for some storytellers, the friar may represent a simpler and somehow more Spanish existence. Their descriptions of him may thus include complaints that contemporary life is not only more complicated or more "artificial" but also less original, less distinctive. The dissatisfaction they express with the consumerist present is often directed as much at its "un-Spanish" character as at its materialism. "I don't really know much about Fray Leopoldo," one man reflects:

> 45. But from what I hear he was very simple, very humble. He wanted nothing for himself. Now then, he lived in other times; they weren't like today. Because today we buy the big cars which the television shows us. Because our women wear jeans and play tennis when ten years ago no one knew anything about this. We have never had money, but yes, we used to have time—time to have another little drink with friends, time to talk. Today, no, not even this is left to us. We live in the land of money, we are more American than you—now there, don't look so sad. Things aren't all *that* bad you know. Waiter, bring more coffee!
>
> *Man, age thirty-seven, born and lives Marbella,*
> *grade school. Married, sells truck parts, rarely*
> *attends mass.*

Not just discontentment but a more profound pessimism and even hopelessness pervade a number of these narratives. "In the past, people wanted to survive. Today we want these things that people even more

33. Woman, age thirty-five, born Granada, high school. Married, linen shop owner, regularly attends mass.

selfish than ourselves stick before our nose. That which Fray Leopoldo did no one does anymore. Who is it today who doesn't think about a TV, an apartment, a nice car?" demands a young magazine seller. "And so these things become more important than our family and friends."[34]

The following speaker—a plainclothesman born in Granada, who has worked for the last few years in the Madrid airport—suggests that today's problems may defy solution. His certainty that "only a true miracle could put things in order" leads him to see people's faith in Fray Leopoldo as a last resort.

> 46. There are so many things in the world that don't make
> sense to me. You see, there are the drug addicts, and behind
> them the pushers, and behind them the doctors, the big
> economic interests. That is, it's something almost without
> solution because everything is related, there isn't anything
> that's not part of the game. So it is that people despair and
> seek a more magic, a miraculous, solution. Like these Hare
> Krishna people. Do you see that girl over there? [He gestures
> to a well-dressed young woman distributing pamphlets and
> long-stemmed red roses.] So then, that's how I understand this
> business of Fray Leopoldo. I myself don't believe in him, but I
> can see why others do.
>
> > *Man, age thirty-one, born Granada (Madrid*
> > *last nine years), some high school. Married, air-*
> > *port security, rarely attends mass.*

Once again, storytellers' depictions of a supposedly simpler, less psychologically demanding era do not necessarily imply emotional instability or dissatisfaction with their own day-to-day existence. Rather, they may be worried about threats to their personal happiness which they feel are posed by the direction being taken by the nation and the world. The following man, for one, is clearly less interested in returning to that time in which the friar made the rounds of Granada counseling the sick and needy than he is in denouncing the threat to the future posed by nuclear weapons.

> 47. Fray Leopoldo, yes, he lived for others. He helped the sick,
> the poor; he gave good counsel to the needy. Today it's very
> different. Because the atomic war is coming in which I'm going
> to die, in which you will die too. So how is it that people like

---

34. Woman, age twenty-seven, born Granada, some high school. Married, sells newspapers and magazines, seldom attends mass. ("Why should I? I don't need someone to help me pray.")

me are going to believe in saints when they can't even believe
in human beings?

> *Man, age twenty-two, born Alfique (Granada*
> *six years), some high school. Single, waiter in*
> *café, "almost never" attends mass.*

Some of the most interesting apparent celebrations of the past center
on the Huerta de la Alegría (garden of happiness), the monastery garden
in which Rosi used to play as a child. ("They had pigs, roosters, rabbits,
vegetables of every sort, and the biggest, sweetest lemons. It was like
another world. I never wanted to go home.") Because, as previously
noted, Fray Leopoldo was responsible for its cultivation during his first
years in the order and continued to spend spare hours there after becoming official alms collector, the garden remains closely associated with
him in the minds of many people.

In some accounts, the Capuchins, despite Fray Leopoldo's protests, insist on selling the land to a developer in order to make money. Sick at
heart, the friar dies soon afterward. In other versions of the story, the
garden flourishes throughout Fray Leopoldo's lifetime. In his final hour,
he gives his fellow friars detailed instructions for its care, but they ignore these, and the fabled fig trees and roses wither. Although these
individuals later repent, they cannot restore the garden to its former
glory. Chagrined, they tear out the remaining roots and pour cement
over the now barren earth.[35]

And yet, while these accounts resemble numerous other Counterlegends in their denunciations of the religious establishment (represented
here as elsewhere by the Capuchins), they may offer a more profound
message about the recent past. The magic quality of the fruits and flowers that Fray Leopoldo cultivates (cherries big as plums, roses that perfume all Granada) is often so pronounced as to effectively situate the
garden within another order of existence in which there is no future. As
such, it becomes a metaphor for a way of life the speaker finds appealing
but fundamentally alien, and therefore, no model for the here-and-now.
The real point of the tale is thus less the friars' ill treatment of the
protagonist than the irreparable loss of Eden that leaves one no choice
but to live in an imperfect present.

In yet more obvious support of this last point, while some storytellers
depict the Capuchins as purposely disregarding Fray Leopoldo's instructions, others suggest that the garden dies despite their best efforts. Sad-

---

35. Holy figures frequently display their displeasure through withering trees and
flowers. See Thompson, *Motif-Index*, D2081 ("land magically made sterile").

dened by their inability to revive its trees and flowers, the friars decide
to convert the site into a home for the elderly (the present Fray
Leopoldo Home in which Doña Hortensia lives). Although the following
storyteller takes obvious pleasure in recalling the fragrant haven over
which the friar presided, its transformation strikes him as inevitable.
The following account and others like it permit individuals to mourn a
past whose perfection isolates it from a present with which their true
allegiance must of necessity lie.

> 48. It was a lovely thing, lovely to behold. But when the
> *Hermanico* died, it quickly went to seed. The other friars did
> everything, everything so that those roses might bloom again,
> but with no luck. They worked hours planting, watering, and
> nothing grew. Where there had been lemons, oranges as big as
> any melon, there was now just stone. So they had no other
> choice but to build that old folks' home. It's sad. But, of
> course, that's how things go. Besides, the home turned out
> very nicely. Today there are more than a hundred old people
> living there.
>
> > *Man, age sixty-four, born Granada, some grade*
> > *school. Widowed, retired government worker,*
> > *attends mass "maybe once a month."*

As already noted in the beginning of this discussion, comparisons of
past to present need not favor one era over the other, and indeed the
great majority of storytellers are quick to point out advantages and disadvantages in each. Although these individuals may lean somewhat
more toward one era than the other, they do not express a definite preference for either. "Before," Doña Hortensia explains, "Spain was a garden for four or five persons. Well, now it has lost a good deal of its
beauty, but today, in turn, thank goodness, there are more people who
can enjoy it."

For some storytellers, the divide between past and present is so great
as to make impossible any sort of qualitative judgment. Readily ac-
knowledging various contrasts between Fray Leopoldo's time and their
own, they nonetheless are careful to avoid terms like "good" and "bad,"
"better" and "worse." "The world today is just different, very different," they may say if pressed. This sort of insistent neutrality, however,
is the exception rather than the rule. Most accounts of Fray Leopoldo
constitute a kind of verbal balance sheet in which storytellers reflect
aloud on collective as well as individual tragedies and triumphs.

Storytellers quite often modify their opinions in the course of these
extended evaluations. A sudden, chance recollection, for instance, may

cause a celebration of the past to change direction in mid-stream. A reference to the rodents who fed on the rotting fruit and refuse, for instance, emphatically breaks the mood created by a lyric evocation of Fray Leopoldo moving beneath a canopy of light and leaves. "It was beautiful to see those plums, pears, and custard apples as far as the eye could see; just beautiful," the speaker, a housewife in her early fifties, assures her listeners. "But to be honest with you, I hated to let the children play outside because there were so many rats."[36]

Manolo's Aunt Mari likewise concludes an initially glowing portrait of Fray Leopoldo's Garden of Happiness with a somber reference to the typhoid epidemic that claimed her grandmother's life. "Of course," she remarks as an apparent afterthought:

> 49. That garden, like all the others in Granada, was watered with dirty water. It was very pretty, but it smelled bad—very bad. Wastes were thrown into the street; there were some seemingly bottomless and filthy wells here. The irrigation ditch was a true pigpen. To the extent that people would pay much more for lettuce if it were from the Albaicín [district of the city] because the water there was from the fountain and was not polluted. There was a lot of disease, a lot of epidemics in the time of the *Hermanico*. My grandmother died of cholera in 1940—she and I don't know how many others.
>
> > *Woman, age sixty-three, born Granada, some grade school. Widowed, works in shoe shop, customarily attends mass.*

Storytellers, to be sure, may take the opposite tack, evincing an unexpected twinge of nostalgia that they initially dismiss. Thus Luís Antonio concludes a denunciation of Franco's disastrous early economic policies with the wish that he could have seen Granada fifty years ago. "What the Albaicín must have been like then!" he exclaims with obvious longing.

In much the same spirit, a countess—who now depends on the income from urban real estate instead of country produce—claims to prefer her bright new fourteenth-story apartment to the drafty old house of her childhood; she remembers the inner courtyard where Fray Leopoldo used to take refuge from the midday sun. "I don't like old things at all," she says:

---

36. Woman, age fifty-one, born Valencia, high-school education. Married, works at home, regularly attends mass.

50. I believe in the present. But to be honest with you, every
once in a while I miss the courtyard—the courtyard in my
parent's house. [Here the speaker pauses, lost in thought.] Do
you see that chair there? It used to be Fray Leopoldo's. He
always sat there in the shade to rest when he came to ask alms.
It's curious. He came to the house all year round, but when I
think of him it's always May. I couldn't bring myself to throw
it out. I know it's very ugly. And yet, even so . . .

> *Woman, age sixty-two, born Granada, high-
> school education. Widow, lives on the proceeds
> from real estate holdings, customarily attends
> mass.*

The same sorts of mixed sentiments are particularly apt to surface in
discussions of the past's supposed simplicity. Affectionate evocations of
Fray Leopoldo and his epoch may conclude with the speaker cautioning
listeners that his or her own preferences are not necessarily shared
by others. Although, for example, Rosi's aunt speaks wistfully of a
more "wholesome" era, her extreme pride in one of her grandniece's
achievements enables her to view her own aversion to the present with a
certain humor. "We had nothing, nothing in Fray Leopoldo's time," she
explains:

51. But we sang, we danced, we ate sunflower seeds in the
plaza, and we entertained each other. Today, no, we have lost
the happiness we used to have. Now, of course, it isn't
everyone who thinks the way I do. My grandniece calls me
outdated. [She chuckles.] I'm so proud of her! Here I am,
almost illiterate, and she is studying philosophy in the
university.

> *Woman, age seventy-one, born Granada, "a
> few months" grade school. Single (fiancé killed
> in civil war), cook and dishwasher in restaurant
> (recently retired), attends mass "when I can."*

A similar self-awareness characterizes the account of an older man
from Maracena, a small town on the outskirts of Granada. His own feelings of discomfort with the present do not prevent him from asserting
that most people are better off today than they once were. His reflections below follow an account of how Fray Leopoldo healed the speaker's
paralytic sister. "Ask anyone about it," the man says:

52. Well, then again, perhaps not anyone. It's that today more
than half of the people who live here were born someplace else.

Today we are no longer a village, but rather, an international village. Everyone is a police lieutenant, a chemist, a furniture salesman, everything except a farmer. If I had to depend on [sales of] fertilizer for a living, I wouldn't eat. Today I no longer know the names of half the streets. And the customs—I'd rather not talk about them. People like me will never adjust. Although I have to tell you that life is better for the majority of people. In those times of Fray Leopoldo people lived very badly.

> *Man, age sixty-four, born Maracena, some grade school. Married, runs small fertilizer supply store, attends mass "maybe once a month."*

Even persons who declare their satisfaction with the present may reveal flashes of yearning for the past. They may begin by decrying the provincialism of an earlier Granada ("life was so boring!" a ninety-three-year-old man exclaims).[37] They then proceed, however, almost involuntarily, to undercut their own position. One older woman shakes her head in amazement on recalling how she had to wait until the age of thirty to see nearby Málaga. She nonetheless goes on to compare Granada to a small town with its attendant charms as well as its frustrations. "Back then," she says, "Granada was the whole world. And the people were like people in a small town. Very backward, knowing nothing, but still innocent and good."[38]

A similarly deep-rooted ambivalence is obvious in Manolo's reactions to the notion that people used to be more interested in the welfare of others. "Of course there was more contact with one's neighbors," he says, "What would you expect when there was only one toilet for thirty people? Or when your neighbor was a nightwatchman who would come home from work at dawn and doze off in the stairwell so as not to wake the children who were still sleeping with their mother in the master bed? All of us tripped over him. More contact, indeed!"

And yet, despite his apparently unequivocal rejection of the idea that relationships among people were somehow better in the past, Manolo goes on to remember how the residents of the tenement-like house in which he spent his childhood took up a collection for the widow of a neighbor, and how the woman and her seven children spent Christmas with his own family. These recollections lead him not just to soften his

37. Man, age ninety-three, born Granada, no formal education ("that is, I can read and write, but all I know I learned at home"). Widowed, retired, does not attend mass.
38. Woman, age fifty, born Granada, some grade school. Married, sells fruit, usually attends mass.

initial stance but ultimately to embrace the position he first mocks. "So then," he concludes a trifle grudgingly, "it's true that misery unites people. And money beats down [*atropella*] people's conscience. I don't like the sort of poverty that was all we had in Fray Leopoldo's time. But where there is poverty there is more union among people."

In summary then, the references to past and present so evident in many of the accounts we have seen here may appear at first glance to indicate a lack of interest in Fray Leopoldo. Much of the friar's power, however, lies precisely in his ability to trigger broader reflections on the past. The tellers' frequently mixed and powerful feelings about the changes they describe unite the most disparate narratives, giving them a bittersweet urgency.

CHAPTER SIX

Conclusion

In the preceding pages we have seen that tales about Fray Leopoldo are united by an essential pluralism, a deeply rooted anti-institutional impulse, and a concern for, when not obsession with, the relationship between the present and the recent past. In all of these respects the stories stand apart from the formal Life, which depicts the friar as traditional exemplar and miracle worker.

The Fray Leopoldo narratives attest to the ability of a seemingly conservative and, for some, even archaic folk form to foster spirited debate about change in present-day Granada. Their ability to highlight the inadequacies of frequently employed oppositions between official and popular, sacred and secular, oral and written, and, ultimately, past and present, gives them an interest and importance that transcends both the saint's legend and contemporary Spain. At the same time, however, the stories remain an especially vivid reflection of the multistranded, uneven, and always time- and place-specific processes customarily subsumed under the label of "modernization." In this conclusion I first recapitulate the ways in which the accounts we have seen in the preceding pages underscore the serious inadequacies of the dichotomies just mentioned.[1] I then briefly suggest key ways in which the narratives diverge from numerous other accounts of holy figures. I conclude by insisting that the stories, as well as the tensions and transformations they reflect, are uniquely Spanish and Andalusian.

---

1. I am by no means the first to call attention to the inadequacies of such dichotomies in relation to religious symbols and saints' cults in particular. See, for one example, Brown, *The Cult of the Saints*, for one discussion of "popular" vs. "official" religious practice.

Official vs. Popular

The opposition between Great Traditions and Little Traditions, closely associated with the writings of Robert Redfield, has come under increasing attack within the last decade by scholars who have pronounced it overly simple and, often, inaccurate.[2] The problems with this division are nowhere more obvious than in the Fray Leopoldo narratives. It is almost impossible to formulate a single definition of "official" and "popular" in regard to the stories we have seen, let alone to separate effectively the two domains.

In the preceding discussion, I have referred to the formal biography of Fray Leopoldo as the fullest and most direct expression of what storytellers themselves regard as the officially legitimated vision of his life. At the same time, however, I have stressed that this text, authored by one of the friar's fellow Capuchins, embodies a perspective on him definitely not shared by all members of the ecclesiastical establishment, even in his own order. We saw in chapter 2 that a number of more radical, action-oriented clerics express definite reservations about, when not objections to, the devotion to Fray Leopoldo. For them, the friar represents an other-worldly orientation and obedience to established authority that they associate with personal conformism and political apathy. Certainly, the parish priests who prepared the highly critical report presented to the current archbishop of Granada on his arrival in the city would in no way endorse the image of the friar either as miraculous intercessor or as embodiment of eternal truths so central to the Life.

I have also emphasized the more subtle, albeit significant, divergences in outlook between the archbishop and the friar's biographer. The former refers repeatedly to Fray Leopoldo as an expression of a bygone era and goes so far as to assert that "different times have different models." The archbishop's support for the friar's cause is above all an acknowledgment of the faith that many Granadans place in Fray Leopoldo and a signal of his own desire to forge a new alliance between the church and a lay population whose members have bitter memories of the hierarchy's support for Franco. Nowhere in his remarks does one find the insistence on timelessness or the interest in Fray Leopoldo as a model of specifically Franciscan values that are hallmarks of the Life.

The Life is also the biographer's personal statement of disappointment intertwined with faith. Fray Angel clearly cannot forget his own experience of Fray Leopoldo and of the civil war. Thus, despite both his studied

2. See Redfield, *Peasant Society and Culture*. Some of the most articulate recent criticism appears in the articles collected in Badone, ed., *Religious Orthodoxy and Folk Belief*.

attempts at objectivity and heavy reliance on time-honored hagiographical conventions, the Life is Fray Angel's story as much as it is the friar's.

If the designation "official" in regard to the Fray Leopoldo phenomenon is therefore relative at best, the term "popular" presents yet more perplexing problems. First, although the tales represent a large cross-section of Granada, they do not reflect all sectors of the population. I made an effort to talk to all sorts of people about the friar, but conspicuously absent from my collection are stories told by factory workers and gypsies. Thus while the tales can be said to fulfill the dictionary definition of popular, "of or relating to the general public," they most definitely reflect the views and values of some people more than others.[3]

Moreover, we have observed at length the often dramatic differences in storytellers' attitudes toward Fray Leopoldo, the supernatural, and recent Spanish history. The essential heterogeneity that is one of the oral corpus's most significant features impedes formulation of a single, collective image of the friar. Just as one encounters clay statuettes of a chubby friar (a hole in the knapsack for toothpicks) along with a variety of wooden carvings and expensive porcelain figurines, so the stories present diverse and often competing portraits of Fray Leopoldo. Which of these is popular? One, all, none? Are some more popular than others? And how does one decide?

We have also noted the class divisions visible in Legends and Counterlegends. Although I have cautioned that each group includes a range of individuals, Legend tellers on the whole are unquestionably more apt than their counterparts to be members of the middle and upper-middle classes. The documented link between social class and participation in formal religious activities in Spain would lead one to expect their stories of Fray Leopoldo to parallel more closely the Life.[4] Indeed, the great majority of Legends appear to resemble the formal biography. More detailed examination, however, reveals a number of critical divergences that make it all but impossible to see them as endorsements of the Capuchins' (or at least one Capuchin's) view.

3. This is the definition given by *Webster's New Collegiate Dictionary*. According to it, "popular" can also mean "suitable to the majority," "having general currency," or "commonly liked or approved."

As previously noted, Granada has relatively few factories and factory workers. I did, however, make a concerted effort to obtain stories of Fray Leopoldo at the Alhambra Beer Factory and was singularly unsuccessful. Although accompanied by a member of the community, I experienced a similar lack of response in the heavily gypsy Sacromonte district. "Fray Leopoldo didn't come this way a lot, I guess," one young man remarked.

4. See, for instance, the previously cited "Asistencia a la Eucaristía dominical, 1983."

And yet, if these stories are not "official," are they necessarily "popular"? And if so, how can we meaningfully compare individual Legends and Counterlegends? Does Doña Hortensia's sudden denunciation of Franco in an otherwise Life-like account of one of the friar's miracles mean that her account is somehow more "popular"—or at least less "official"—than Dori's conventional version of the same incident? Or is popularity a function of class identity, so that anything that Dori says is "popular," while Doña Hortensia's accounts must necessarily be assigned some other label? And if the tellers' social class is to be the criterion for cataloguing stories, how does one deal with the obvious differences in the tales related by Dori and by Manolo or Rosi? And what about Luís Antonio and Ernesto, who claim simply to be repeating what others have told them? Although absurd in one respect, these questions are nonetheless effective in demonstrating the difficulties engendered by any attempt to compartmentalize the tellers, let alone their stories.

The lack of any single definition of the "official" and the "popular" does not, to be sure, negate the existence of discernible differences among the persons and groups competing for possession of a common symbol. It does, however, force one to see existing demarcations as manifold and, above all, fluid. For although the stories represent the continuation of the struggle between the church and the lay population for control of a long-contested space, neither its parameters nor the identity of the combatants can be regarded as fixed.

Sacred vs. Secular

The same sorts of difficulties inherent in potential divisions between the official and the popular resurface in attempts to divorce the sacred from the secular. We have observed that the figure of Fray Leopoldo often serves as a springboard to discussion of far broader, apparently nonreligious concerns. In addition, he embodies hierarchical personal relationships found in both the family and the church.

Even those tales that address most directly questions about miracles and sanctity in an increasingly technological society are apt to contain references to an earlier era. Moreover, storytellers as a whole would appear at least as interested in evaluating recent changes affecting both the individual and the community as in debating whether Fray Leopoldo does or does not fit conventional definitions of a saint. A sizable number of narratives devote considerably less time to the friar than to his times. Then too, were I to eliminate from my collection any tale that commented on the Franco years, no more than a handful of stories would remain.

But the past itself reveals a deliberate blurring of "sacred" and "secular" concerns. One could argue that, particularly during the first half of his regime, Franco attempted nothing less than to resacralize Spanish society by celebrating the nation's religious heritage and empowering its ecclesiastical institutions.[5] His National Catholicism was a methodical attempt to use religious symbols to describe and justify an array of political decisions.

In addition, one could argue that Spain's economic modernization and accompanying social transformations (often referred to as "secularization"), which began in the mid-1950s, are themselves a dominant theme of the Fray Leopoldo stories. "What does it mean to live in a present where people believe different things or nothing at all?" storytellers often appear to be asking. "How can I believe in miracles when I believe in science?" Or "How could Fray Leopoldo have performed this seemingly impossible action which my mother—and she taught us to always tell the truth—says she saw with her own eyes?"

The difficulty of divorcing the sacred from the secular is further compounded by the fact that tales of the friar are often debates about, or emphatic rejections of, a type of patriarchal authority closely associated with, but in no way the exclusive province of, the Catholic church. Like so many other Spanish and Andalusian holy figures, Fray Leopoldo embodies fundamental ideas about the family and society at large. He emphasizes both how familial interactions provide the framework for the conception and interpretation of religious symbols and how ambiguous feelings that cannot always be manifested within the family circle may find expression in the religious domain.

In chapter 1 I talk about the many persons who call the friar *abuelito*, or grandfather. This makes Fray Leopoldo the titular head of a family in which supreme authority is vested in the father. As both an approachable father emeritus and a parent who almost certainly has been (and may still be) stern and overbearing with his own sons and daughters, he suggests criticism as well as endorsement of the sort of authority Andalusian fathers have customarily been expected to exert. At the same time, the popularity of this "grandfather saint" underscores the remoteness of a divine Father whom storytellers may consider too important to be bothered with the ups and downs of their own lives.

The same sort of intermingling of religious and family symbols (and thus "sacred" and "secular" concerns) is obvious in Fray Leopoldo's identity as a *hermano* or *hermanico* (friar or brother), rather than a

---

5. Berger makes this point in *The Sacred Canopy* when he compares postwar Spain to postwar Israel in the attempt to return to religious traditions.

padre (priest or father). As a lay member of a religious order, Fray Leopoldo did not rankle people through formal preaching or stand in judgment as a confessor, but rather, inspired in them the affectionate protectiveness customarily associated with younger siblings. As a result, he provides an effective foil to those other members of the religious hierarchy—including ordained members of his own order—whom many tales portray as arrogant and uncomprehending. And yet even while Fray Leopoldo is perceived as being more approachable than his fellow clerics, he undeniably remains a member, and thus implicit supporter, of an institution in which, as in the nuclear family, authority is directed downward from above.

Oral vs. Written

At first glance, the distinction between the oral and the written in relation to the Fray Leopoldo stories would appear mercifully simple. After all, the Life is indisputably a printed composition; the stories, oral performances. This seemingly straightforward division is nonetheless complicated by the pointed reliance of the friar's biographer on oral testimony, as well as by the multifaceted and often indirect relationship between the stories and the Life.

Hagiographers throughout the ages, to be sure, have depended to varying extents on oral sources. As these sources, in turn, reflect centuries of interchange with a literary tradition, the saint's legend is, in many ways, a hybrid form.[6] The Life, for its part, reveals a particularly close relationship with the oral tradition. As vice-postulator of Fray Leopoldo's canonization process, its author had no other choice but to collect many personal testimonies, which have influenced his account, albeit in a less obvious manner than written models such as the *Fioretti*.

Fray Angel's concerted effort to seek out oral sources does not mean he did not transform them. As Fray Leopoldo's friend and official spokesman for his cause, he undoubtedly wanted to hear some things and did not want to hear others. Then too, one would not expect people to have shared some sorts of information with him. It is difficult, for instance, to imagine the mayor of Alpandeire boasting to Fray Angel (as he did to me) about how he tricked the Capuchins into building the road the community needed rather than the one which would have led from the town to Fray Leopoldo's ancestral plot. One should also note that

---

6. See Utley, "Oral Genres," for a discussion of the relationship between various folk-literary and literary forms.

Fray Angel did not own a tape recorder ("they make me nervous," he explained). As a result, there must therefore have been many occasions on which he jotted down half of what he heard, hoping to rely on memory, or slowed down the storytellers, therefore modifying their presentation. Unlike most contemporary folklorists and anthropologists, he quite often asked informants to give him a written account of their experiences or interviewed them in his office, thus removing them from a more natural performance setting.

All the same, Fray Angel did set out to record oral testimony and to faithfully transmit this in his biography of Fray Leopoldo. In the juridic document known as the Articles of Canonization, he routinely omits or transforms material that might hinder Fray Leopoldo's cause. But in the Life, he quite often allows his sources to directly influence his writing.

We have noted, for instance, that the incident in which the young Leopoldo gives away the money intended by his mother for cooking oil appears in the Articles as an illustration of his charity from an early age. In the Life, however, the coins he offers to the souls mysteriously find their way back into his pocket. The author distances himself from this apparently miraculous, if not frankly magic, occurrence by naming his sources (and thereby transferring the burden of responsibility for the truth of the account to them). He also leavens his account with humor, noting that the heavens were not always so quick to show approval of Fray Leopoldo's generosity. Nonetheless, he has retained the outlines of the story essentially as it appears in the notes he took in Alpandeire. This fidelity to what he heard, or thought he heard, from three old men there gives the incident a peculiar flavor. The palpable presence here and elsewhere of an oral substratum gives a sometimes unexpected dimension to this often self-consciously "literary" work.

If the Life's debts to oral sources are clear on numerous occasions, storytellers' relationship to it—as well as to a more diffuse and generalized hagiographic tradition—is considerably more complicated. I have pointed out that although people quite frequently talk as if they were thoroughly familiar with the biography, my pointed questioning about specific incidents often revealed that they actually had not read so much as the first page. A sizable number of storytellers, to be sure, are acquainted with abridged versions of the text and are almost certainly responding to what they have heard about the friar from other people. As one might expect, their own feelings toward these human sources cannot help but influence their own assessments of Fray Leopoldo.

The storyteller's source might be a cherished relative, such as Dori's grandmother, who recounted the friar's miracles for the children every time she came to visit. It might be an employer who gave everyone the day off on the anniversary of the friar's death (Rosi's uncle), or a customer who regularly spends large amounts of money on flowers for the crypt but who is horrified when a tradesman (Manolo) is forced to raise his rates. Storytellers may likewise have in the back of their minds a next-door neighbor who is certain Fray Leopoldo will find her youngest son a job (Ernesto's mother) or the classmate of a girlfriend who brags that the friar has gotten her through an exam for which there was no time to study (Luís Antonio). Sometimes, indeed, they are not even responding to what so-and-so told them, but rather to what they imagine so-and-so *would* say if asked. ("How do I know? I know!" one man assured me. "Haven't I lived next door to him for almost twenty years?")[7]

Thus despite the existence of a certain consensus among storytellers about what constitutes the authoritative or "official" vision of Fray Leopoldo, only some are actually responding to a specific, literary representation. For this reason, I have in most cases actively avoided suggesting a direct correspondence between the stories and the Life. Then too, while I have regularly discussed contrasting presentations of Fray Leopoldo, I have offered very few one-to-one textual comparisons.

The stories also raise doubts about what is a function of oral vs. written composition and what must be attributed instead to differences in motivation on the part of storytellers and the friar's biographer. The "performance character" of the tales—how and to whom a story is actually recounted—is undoubtedly significant. So is the Life's identity as one in a long line of hagiographical texts. Nevertheless, while in no way seeking to deny the importance of the mode of transmission, I would insist that the more immediate goals of the storytellers and the friar's biographer are at least as deserving of attention.

The abundant detail evident in the Fray Leopoldo tales is, for instance, an obvious feature of many kinds of oral narrative. And yet, storytellers' intense concern for particulars unquestionably reflects a desire to personalize and relive a specifically Spanish past. As I shall shortly reiterate, the type of detail in the Fray Leopoldo stories differs markedly from that found in a number of other saints' tales; the tellers' almost overwhelming desire to document change is in no way characteristic of legends as a whole.

---

7. Man, age fifty, born Granada, some grade school. Married, taxi driver, does not attend mass.

By the same token, although the friar's biographer is certainly aiming for concision, we have no reason to believe that he would have included more details had he written a longer work. The pared-down, exemplum-like incidents in the Life strongly suggest Fray Angel's loyalty to a vision of the friar as Franciscan archetype rather than to a unique personality located in a specific place and time. This vision must have been more compelling to the friar's biographer than specific literary forebears or the need for brevity.

Past vs. Present

Before leaving the subject of dichotomies, it seems appropriate to touch on the difficulties potentially associated with yet another opposition. Perceived differences between the past and present are at the very heart of the Fray Leopoldo tales. And yet, while I myself have followed their tellers' lead in regularly juxtaposing two, ostensibly separate time periods, any such division is relative at best.

I suggest in chapter 5 that separating "was" from "is" even in the most objective terms raises various problems. Where exactly does the Spanish past leave off and the present begin? The day of Fray Leopoldo's death? The hour after Franco's funeral? Does it start with Vatican II? Or with the election of the Socialists almost twenty years later?

Clearly, none and all of these answers are acceptable. What we conveniently refer to as "the past" is multiple and fluid, a series of at times apparently contradictory and partial processes that different people define in different ways. Thus, for instance, although Franco is dead, Francoism has not necessarily vanished. And while one can certainly speak of a "post–Vatican II mentality," there were progressive Spanish priests long before John XXIII, just as there are others who continue to think as they did a half-century before. In short, despite my own efforts to document the ways in which storytellers regularly contrast Fray Leopoldo's era with the present, the relationship between his time and theirs is necessarily more complex and ambiguous than individual comparisons would suggest.

Then too, one must ask not only, what past? but also, whose? The stories we have seen routinely commingle personal, communal, and even national experience in the figure of Fray Leopoldo. But Doña Hortensia's conception of the friar is not Ernesto's or Manolo's, not simply because they have different attitudes toward him or toward organized religion, but also because they are different people who have led quite different lives. These experiential differences prompt them at least in part to invent a past that will be true to their own vision of the present and to their larger sense of what life means.

Saints' Lives as Contemporary Legends

The staunch resistance of the Fray Leopoldo narratives to various forms of dichotomization is in no way uncharacteristic of folk forms in general or of saints' legends in particular. In their essential abiguity and twin potential for accommodation and subversion, they resemble a long line of literary forebears.[8]

But the accounts relayed in this study do stand out from the majority of oral and written saints' tales available in library collections.[9] I would suggest by way of conclusion that tales about Fray Leopoldo are considerably more open-ended than many stories about holy figures. Their very specific use of time and their range of attitudes toward belief further distinguish them from various other hagiographic narratives and ally them to a number of conspicuously secular and contemporary legends.[10]

On the whole, the legend tends to be loosely structured. "Endless in bulk and variety" and "often so short and formless as to defy classification," the genre has long exasperated specialists.[11] The extreme flexibil-

---

8. Bollème underscores the essential ambiguity of folk forms in her discussion of French chapbook accounts of holy figures as an ongoing movement between the text as lived performance and written "prise de pouvoir unique et délibérée." See her "Religion du texte et texte religieux," p. 75.

9. There may well be other stories much like those of Fray Leopoldo, particularly within modern, urban settings. I base this statement on the narratives available in print in research collections.

10. The difficulty of generic definitions, the varying use of time in legends, and the question of belief are all discussed in general terms in Georges, "The General Concept of Legend."

For a good sense of the wide variety of approaches to the legend see Hand, ed., *American Folk Legend*, and Petzoldt, ed., *Vergleichende Sagenforschung* (the latter volume brings together a number of now-classic pieces on the subject by important theorists such as Lutz Röhrich, Carl-Herman Tillhagen, and Friedrich Ranke). A sampling of more recent thinking of the legend can be found in Smith, ed., *Perspectives on Contemporary Legend*, and Bennett, Smith, and Widdowson, eds., *Perspectives on Contemporary Legend*, vol. 2. Other important book-length works on legend include Rosenfeld, *Legende*; Röhrich, *Sage*, and *Sage und Märchen*.

11. The quotations are from Hand, "Status of European and American Legend Study." For an overview of some of the problems inherent in generic classifications of folk forms including the legend see Dan Ben-Amos, "Analytical Categories and Ethnic Genres." For a series of essays specifically on legend classification see Peeters, ed., *Tagung der "International Society for Folk-Narrative Research" in Antwerp (6.–8. Sept. 1962): Bericht und Referat.*

The apparent formlessness of legends has led some scholars to look to psychological factors of their mode of transmission in an attempt to define the genre. A good example of the psychological approach is Dundes, "On the Psychology of the Legend." Dégh and Vázsonyi propose a communication-oriented approach in "Hypothesis of Multi-Conduit Transmission in Folklore."

ity of form that has proved the despair of numerous legend theorists, however, is hardly true of the saint's tale.[12] On the contrary, nearly all accounts of holy figures are based on a finite number of readily recognizable folk motifs.[13] Furthermore, most accounts focus on a description of a single protagonist who, although defined through interactions with other persons—including the narrator—nonetheless remains the undisputed center of the tale.

The Fray Leopoldo stories, for their part, are considerably less tightly structured than many of their counterparts. Although some accounts reveal an easily identifiable beginning, middle, and end, many others are little more than offhand comments. In other cases, bits and pieces (or large chunks) of personal experience or oral history intermingle with readily recognizable folk-literary themes. Time and again, we have observed a storyteller interrupt an account of how the friar helps—or refuses to help—a needy child or struggling worker in order to describe a long list of vanished landmarks or an incident from the civil war. Even those stories that focus most intently on Fray Leopoldo and his exploits often include more or less elaborate tangents. The teller, for instance, may observe how a café the friar supposedly frequented has long since gone out of business, while another may point out the lack of even the simplest labor-saving devices ("people had to work like burros during Fray Leopoldo's time"). Individuals may allude to the intense hunger experienced in both the city and the countryside following the civil war or to a time before modern highways had replaced winding country roads.

As noted in an earlier chapter, Spanish storytellers' propensity to digress contrasts markedly with the distinctly more focused presentations I encountered in the northeastern Brazilian backlands.[14] Those who talk about Fray Leopoldo not only engage in far more asides and afterthoughts, but even more significantly, their listeners rarely prod them back to the topic at hand. Unlike the members of Brazilian audiences, who were often visibly irritated by such departures ("and so *then* what happened?" someone inevitably demanded), those in Granada very rarely registered disapproval.

---

12. For one attempt at a generic definition of the saint's tale see Olsen, " 'De Historiis Sanctorum.' " The author deals primarily with medieval texts. A much earlier attempt to classify hagiographical narratives is Gerould, *Saints' Legends.*

13. For a discussion of recurring themes in Christian saints' legends see Loomis, *White Magic.*

14. See Slater, *Trail of Miracles.* I am in no way claiming that the stories I collected in the Brazilian backlands are characteristic of all, or most, traditional saints' tales. I would nonetheless suggest that they are closer than the Fray Leopoldo stories in a number of important respects to a large portion of the oral and written models most familiar to scholars.

In addition to stories that incorporate an abundance of seemingly unrelated material, we encountered various others in which the friar himself often appears almost extraneous to the narration as a whole. Quite
often, storytellers do more than digress, cheerfully abandoning the friar
for other themes. The extreme looseness of a good portion of the Fray
Leopoldo stories suggests that despite the wide array of attitudes toward
sanctity and the supernatural evident within them, the holy figure himself has ceased to be the prime concern for many tellers. A number of
the examples we have seen lead one to ask, "Is this story really about
Fray Leopoldo?" Although the answer is not always clear, the tellers as a
group undoubtedly have pushed the saint's legend well beyond its customary limits. Although the friar's presence unites the most disparate
stories (sometimes, indeed, it would appear to be the only common de-
nominator), his varying role within the corpus provides a striking contrast to that of holy figures in many other narratives. Thus, even
though the tales are not as numerous or varied on the surface as those
found in other collections, they are set apart by their emphatic lack of
closure.

These frequent digressions and departures in the Fray Leopoldo stories bring me to my second point, which has to do with time. Although
legends as a body deal with the historical past, they may reveal considerable variation in how they define and present their subject. "For while
a legend is *set* in the past," observes the author of an often-quoted essay
on the problems of definitions of the genre, "that past may be conceived
to be *either historical or antihistorical;* and while a legend is set in the
past, it might really be conceived to be *in* and *of* the *present* (and perhaps the *future*) as well."[15]

Saints' legends as a subgroup tend to be antihistorical. Even when
they deal with readily recognizable historical events—a war, a drought,
a particularly fateful political or economic decision—they regularly
transpose these specific instances to an eternal present and a seemingly
unending struggle between good and evil. The storytellers I recorded in
Brazil, for instance, inevitably transformed particular historical person-
ages and events into illustrations of the undeserved suffering and humiliation of the just man and his eventual dramatic triumph over his
oppressors. This dedication to a larger principle recalls the Life of Fray
Leopoldo, but it is decidedly uncharacteristic of the stories recounted in
the city's streets.

15. Georges, "The General Concept of Legend," p. 15.

I have noted that attempts to separate accounts of Fray Leopoldo from more all-encompassing descriptions of the recent past fail to see his importance as a gateway to an era about which many residents of Granada—and Spaniards as a whole—have strong and often contradictory feelings. By the same token, if judged by the largely literary standards of what we have come to know as the saint's legend, the stories appear to suggest a genre in the process of dissolution. But the very elements that might suggest the genre's imminent demise to an outsider (the open-endedness of the tales and their tendency to use the protagonist as a mere springboard) are precisely those features that excite the enthusiasm and approval of those most directly involved. Tales that lack the detailed and, to the outsider, extraneous considerations of the early Franco years often strike both listeners and tellers as less interesting or somehow less complete.

A third major distinguishing feature of the Fray Leopoldo stories is their often explicit attempt to grapple with the slippery question of belief.[16] Their intense and at times conscious pluralism makes the tales an excellent example of the contrapuntal interplay of "question, answer, statement, denial, and doubt," which some writers have identified as the very essence of the legend.[17]

This sort of self-conscious questioning is evident in various representatives of the genre, but it once again is hardly characteristic of the saint's tale per se. Nearly all narratives available to the scholar insist on the truth of the event described. The Brazilian storytellers, for instance, summarily rejected the notion that any right-minded person could disagree with their assertions. Not only do they wholeheartedly affirm the veracity of their accounts, but often they also spell out the dire consequences of disbelief. Should their listeners express doubts about the narrative—and by extension, the power of its protagonist—they cannot claim that they were not amply and graphically forewarned.[18]

The Fray Leopoldo storytellers, in contrast, appear to expect uncertainty if not outright opposition from the listeners. Their seemingly casual attitude toward religious matters is also distinctive as is the insistence on the subjective quality of faith. ("Well, it's true for me," people often said. Or, yet more frequently, "There is no arguing about

16. The question of belief has long been central to legend theorists. For a historical overview see Dégh and Vázsonyi, "Legend and Belief," and Dégh, "The 'Belief Legend' in Modern Society." Another useful discussion is Blehr, "The Analysis of Folk Belief Stories."

17. See Dégh and Vázsonyi, *Dialectics of the Legend*, p. 42.

18. For a discussion of these sorts of retaliatory actions see Halpert, "Supernatural Sanctions and the Legend."

belief.") The storytellers expect their listeners to question their assertions, and they express reservations themselves about the events they
are describing. Although some skirt the issue of truth ("this is what my
mother told me"), others voice their doubts directly ("is this story true?
I'm not really sure"). Still others go so far as to dismiss their own accounts as patently untrue. ("It's a pretty story, but I don't believe it,"
they might declare. Or "This is a good example of the sort of nonsense
one hears in the streets of Granada.") In a number of cases, belief itself—and not the friar or even the larger relationship between past and
present—emerges as the ultimate subject of the tale.

As even this very brief discussion should suggest, the Fray Leopoldo
stories depart in key ways from a number of accounts of holy figures,
particularly those associated with the past and the countryside.[19] The
open-endedness, the intense engagement with a recent and historically
specific past, and the deep sense of relativity that set apart these accounts from more traditional saints' narratives are characteristic of many
contemporary legends on superficially very different themes.[20]

And yet, if the Fray Leopoldo stories resemble present-day legends
from a wide variety of contexts, there is no mistaking their distinctly
Spanish and Andalusian character. They focus, after all, on a local Capuchin friar. Fray Leopoldo speaks with a distinctly regional accent, eats
fried crumbs and drinks *cortados*, and moves with ease about a city he
knows and loves. His deeds regularly trigger commentary on Spain's
present in light of its past and, more particularly, on the bitter legacy of
the civil war.

19. Some of the numerous difficulties associated with distinguishing contemporary
from noncontemporary or traditional legend are discussed in Williams, "Problems in Defining Contemporary Legend."

20. In their association with a long written as well as oral tradition they are much like
the Mexican treasure tales discussed in Shirley Arora's "Memorate and Metaphor."

The distinctly present-day character of these, in some ways, highly traditional stories
seriously challenges the wisdom of any attempt to divorce religious narratives from other
sorts of legends. Accounts of the friar clearly do not just allow, but actively encourage,
debate that at least one pair of scholars asserts "is not under normal conditions found in
legends of sacral character" (Dégh and Vázsonyi, "Dialectics of the Legend," p. 8). These
authors argue for a division between "religious" or "hagiographic" legends and "folk legends" on the grounds that religious legends supposedly "do not evoke and do not even
permit" that expression of varying viewpoints that they find fundamental to the legend as
a genre.

To be sure, not all scholars would concur with this attempt to place religious legends in
a separate compartment. For one example of a highly successful study dealing with saints'
tales as legends see Schmitt, *The Holy Greyhound*. See also Yoder, "The Saint's Legend in
the Pennsylvania German Folk-Culture," as well as a number of the articles in Schmitt,
ed., *Les Saints et les stars*, and in Wilson, ed., *Saints and their Cults*.

To be sure, this local figure is credited by some people with performing supernatural actions that have been attributed to Christian saints for many centuries. The use of a clearly and even exaggeratedly traditional religious idiom by both believers and nonbelievers to talk about a wide variety of social, political, and economic—as well as more narrowly religious transformations—is in no way a constant of what has been termed "the modernization process." Nor, as we have seen, is anti-institutionalism a novelty in Spain. In addressing the near-universal theme of change in the face of new technologies, the tales we have examined employ tropes and play on conflicts with a long and specifically Spanish history. The Fray Leopoldo stories thus call into question not just what "secularization" may mean in a particular local and national context, but also in what ways the tensions it underscores may be considered peculiarly modern.

"How different are two sets of narratives descended from a single literary tradition?" I asked at the beginning of my research. My final answer is "As different as Spain and Brazil." Although this may sound facile, the discovery is hardly that: many individual stories are virtually identical. Were proper names to be removed and the texts translated into English, it would be impossible in many cases to ascertain their origin. While it is true that these narratives draw on a common store of folk motifs and, often, on a common literary language, their intimate if constantly shifting relationship with the world around them makes all one-to-one comparisons limited if not misleading. In the last analysis, the Spanish and Brazilian stories are as alike as apples and oranges or, as residents of Granada would say, chestnuts and eggs ("se parecen como un huevo a una castaña").

In their familiarity as much as their essential multiplicity, the Fray Leopoldo stories resemble the popular pastry called *mil hoja*. Though compact to the eye, it splinters upon touch into many layers. Generally short on the sort of passionate conviction that illumines a number of other saints' tales, the stories are, in turn, long on nuance and intensely multivocal. In them, one experiences vicariously the jagged course and individual psychic costs of social movements customarily described in the most general and schematic terms. One also comes to appreciate the considerable flexibility of the most outwardly traditional folk-literary forms. The tales are of particular interest in that there is no guarantee that the oppositions they encapsulate will be those in play tomorrow. The stories' continued interest for the residents of Granada suggests a struggle for symbolic possession that has not yet been, and may never be, resolved.

In the introduction to this study, I noted it would be quite possible to spend a long time in Granada without ever hearing Fray Leopoldo's name. The devotion itself is hardly obvious. There are no elaborate, eye-catching processions like those that enliven Holy Week, no curious rites that make good copy for glossy tourist magazines. Only an occasional traffic jam, a greater-than-usual number of single carnations tucked into a drinking glass on a manicurist's table or a carafe atop a café counter marks the ninth of the month. It would be easy to overlook the little statue of the friar tucked in between a bottle of Parfaite Amour and another of Johnny Walker in the home of a friend's mother, the familiar face stamped onto a decorative linen towel in a modest "one-fork" restaurant. One could just as readily skip over the letter in a local newspaper from a resident of the Realejo district who complains about the inconveniences caused by the rerouting of the Number 6 bus ("and what about the old lady accustomed to visiting Fray Leopoldo's crypt every morning?" the writer demands as a parting shot).[21]

And yet, the largely unsensational nature of the Fray Leopoldo phenomenon in no way obviates its importance. Accounts of the friar's life may appear at first glance simple and repetitive. "Yet another miracle!" the casual observer is apt to exclaim. But the tales are not all alike. Initially straightforward, seemingly otherworldly, they are in the end oblique and extraordinarily human.

21. "Letters to the editor," *El Ideal*, 18 May 1984, p. 12.

Appendix A

Comparison of Extraordinary Events in the Life, the Articles of Canonization, and the Oral Tradition

The following table lists the miraculous or near-miraculous events that appear in the Capuchins' biography of Fray Leopoldo, together with appropriate page numbers. Each incident is classified as prophecy, clairvoyance, cure, divine intervention, physical impossibility, or satisfaction of psychic need (some events, to be sure, suggest more than one such category). I have gone on to indicate wherever there is a correlate in the official canonization papers, as well as the number of times the incident was recounted to me.

Only obvious versions of a single story are reflected in these calculations. For instance, the tales I heard are replete with examples of bilocation, clairvoyance, and cures of mortal afflictions, but they do not necessarily correspond to the specific incidents reported in the friar's biography. The cases of the stubborn stone and the trapped mules, both discussed at length in the body of this study, are the most frequently repeated of those actions that appear in the Life.

Incident in Life	Classification	Correlate in Articles	Times Recorded in Oral Tradition
1. Mute child speaks as foretold on FL's death (p. 14)	prophecy/cure	—	16
2. Money given to poor reappears in FL's pocket (p. 27)	divine intervention/ physical impossibility	—	4

Incident in Life	Classification	Correlate in Articles	Times Recorded in Oral Tradition
3. FL prays for protection against storm; child who mocks him struck by lightning (p. 29)	divine intervention/ physical impossibility	No mention of money's reappearance (p. 25)	4
4. FL almost trampled by holiday crowd; saved from certain death by mysterious soldier (p. 71)	divine intervention	—	2
5. FL expresses hope for unborn child although expectant mother has told no one of pregnancy; child goes on to join religious order (p. 131)	clairvoyance/ prophecy	—	1
6. FL heals fractured arm (p. 131)	cure	—	3
7. FL warns family never to allow operation on child; parents later permit surgery, child saved from death when they call on FL (p. 133)	prophecy/cure	—	—

Incident in Life	Classification	Correlate in Articles	Times Recorded in Oral Tradition
8. FL causes tumor in boy's knee to vanish (p. 138)	cure	—	3
9. FL arranges husband for young seamstress eager to marry (p. 138)	satisfaction of psychic (and possibly economic) need	—	2
10. FL assures landlady poor tenant will pay rent by 3:00 next day; tenant does (p. 141)	prophecy	—	—
11. Christ-like figure suddenly appears, seemingly from nowhere, to absolve remorseful husband who has asked FL's help (p. 143)	divine intervention/ physical impossibility	—	—
12. Hospital aide discovers FL hovering inches above bed (p. 154)	physical impossibility	Incident mentioned, but no details provided (p. 23)	6
13. FL emerges unscathed when he places self between two fighting men (p. 155)	physical impossibility (or strong improbability)	—	9

Incident in Life	Classification	Correlate in Articles	Times Recorded in Oral Tradition
14. FL cures sick child with bowl of chicken soup (p. 172)	cure	—	4
15. FL knows servant is lying when she claims her employer cannot receive him (p. 189)	clairvoyance	Realizing that girl is lying, FL stresses importance of truth (p. 29)	2
16. Angel-like figure enters locked gate to ask FL for food (p. 192)	divine intervention/ physical impossibility	—	—
17. Dove singles out FL from others in a crowd (p. 199)	divine intervention	—	5
18. FL sighted in two places at same time (p. 203)	physical impossibility	—	15
19. FL knows young man has something to tell him (p. 205)	clairvoyance	—	—
20. FL advises woman to follow advice regarding lawsuit; she avoids trouble by following his advice (p. 205)	prophecy	—	—

Incident in Life	Classification	Correlate in Articles	Times Recorded in Oral Tradition
21. FL reads mind of nun considering withdrawing from order (p. 206)	clairvoyance	—	3
22. FL cautions family not to travel without consulting him; they escape disaster through compliance (p. 206)	clairvoyance	—	—
23. FL reads mind of young friar tempted to abandon studies (p. 208)	clairvoyance	Incident summarized with proper names (p. 45)	—
24. FL reads mind of woman ashamed to discuss problem (p. 209)	clairvoyance	Incident summarized (p. 45)	2
25. FL foretells happy outcome of financial matter (p. 209)	prophecy	Incident summarized (p. 45)	—
26. FL reads mind of woman worried about father (p. 210)	clairvoyance	—	—

Incident in Life	Classification	Correlate in Articles	Times Recorded in Oral Tradition
27. FL reads minds of two women worried about dead brother (p. 211)	clairvoyance	—	—
28. FL foretells death of daughter of monastery organist (p. 211)	prophecy	—	—
29. FL foretells saintly future of Conchita Barrecheguren (p. 211)	prophecy	Incident noted briefly (p. 47)	3
30. FL warns of fatal consequences of apparently minor ailment (p. 212)	prophecy	Incident stresses conformity to divine will (p. 43)	8
31. FL assures family that mortally ill woman will recover (p. 213)	prophecy	—	11
32. FL appears in convent precisely at hour of mother superior's death (p. 213)	clairvoyance	—	4

Incident in Life	Classification	Correlate in Articles	Times Recorded in Oral Tradition
33. FL intervenes to save young man unintentionally poisoned by fellow theology student (p. 214)	cure	—	1
34. FL instrumental in child's dramatic recovery from typhus (p. 215)	cure	—	6
35. Bread vendor encounters new prosperity after giving FL loaf of bread (p. 252)	satisfaction of psychic (as well as economic) need	Brief allusion to incident (p. 49)	12
36. FL plows a field faster than a whole group of strong young men (p. 272)	physical impossibility	—	11
37. FL singlehandedly extricates mules from rut (p. 276)	physical impossibility (or strong improbability)	Incident repeated with emphasis on friar's horror of blasphemy (p. 24)	34
38. FL assists in moving heavy stone that workers could not budge (p. 279)	physical impossibility (or strong improbability)	Incident repeated with emphasis on horror of blasphemy (p. 24)	41

Incident in Life	Classification	Correlate in Articles	Times Recorded in Oral Tradition
39. FL restores crushed skull (p. 283)	cure	—	1
40. FL promises woman that house will be hers; ownership papers arrive two hours later (p. 295)	prophecy	—	2

Appendix B

Spanish Originals of Stories in the Text

The following texts correspond to the English translations that appear in the body of the study. Because of the background noise that reduces the sound quality of a portion of the tapes, I have not attempted a phonological transcription. The reader nonetheless should be aware that the taped originals reveal a high degree of regional pronunciation (*pa* instead of *para*, *cantao* instead of *cantado*, etc.).

1. Ella le mandó una visión en que se veía al hijo haciendo todo tipo de escándalos. Pero la madre no le hizo caso, todavía quería su hijo de vuelta. Entonces el muchacho vuelve a la vida y le trae un sufrimiento tras otro; por el mal que él hacía, ¿ves? Entonces fray Leopoldo le contó a mi hermana este ejemplo, que no sabía ella lo que iba a pasar con esta hija. Pero ella también insistía, insistía, hasta que por fin él mandó que la niña se levantara de la cama. Pero luego después, ella comenzó con todo tipo de desgracias. . . .

2. Una vez allí en Láchar, había un matrimonio extrema[da]mente bueno, pero pobre, pobre. Así que cuando el Hermanico vino a pedirles una limosna, no tenían nada en casa para darle fuera de unas pocas almendras. La señora le explicó que ellos tenían vergüenza de ofrecerle tan poca cosa pero no había más comida en casa. Que corría mucha hambre en estos tiempos, ¿entiendes? Pues entonces, él les agradecía las almendras e iba andando para otra casa. Momentos después la señora abre la puerta y ve un almendro de esos grandes lleno, pero lleno de flores muy bonitas, perfumadas. Igual a una nube grande, rosada. Todavía se puede ver allí, yo misma lo he visto muchas veces.

3. Este carretero era honesto pero pobre, muy pobre. Tenía la esposa enferma desde hacía muchos años y varios chiquillos. Vivía de cargar

ladrillos, arena, lo que fuera—una persona excelente. Entonces un día iba pasando por una de esas calles no adoquinadas, que había muchas en la época, y se le volcó el carro: se metió en un bache enorme de grande. Así comenzó a pensar en la familia, lo que iba a sufrir. Pues la gente pasaba mucha hambre entonces, no era como ahora. Así que en el mismo momento llega fray Leopoldo y le dice, "Amigo, ¿qué le pasa?" El otro dice, "Ay, Hermano, es que no puedo sacar el carro de aquí." "No se preocupe," le dice el Hermanico Leopoldo. "Que Dios siempre ayuda a los buenos." Y así fue. Salieron los animales al instante y él no perdió nada.

4. Años atrás una señora presentó su hija a este Siervo de Dios para que rogara por ella, pues tenía ya siete años y no articulaba palabra, a pesar de oír perfectamente. La respuesta de fray Leopoldo fue algún tanto enigmática:

—Señora, hablará su hija cuando yo calle.

Pues bien: aquella mañana rompió a hablar, y no como el que está aprendiendo, sino como el que sabe hacerlo desde los primeros años.

Su madre, en medio de la alegría familiar, recordó la predicción imprecisa del venerable capuchino. Llamó por teléfono al convento:

—Sí, falleció anoche—fue la respuesta.

5. Iba por los cortijos, mucho por los cortijos; muy pobre, muy delgado, pues casi no comía. Aquellos eran tiempos muy malos, la gente pasaba mucha hambre, así que él iba pidiendo y repartiendo todo lo que la gente le daba. Entonces el primer milagro que hizo era en uno de los cortijos en el camino del Padul. La madre de una niña ciega le pedía que le ayudara y él tuvo mucha pena de ella, una niña tan bonica que no podía ver las cosas tan lindas que hay para ver en este mundo. Dolores, se llamaba Dolores la niña. Yo conocí a la abuela de ella en casa de mi suegra hace mucho tiempo, cuando ella todavía vivía en la Calle del Aire. Bueno, entonces él pasó la mano por la cabecita de la niña y le dijo a la madre, "Ella verá cuando yo no vea más." Así. "Ella verá cuando yo no vea más." Bueno, pasaron los meses, pasaron los años, ella casi no se acordaba más de lo que él le había dicho. Hasta que el día en que la niña comienza a ver bultos. Y luego después sigue viendo de verdad. Así que la madre se acuerda de fray Leopoldo y llama por teléfono al convento, a Granada. "¿No hay un frailecico que antes andaba mucho por los cortijos? Pues yo quería hablar con él." Entonces le dijeron, "Lo sentimos mucho, señora, pero hace un par de días que se murió."

6. Es que yo, sí, creo mucho en los milagros. Porque acontece que cuando yo tenía mis catorce años, fuimos a Lourdes. Y allí había una señora todo torcida, no podía caminar de manera alguna, la pierna estaba

totalmente hinchada, ¿no sabe Ud.? Así que entró en el agua y luego después comenzó a gritar, "¡Gracias a la Vírgen santísima! Gracias a la Vírgen santísima!" Así. Y ella estaba llorando, todo el mundo lloraba. Y yo, pues, yo me eché a llorar también—pues bien, así que yo creo que los santos obran milagros. Y fray Leopoldo era un hombre muy santo, todo el mundo lo sabe.

7. Había pues una señora muy rica que vivía por aquí en una casa en una transversal de Gran Capitán. Una casa muy bonita de tres pisos, tenía un patio precioso lleno de plantas de todo tipo. Entonces él iba siempre allí a pedir para los pobres. Así que un día él fue detrás de un poco de aceite. Que hoy en día este convento es rico pero en aquel tiempo era pobre, pobre: los frailes tenían una huerta y vivían de ella. Pues bien, cuando pidió el aceite, la criada—Emilia se llamaba, todavía vive, la señora no, pero ella sí—entonces ella fue a buscar el aceite en el cacharro donde se lo guardaba. Pero no había nada, el cacharro estaba totalmente vacío. Entonces la señora le dijo que viniera más tarde, que iba a mandar buscar aceite en el cortijo. Pero él dijo que no, que ya había aceite en el cacharro y que no valía la pena mandar buscar más. Así que la criada, muy extrañada, fue a ver de nuevo. Y el cacharro estaba lleno, lleno.

8. Lo que sé de fray Leopoldo es esto: que un día todo el mundo estaba rezando en la catedral, todo el mundo de rodillas, rezando, y él también, los ojos cerrados, de rodillas. Y de repente comenzó a subir, a subir para arriba sin que él se diera cuenta de nada. Todo el mundo lo vio. El no se dio cuenta de nada hasta que la cabecilla casi rozaba el techo. Pero los de abajo sí, quedaron atónitos. "Mire al Hermanico," se dijeron. Y el obispo tuvo que parar la misa hasta que él volvió a la tierra. Fue mi madre quien me lo contó pero todo el mundo lo sabe. Quiero decir, yo no lo ví pero sé que es verdad, sí, es verdad para mí.

9. Es un misterio, ¿no sabes? Porque estaba haciendo un frío de morirse y el árbol lleno de fruta y de flores. De repente, sin más nada, pues él era así. Parecía ser una de estas personas sin la menor importancia pero cuando él pasaba por la calle la gente veía cosas realmente maravillosas. No sé explicártelo, nadie lo explica. Pero que acontecía, acontecía. Puedes confiar, que es verdad.

10. Había pues un pedrusco en medio del camino cerca del Triunfo. Y había cinco obreros, uno de ellos conocido nuestro, por nombre de Antonio, Antonio Gómez. En aquella época casi no había nada motorizado, la gente se peleaba para sobrevivir. Así que estos obreros habían estado luchando con ese pedrusco la mañana entera. Estaban cansadísimos, a punto de más no poder, cuando llegó fray Leopoldo. Así que él les

calmó. "Descansen un poquito," les dijo, "pues la piedra está para salir." Y fue así. Uno de ellos se fue, pero los otros siguieron su consejo. Y el pedrusco les salió sin más problemas.

11. Yo veía mucho a fray Leopoldo cuando chiquilla. Mi padre tenía un depósito de botellas de refrescos en la Calle San Isidro y él pasaba mucho por el barrio. La gente le tenía muchísima confianza. Si un niño se enfermaba no era al médico o al cura a quien se llamaba, era a fray Leopoldo. Yo lo vi pasar una mañana entera al lado de un muchacho enfermico. Para ver si la fiebre no se pasaba, ¿sabe Ud.? Ahora no le digo que era un San Juan de Dios, una Santa Teresa, yo no lo digo. Pero el niño se mejoró. Esto sí.

12. Soy extremeño, no soy de aquí, así que no llegué a conocer a San Leopoldo. Pero tengo muchos amigos que me han contado como él pasaba por aquí con su burrico pidiendo y repartiendo todo lo que recibía con los pobres.

13. Para decirte la verdad, yo confío mucho más en los reflejos de mi hermano que en el santo. Pero no voy a decirles nada, ¿para qué? Además es cierto que pudiera haber acontecido algo mucho más feo. Pues el coche salió muy mal pero no les pasó nada. No me parece ningún milagro, pero aún así, hay cosas en la vida que no se explican fácilmente.

14. Claro que yo no creo que se puede cambiar un pedrusco en una piedrecita. Es sólo una manera de hablar. Que fray Leopoldo tenía mucha mano con la gente, conseguía hacer cosas que una persona más instruída nunca pudiera haber hecho. Así que cuando la gente te dice que él cambiaba las piedras en piedrecitas están diciendo que él era una persona fuera de lo común; que él era extraordinariamente bondadoso, tal vez, extraordinariamente bueno.

15. No digo que los jóvenes, que yo, no creemos en nada. A lo mejor todos creemos un poco en esto de los santos por si acaso hay Dios. Pues habiendo Dios, no queremos ir al infierno. Es que nadie sabe del otro mundo, si hay o no hay, ¿ves?

16. Era una vida dura hasta más no poder. Y allí fray Leopoldo, andando por las calles todos los días con su cesta, pidiendo para el convento. Era para los frailes, ¿entiendes? sólo para ellos. "En la casa del cura siempre hay hartura," como dice el refrán. Para la gente de la calle, nada. Nada en absoluto. Nosotros nos moríamos de hambre pero no nos hacían caso. Mira, había una niñita de ocho años que les pidió comida un día y le dijeron que no había nada para comer en el convento. ¡Nada para comer! ¿Entonces cómo se explica que los frailes todos andaban tan gorditos? Sin duda se nutrían de aire. De aire y de rezos.

17. Así que él vivía para servir a los más necesitados. Fray Leopoldo, no, sólo pensaba en llenar la barriga, él y los otros frailes, no pensaban en otra cosa. Mira, hoy en día hablan de como él andaba por las calles descalzo en el invierno, pero yo mismo solía arreglarle las alpargatas, y tenían la suela bien gruesa, ¡puedes confiar!

18. Dicen que se acostaba con todo el barrio de San Lázaro pero yo no sé. A lo mejor es mentira pero dicen que en su día era muy amigo de esas mujeres que, que . . . A lo mejor se arrepintió de haberse acostado con tantas mujeres al fin de la vida y así quedó haciendo penitencia como limosnero. A lo mejor. Pero dicen que quedaba en la calle hasta las cuatro de la mañana a tomar y a hacer todo tipo de escándalos. Es lo que dicen por aquí.

19. Es que fray Leopoldo andaba mucho en la zona. Confesaba a las prostitutas, les ayudaba mucho. Les enseñaba a leer y a escribir, les traía comida, y luego después . . . no, no, estoy bromeando. Te juro que estoy bromeando. Les ayudaba de veras. Les ayudaba, sí. Que un amigo mío me contó como era: él iba por las calles, descalzo, entre las mujeres de mala vida de quienes nadie quería saber. Menos que todos, los capuchinos. Eran ellos mismos los que comenzaban a decir cosas feas de él, ¿sabes?

20. El tenía que traerles una cierta cantidad de dinero—digamos treinta duros—todos los días. Sin faltar. Y si no lo tenía, los otros frailes no lo dejaban entrar. Le obligaron a dormir allí en el portón, ¡pobrecito! Así que la gente tenía pena de él porque era uno de esos viejos limpios, bien bonicos. Y le daban unos céntimos para que él pudiera dormir en su propia cama.

21. Yo, sí, creo en los santos, y creo en los milagros, eso, sí. Ahora esto de fray Leopoldo no pasa de habladurías. A fray Leopoldo, pobretico, los otros frailes no le hacían caso en absoluto. Incluso había más de uno que se burlaba de él. Hoy no, claro que no. Le tienen en un trono. Pues eso de los milagros es un señor negocio. ¡Tanta vela, tanta flor, tanta cosa!

22. Pues bien, entonces fray Leopoldo hacía muchos milagros, mucha cosa buena por aquí. Curaba a los enfermos, a los ciegos, hasta se quitaba los zapatos para dárselos a los más necesitados. El regalaba tantos pares de zapatos así a los pobres que los capuchinos le dijeron, "Mire, Fray Leopoldo, no vamos a darle más zapatos si Ud. continúa de esta manera." Hoy ellos dicen que fray Leopoldo solía andar descalzo aún en invierno por ser tan humilde, cuando la verdad es que ellos no querían darle ni un par de alpargatas. Claro que andaba descalzo. ¿Qué otra cosa podría hacer el pobrecillo?

23. El era el pobre del convento; los demás eran ricos, tenían dote. Y él era lego, pobrecito, así que tenía que servirles. Que esta gente es así. Ud. sabe, siempre quieren mandar en los demás. Pues entonces él barría los patios, hacía todo lo de la cocina. Tenía que limpiar los zapatos de los demás todos los días. Lavaba la ropa de cama y fregaba el suelo. Todo lo que los otros no querían hacer. Pues él era pobre, no sabía leer, así que se reían de él y le trataban como si fuera empleado suyo.

24. A fray Leopoldo le odiaban, por eso le mandaban a pedir a los señoritos, a la pompa de Granada. (¿Qué quiere decir pompa? Pues pompa es millonario, es quien tiene un banco, quien tiene mucha tierra.) Entonces él iba a pedir a estas casas en que la señora solía dar las flores para el altar y estas cosas. Iba la tarde entera a pedir limosna, descalzo, con sol o con lluvia, con mucha humildad. Y cuando regresaba al monasterío tenía que aguantar la risa de los demás. Comían el pan que él les había conseguido pero se reían de él. Aunque él hacía muchos milagros. Por ejemplo, eso de la moneda de oro.

25. Durante la vida fray Leopoldo hacía mucho, mucho, para los pobres de Granada pero aquellos otros frailes capuchinos no le hicieron caso. Dijeron que todo era mentira, fanatismo, y después de muerto le echaron en el cementerio, bien lejos de todo. Los frailes y las monjas se juntaron todos para enterrarle. Con la cara triste pero por dentro muy alegres. Querían olvidarse de él. Estaban hartos de aquellos milagros suyos que les habían dado tanto trabajo.

26. A ninguno de los capuchinos les gustaba el Hermanico Leopoldo. El jefe del monasterio sobre todo, éste vivía diciendo cosas horrorosas de él. Mentira, pura mentira, ¿comprendes? Hasta que un día éste enfermó, quedó muy enfermo, estaba para morir. Pues bien, a estas alturas piensa de repente en el hermanico, hace promesa con él para no morir e irse al infierno. Y se salva. Se salva, sí, señor. Así que queriendo reconocer tan gran milagro manda construir una iglesia. La iglesia del Triunfo. Cosa muy de lujo, todo el mundo la conoce.

27. En el pasado había mucha gente mala, realmente muy mala. Y los pobres todos muy inocentes, no sabían defenderse. Hoy no, es diferente. Todo el mundo tiene un nieto abogado que le dice, "Oye, abuelito, deja esta vida sacrificada y vente a vivir en la ciudad, que aquí es mucho mejor." Pero en aquellos tiempos, por ejemplo, había un señorico de la tierra de esos muy malos, muy poderosos, que quería sacarle el terreno a uno de sus trabajadores. Insistía e insistía tanto que el pobre casi se lo entrega. Pues le hacía unas amenazas tan terribles que el hombre casi se muere de miedo. Así que el sinvergüenza le habría robado por seguro si fray Leopoldo no hubiera aparecido por ese pueblo en el momento cierto. Era un fraile muy milagroso.

28. El venía por el campo con la cesta llena de trigo. En tiempo de la cosecha, el sol en la cara, el campo todo dorado de sol, dorado de trigo. Hoy hay una carretera buena pero en aquella época había sólo un camino de tierra. Solía pasar el día entero pidiendo comida y repartiéndola en el camino pues había mucha hambre en aquellos días, la gente sufría mucho. Así que era sólo cuando comenzaba a atardecer que se acordó de repente de los frailes que estaban esperándole en el convento. Pues ellos tenían vergüenza de pedir, dependían de él para comer. Así que él no sabía qué hacer. Corría para el convento, muy preocupado pues no le quedaban más que unos granillos que ni daban para un pajarillo llenar el estómago. Pero cuando abre la puerta del convento de repente siente la mochila muy pesada, pues se había llenado de pan. Así. Entonces corre para servirles a los capuchinos que ya estaban en la mesa. "¡Por fin!" le dicen. "Tardaste mucho en el camino. Y nosotros aquí muriéndonos de hambre. ¡Que egoísmo!"

29. Encendieron las luces y quedaba una cosa de ensueño, con aquel cantillo del agua. Había vino de lo más fino que hay en toda España, carne de toda especie. . . . Al fin del banquete les pusieron una tarta de helado que era tan bonita que daba pena comerla, era como un castillo pero todo de helado, ¡qué maravilla!

30. Fray Leopoldo, sí, lo conocía mucho. Era el que venía siempre en una furgoneta llena de pieles. Nosotros antes teníamos una fábrica de cueros y comprábamos las pieles a los capuchinos, que en aquella época tenían muchas reses; no sé bien por donde, pero ellos se comían la carne y nos vendían las pieles. Pues bien, entonces hicimos la cuenta y si fuera una cosa de 300, fray Leopoldo siempre decía, "No, no, 500, 500," así, de broma ¿no sabe Ud.? Y se reía mucho, mucho. Que él era santo pero también andaluz, entiendes, y hasta a nuestros santos les gusta regatear.

31. Ahora, esto de los milagros no pasa de pura invención. El no hacía nada, quiere decir, nada del otro mundo. Además yo no creo en los milagros. Al fin y al cabo, ¿para qué sirven, pues? A mi ver sólo existe lo humano. El bien que hacemos, el mal que hacemos, todo queda aquí en la tierra. Y si nosotros todos nos hiciéramos el bien uno al otro, este mundo sería una balsa de aceite.

32. Entonces, fray Leopoldo se sentaba con ellos, les dio pan, les dio morcilla, lo que él pudiera tener. Sólo no les daba dinero, pues el dinero que recibía era todo para el convento. ¡Ahora si hubiera sido por él, puede Ud. creer que aquellos viejitos habrían quedado con el dinero también!

33. Es que hemos pasado de una esclavitud a otra. La del analfa-betismo y de la pobreza a la de la televisión y estas cosas que no dejan a

212 / Appendix B

nadie pensar. Mi hija aquí sólo puede hablar de las últimas cositas:quiere este disco, aquellos zapatos de tenis, aquella muñequita. Mira, me gustaría creer que estamos mejor ahora que en la época de fray Leopoldo. Pero a mi ver, las cosas me parecen muy iguales, demasiado iguales. ¿Y el gobierno? Mejor ni hablar. Todos estos políticos dicen una cosa y corren a hacer otra.

34. Tienes que entender que en la época de fray Leopoldo corría mucha hambre. Eramos ocho hermanos y teníamos que irnos a la estación con mi madre para esperar el vagón de carbón que pasaba por Granada todos los días. No tenía hora cierta, así que siempre salíamos de casa a las cuatro de la mañana, con un frío de pelar. A veces el vagón llegaba sin tardar pero a veces teníamos que esperar hasta las ocho o las diez de la mañana. Ay, ¡qué vida más dura!

35. Y así que cuando ella por fin llegó a casa, los vecinos estaban esperándole. Una cola enorme frente a la puerta, la gente casi se mataba para comprar un trozo, que no había carne alguna en la calle para vender, ¿ves? Pero aún así mi madre obligó a todo el mundo a esperar. La carne olía tanto, tanto que tenía que bañarse primero. ¡Qué vida más sacrificada! Por Dios, ¡qué olor!

36. Pues todo ¿me entiendes? era tan difícil. Mira, hoy mi sobrino le pide pan con mermelada a mi madre de merienda y ella quiere saber qué clase de mermelada quiere, ¿melocotón, uva, naranja? Pero en aquel tiempo cuando fray Leopoldo iba andando por Granada pidiendo, ¿cuál era el niño que se atrevía a pensar en mermelada? ¡Qué va! Que no había ni pan.

37. Yo era todavía muy chaval cuando asesinaron a mi padre. Era republicano, así que le mataron en medio de la calle. Después nadie quería hablar con nosotros. Bajaban los ojos cuando pasábamos cerca, pues todo el mundo sabía que mi padre había sido un rojo. Nadie nos dijo nada. Por miedo, ¿ves? Sólo fray Leopoldo cruzaba la calle para saludarnos. Los guardias y la gente de la calle todos mirándonos, un silencio terrible, enorme. Así que él pasó la mano por mi cabeza y me dijo en voz alta, "No te aflijas, muchachito. Tu padre era un hombre bueno y por cierto está con Dios."

38. Este sí, asesinó a muchísima gente. Se lo digo yo, que él mató a dos hermanos míos, más una cuñada y un sobrino mío que quiso defender a la madre. Nosotros vimos todo sin poder hacer nada, nada. Así que le digo que el mundo tiene sus santos y tiene sus asesinos. Los dos juntos. ¿Pues el fray Leopoldo no vivía justo en la época de Franco?

39. En la época de fray Leopoldo los padres pensaban que los hijos iban a ser igual a ellos. Nunca les pasó por la cabeza que el mundo

pudiera cambiar. Así que los padres no mandaban a los hijos a estudiar. ¿Para qué? ¿La vida de ellos no iban a ser la misma cosa? Habían nacido para trabajar, para ser brazos para los gordos.

40. Tenía yo ¿Ud. comprende? profesores muy buenos. Pero el más grande de todos ha sido el propio Generalife. Antes de ser patrimonio del Estado era propiedad particular de unos duques. Quien quisiera pintar allí tocaba a la puerta y venía una criada a abrir. Hoy día los pintores trabajan de fotografías pero no es igual. La propia naturaleza te enseña tanto. Parece que un ciprés verde no pudiera tener una sombra violácea, pero lo he visto, lo he visto y entonces sí, puede ser. Tanto valor estético tenían las huertas regadas, las coles enormes y bermejas, como los cármenes. Y hoy no hay más, no hay más. Han derrumbado la casa en la cual yo conocí a fray Leopoldo. ¡Esa y tantas otras!

41. El convento tenía una portada muy sencilla, carril de cipreses, un Cristo a la izquierda. Y frente al Cristo había la entrada principal. Por encima se leía, "¡oh dichosa soledad!, ¡oh sola felicidad!" Y en el fondo del carril había la entrada de la iglesia. Una iglesia muy antigua, muy sencilla. Era bonita y en fin tenía un espíritu seráfico. *Era como entrar en otro mundo.*

42. Hoy no hay más, pero en aquella época en el corazón se vivía con más sencillez. Una pobreza muy grande, una falta de cultura muy grande, pero en el momento en que te pones a recordar, todo te parece una cosa tan sencilla, tan bonita, tan buena. Y ahora la vida es tan diferente, tan complicada. Que tenemos muchas cosas, pero vivimos más apartados.

43. Este fraile era muy sencillo. Comía lo necesario, bebía lo necesario, y ya está, no quería otra cosa para sí. Hoy no, estamos muy mal, el mundo es una desgracia porque la gente no se habla, no se ayuda más. No era así en los tiempos de fray Leopoldo, ¿me entiendes? El ayudaba a los gitanillos, fundaba un colegio para ellos, les daba comida, ropa, zapatos. Pero hoy todo el mundo corre detrás del dinero, todo el mundo vive con miedo del otro, y nadie disfruta de lo que tiene.

44. Fray Leopoldo sabía enseñar a los ricos. Sabía mostrarles que la riqueza no puede ser el fin de la vida. El pedía limosnas a los ricos para dar a los pobres. Sabía que los ricos deben ser más pobres y los pobres más ricos. Sabía que el mundo sería mejor si fuéramos un poco más iguales. Pero, claro, él era santo. Y yo, bueno, yo tengo que pensar en el dinero.

45. Yo realmente sé muy poco de fray Leopoldo. Pero de lo que entiendo él era muy sencillo, muy humilde. No quería nada para sí. Ahora, vivía en otros tiempos, no eran como hoy. Que hoy compramos

los coches grandes que la televisión nos enseña. Que las mujeres se ponen de "jeans" y juegan al tenis cuando hace diez años nadie sabía de que se trataba. Nosotros nunca hemos tenido dinero pero sí, teníamos tiempo—tiempo para tomar una copita más con los amigos, tiempo para conversar. Hoy no, ni eso nos queda. Vivimos en el país del dinero, somos más americanos que vosotros. . . . Ahora, no te pongas tan triste. Las cosas no son para tanto. Mozo, ¡traiga más café!

46. Hay tantas cosas en el mundo que no me explico. Ud. ve que hay los drogadictos y por detrás de ellos los camellos y por detrás de ellos todavía los médicos, los grandes intereses económicos. Quiero decir, es una cosa casi sin solución, que todo está relacionado, no hay nada que no entre en el juego. Así es que la gente se desespera y busca una salida más bien mágica, milagrosa. Como los Hare Krishna, ¿no ves esa joven bonita allí? Pues es así que yo entiendo esto de fray Leopoldo. Yo mismo no le tengo fe pero, entiendo, sí, por que la gente cree en él.

47. Fray Leopoldo, sí, vivía por los demás. Ayudaba a los enfermos, a la gente pobre, les daba buenos consejos a los necesitados. Hoy en día es muy diferente. Pues viene la guerra atómica en que me muero, en que te mueres tú. Así, ¿cómo es que la gente como yo va a creer en los santos cuando ni cree en el hombre?

48. Era una cosa linda, linda de verse. Pero cuando el Hermanico se murió, se echó a perder rápido. Los otros frailes hicieron todo, todo para que aquellas rosas volvieran a florecer, pero nada. Trabajaron horas plantando, regando y no les nació cosa alguna. Donde había limones, naranjas tan grandes como melones ya había piedras. Así que no les quedaba más remedio que construir un hogar de ancianos. Una pena. Pero claro, el mundo es así. Además el hogar les quedó muy bonito. Hoy viven más de cien viejecitos allí.

49. Claro, aquella Huerta, como todas de Granada, se regaba con agua sucia. Sí, pues Granada era todo un jardín pero se echaban los excrementos en la calle, había unos pozos ciegos, inmundos, por aquí. Así que la acequia era un verdadero estercolero. Tanto que la gente pagaba mucho más por la lechuga si ésta fuera del Albaicín pues el agua venía de la fuente, no estaba sucia. Había mucha peste, mucha epidemia, en el tiempo del Hermanico. Mi abuela se murió de cólera en 1940, ella y no sé cuantos más.

50. No me gustan para nada las cosas antiguas. Creo en el presente. Pero para serle muy honesta, de vez en cuando echo de menos el patio, el patio de la casa de mis padres. ¿Ve Ud. esa silla? Era de fray Leopoldo. Siempre se sentaba en la sombra a descansar cuando venía a

pedir. Es curioso. Venía a casa el año entero, pero cuando pienso en él es siempre mayo. Así que yo me quedé con la silla. Sé que es muy fea. Pero aún así. . . .

51. No teníamos nada, nada en aquella época de fray Leopoldo. Pero cantábamos, bailábamos, comíamos pipas en la placeta, nos divertíamos entre nosotros. Hoy no, hemos perdido aquella alegría. Ahora, no todo el mundo piensa como yo. Mi sobrina me llama de anticuada. ¡Estoy tan orgullosa de ella! Aquí estoy, casi analfabeta, y ella estudiando filosofía en la universidad.

52. Pregúntale a cualquiera. Bueno, tal vez no a cualquiera. Es que hoy más de la mitad de las personas que viven aquí nacieron en otro lugar. Hoy no somos más un pueblo sino un pueblo internacional. Todo el mundo es teniente, es químico, es vendedor de muebles, todo menos agricultor. Yo si tuviera que vivir de los abonos no comía. Hoy no conozco los nombres de la mitad de las calles. Y las costumbres, mejor ni hablar. Gente como yo no se acostumbrarà jamás. Ahora, aún así, tengo que decirle que la vida es mejor para la mayoría de la gente. En aquellos tiempos de fray Leopoldo se vivía muy sacrificado.

References Cited

Aceves, Joseph B., and William A. Douglas, eds. *The Changing Faces of Rural Spain*. Cambridge, Mass.: Schenckman, 1976.

Acosta Sánchez, José. *Andalucía. Reconstrucción de una identidad y la lucha contra el centralismo*. Barcelona: Anagrama, 1978.

Aguilar Criado, Encarnación. *Las hermandades de Castilleja de la Cuesta. Un estudio de antropología cultural*. Seville: Servicio de Publicaciones del Ayuntamiento de Sevilla, 1983.

———. "Los primeros estudios sobre la cultura popular andaluza. Los orígenes de la antropología en Andalucia." Ph.D. diss., Universidad de Sevilla, 1988.

Aguilera, Francisco Enrique. *Santa Eulalia's People: Ritual Structure in an Andalusian Multicommunity*. St. Paul, Minn.: West, 1978.

Aigrain, René. *L'Hagiographie. Ses sources, ses méthodes, son histoire*. Paris: Bloud et Gay, 1953.

Altman, Charles F. "Two Types of Opposition in the Structure of Latin Saints' Lives." In *Medieval Hagiography and Romance* (*Medievalia and Humanistica* n.s. 6), edited by Paul Maurice Clogan, pp. 1–11. Cambridge: Cambridge University Press.

Arora, Shirley L. "Memorate and Metaphor: Some Mexican Treasure Tales and Their Narratives." In *Perspectives on Contemporary Legend*, vol. 2. *See* Bennett, Smith, and Widdowson 1987.

Artigues, Daniel. *L'Opus Dei en Espagne: son évolution politique et idéologique*. N.p.: Ruedo Ibérico, 1968.

"Asamblea de vecinos de S. Ildefonso contra el traslado de su párroco," *El Ideal*, 20 March 1984, pp. 1 and 20.

Asistencia a la Eucaristía dominical, 1983." Granada: Diócesis de Granada. Mimeo.

217

Badone, Ellen, ed. *Religious Orthodoxy and Folk Belief in European Society.* Princeton: Princeton University Press, forthcoming.

Bataillon, Marcel. *Erasmo y España, estudios sobre la historia espiritual del siglo XVI,* 2 vols., translated by Antonio Alatorre. Mexico City: Fondo de Cultura Económica, 1950.

Bauman, Richard. *Story, Performance, and Event: Contextual Studies of Narrative.* Cambridge: Cambridge University Press, 1986.

Behar, Ruth. *Santa María del Monte: The Presence of the Past in a Spanish Village.* Princeton: Princeton University Press, 1986.

————. "The Struggle for the Church: Popular Anticlericalism and Religiosity in Post-Franco Spain." In *Religious Orthodoxy. See* Badone forthcoming.

Belda, Rafael, et al. *Iglesia y sociedad en España, 1839–1975.* Madrid: Editorial Popular, 1977.

Bellah, Robert, et al. *Habits of the Heart: Individualism and Commitment in American Life.* Berkeley and Los Angeles: University of California Press, 1986.

Ben-Amos, Dan. "Analytical Categories and Ethnic Genres." In *Folklore Genres. See* Ben-Amos 1976, pp. 215–42.

————. "Narrative Forms in the Haggadah: Structural Analysis." Ph.D. diss., Indiana University, 1967.

————, ed. *Folklore Genres.* Publications of the American Folklore Society Bibliographical and Special Series 26. Austin and London: University of Texas Press, 1976.

Ben-Amos, Dan, and Kenneth Goldstein, eds. *Folklore: Performance and Communication.* The Hague: Mouton, 1975.

Bennett, Gillian. "The Phantom Hitchhiker: Neither Modern, Urban, nor Legend?" In *Perspectives on Contemporary Legend* (vol. 1). *See* Smith 1984.

Bennett, Gillian, Paul Smith, and J. D. A. Widdowson, eds. *Perspectives on Contemporary Legend,* vol. 2. Cectal Conference Papers Series 5. Sheffield (England): Sheffield Academic Press, 1987.

Berger, Peter. *The Sacred Canopy: Elements of a Sociological Theory of Secularization.* Garden City, N.Y.: Anchor Books, 1969.

Bernal, Antonio Miguel. *La propiedad de la tierra y las luchas agrarias campesinas del XIX.* Barcelona: Ariel, 1979.

Bilinkoff, Jodi Ellen. "The Avila of St. Teresa: Religious Reform in a Sixteenth-Century City. Ithaca: Cornell University Press, 1989.

Blehr, Otto. "The Analysis of Folk Belief Stories and Its Implications for Research on Folk Belief and Folk Prose." *Fabula* 9 (1967): 259–63.

Boggs, Ralph S. *Index of Spanish Folktales Classified According to Antti Aarne's Types of the Folktale.* Translated and enlarged by Stith Thompson. Folklore Fellows Communications 74. Helsinki: Suomalainen Tiedakatemia, Academia Scientiarum Fennica, 1930.

Boissevain, Jeremy. "When the Saints Go Marching Out: Reflections on the Decline of Patronage in Malta." In *Patrons and Clients in Mediterranean Societies*, edited by E. Gellner and J. Waterbury, pp. 81–96. Hanover, N.H.: Center for Mediterranean Studies of the American University Field Staff, 1977.

Bollème, Geneviève. "Religion du texte et texte religieux." In *Les Saints et les stars*. See Schmitt 1983.

Brandes, Stanley. *Metaphors of Masculinity: Sex and Status in Andalusian Folklore*. American Folklore Society New Series 1. Philadelphia: University of Pennsylvania Press, 1980.

————. "The Priest as Agent of Secularization in Rural Spain." In *Economic Transformations and Steady-state Values: Essays in the Ethnography of Spain*, edited by Joseph B. Aceves, Edward C. Hansen, and Gloria Levitas, pp. 22–29. New York: Queens College Press.

Bremond, Claude, Jacques Le Goff, and Jean-Claude Schmitt. *L'Exemplum*. Typologie des Sources du Moyen-Age Occidental 40. Brepols: Turnhout-Belgium, 1982.

Brenan, Gerald. *South from Granada*. New York: Farrar, Straus and Cudahy, 1957.

Brewer, E. Cobham. *A Dictionary of Miracles. Imitative, Dogmatic, and Realistic*. Philadelphia: J. B. Lippincott, 1884; rpt. Detroit: Gale Research, 1966.

Briones Gómez, Rafael. "La semana santa andaluza." *Gazeta de Antropología* 2 (1983): 4–10.

Brown, Peter. *The Cult of the Saints: Its Rise and Function in Latin Christianity*. The Haskell Lectures on History of Religions n.s. 2. Chicago and London: University of Chicago Press, 1981.

————. *Society and the Holy in Late Antiquity*. London: Faber and Faber, 1982.

Brunvand, Jan. *The Choking Doberman and Other "New" Urban Legends*. New York and London: W. W. Norton, 1984.

————. *The Mexican Pet: More New Urban Legends and Some Old Favorites*. New York and London: W. W. Norton, 1986.

————. *The Vanishing Hitchhiker: American Urban Legends and Their Meaning*. New York and London: W. W. Norton, 1981.

Bustamante, Crisóstomo de. *Mártires capuchinos de Castilla*. La Coruña: Imprenta Moret, 1962.

Butler, Alban. *Lives of the Saints*. Rev. ed., 4 vols. Edited by Herbert Thurston and Donald Attwater. New York: P. J. Kenedy and Sons, 1956.

Caesarius of Heisterbach. *Dialogue on Miracles*. 2 vols. Translated by H. von E. Scott and C. C. Swinton Bland. New York: Harcourt, Brace, 1929.

Callahan, William J. *Church, Politics, and Society in Spain, 1750–1874.* Harvard Historical Monographs 73. Cambridge and London: Harvard University Press, 1984.

Caro Baroja, Julio. *Introducción a una historia contemporanea del anticlericalismo.* Madrid: Istmo, 1980.

Carr, Raymond, and Juan Pablo Fusi Aizpura. *Spain: Dictatorship to Democracy.* London: George Allen and Unwin, 1979.

Carroll, Michael P. *The Cult of the Virgin Mary: Psychological Origins.* Princeton: Princeton University Press, 1986.

Castón Boyer, Pedro, et al. *La religión en Andalucía. (Aproximación a la religiosidad popular).* Biblioteca de la Cultura Andaluza. Seville: Editoriales Andaluzas Unidas, 1985.

Cazorla Pérez, José. "Cambio social y cultura politica." *Documentación Social* 73 (1988): 73–85.

———, ed. *Problemas de estratificación social en España.* Madrid: Cuadernos para el Diálogo, 1973.

Centro de Investigaciones Sociológicas. "Iglesia, religión y política." *Revista española de investigaciones sociológicas* 27 (1984): 295–328.

Christian, William A., Jr. *Apparitions in Late Medieval and Renaissance Spain.* Princeton: Princeton University Press, 1981.

———. "Folk Religion: An Overview." In *Encyclopedia of Religion,* edited by Mircea Eliade. New York: Macmillan, 1987.

———. "Holy People in Peasant Europe." *Comparative Studies in Society and History* 10, no. 1 (1973).

———. *Local Religion in Sixteenth-Century Spain.* Princeton: Princeton University Press, 1981.

———. *Person and God in a Spanish Valley.* New York: Seminar Press, 1972.

———. "Secular and Religious Responses to a Child's Potentially Fatal Illness in the Canary Islands." Paper presented at the Conference on Religious Regimes and State Formation, Free University, Amsterdam, June 22–26, 1987.

———. "Tapping and Defining New Power: The First Month of Visions at Ezquioga, July 1931." *American Ethnologist* 14, no. 1 (1987): 140–66.

Christiansen, Reidar Th. *The Migratory Legends, a Proposed List of Types with a Systematic Catalogue of the Norwegian Variants.* Folklore Fellows Communications 71. Helsinki: Suomalainen Tiedakatemia, 1958.

Collier, George A. *Socialists of Rural Andalusia: Unacknowledged Revolutionaries of the Second Republic.* Stanford: Stanford University Press, 1987.

Collier, Jane F. "From Mary to Modern Woman: The Material Basis of

Marianismo and Its Transformation in a Spanish Village." *American Ethnologist* 13 (1986): 100–107.

Cuenca Toribio, José Manuel. *La Andalucía de la transición (1975–1984): política y cultura.* Madrid: Mezquita, 1984.

————. *Estudios sobre la iglesia andaluza moderna y contemporanea.* Publicaciones del Instituto de Historia de Andalucía 16. Córdoba: Publicaciones del Instituto de Historia de Andalucía, 1980.

————. *Relaciones Iglesia-Estado en la España contemporanea, 1833–1985.* Madrid: Alhambra, 1985.

D'Alatri, Mariano, ed. *Santi e santità nell'Ordine cappuccino,* 3 vols. Rome: Postulazione Generale dei Cappuccini, 1980–82.

Dégh, Linda. "The 'Belief Legend' in Modern Society: Form, Function and Relationship to Other Genres." In *American Folk Legend. See* Hand 1971.

Dégh, Linda, and Andrew Vázsonyi. *The Dialectics of the Legend.* Folklore Preprint Series 1, no. 6. Bloomington, Ind.: Folklore Institute Publications Group, 1973.

————. "Hypothesis of Multi-Conduit Transmission in Folklore." In *Folklore. See* Ben-Amos 1973.

————. "Legend and Belief." In *Folklore Genres. See* Ben-Amos 1976.

————. "The Memorate and the Proto-Memorate." *Journal of American Folklore* 87 (1974): 225–39.

Delehaye, Hippolyte. *Cinq leçons sur la méthode hagiographique.* 2d ed. Subsidia Hagiographica 21. Brussels: Societé des Bollandistes, 1968.

————. *The Legends of the Saints.* Translated by Donald Attwater. New York: Fordham University Press, 1962.

Delooz, Pierre. *Sociologie et canonisation.* Collection scientifique 30. Liege: Faculté de Droit, 1969.

————. "Towards a Sociological Study of Canonized Sainthood in the Catholic Church." In *Saints and Their Cults. See* Wilson 1983.

Díaz del Moral, Juan. *Historia de las agitaciones campesinas andaluzas,* 4th ed. Madrid: Alianza, 1984.

Díaz Viana, Luís. *Canciones populares de la Guerra Civil.* Madrid: Taurus, 1985.

Divinus Perfectionis Magister. (Apostolic Constitution, 26 February 1983.)

Domínguez Ortiz, Antonio. *Andalucía ayer y hoy.* Barcelona: Editorial Planeta / Instituto de Estudios Económicos, 1983.

Douillet, Jacques. *What Is a Saint?* Translated by Donald Attwater. New York: Hawthorn Books, 1958.

Drain, Michel, et al. *Los andaluces.* Coleccíon Fundamentos 68. Madrid: Ediciones ISTMO, 1980.

Driessen, Henk. "Religious Brotherhoods: Class and Politics in an Andalusian Town." In *Religion, Power, and Protest in Local Communities: The North Shore of the Mediterranean*, edited by Eric Wolf, pp. 73–91. Berlin and New York: Mouton, 1984.

Dunaway, David K., and Willa K. Baum, eds. *Oral History: An Interdisciplinary Anthology*. Nashville, Tenn.: American Association for State and Local History, 1984.

Dundes, Alan. "On the Psychology of Legend." In *American Folk Legend*. See Hand 1971.

Duocastella, Rogelio. *Análisis sociológico del catolicismo español*. Barcelona: Nova Terra, 1967.

———. *Cambio social y religioso en España*. Barcelona: Nova Terra, 1975.

Elliott, J. H. *Imperial Spain: 1469–1716*. New York: Meridian, 1963.

Estudio sobre la renta. Granada: Banco de Bilbao, 1985.

Fernandez, James W. *Persuasions and Performances. The Play of Tropes in Culture*. Bloomington: Indiana University Press, 1986.

———. "Consciousness and Class in Southern Spain." *American Ethnologist* 10 (1983): 165–73.

Fernández Catón, José María. *El patrimonio cultural de la Iglesia en España y los acuerdos entre el Estado español y la Santa Sede*. León: Centro de Estudios e Investigaciones "San Isidro," 1980.

Fine, Elizabeth C. *The Folklore Text: From Performance to Print*. Bloomington: Indiana University Press, 1984.

Finnegan, Ruth H. *Oral Poetry: Its Nature, Significance and Social Context*. Cambridge and New York: Cambridge University Press, 1977.

La Fonction du miracle dans la spiritualité Chrétienne. (Special issue, *Revue d'Histoire de la Spiritualité* 48 [1972].)

Francis of Assisi. *The Little Flowers of Saint Francis. With Five Considerations on the Sacred Stigmata*. Translated by Leo Sherley-Price. The Penguin Classics 91. Baltimore: Penguin Books, 1959.

"Francisco Llop: antropólogo valenciano que escribe una tesis doctoral sobre los toques de campaña." *El País*, 11 June 1984, p. 56.

Fraser, Ronald. *Blood of Spain: An Oral History of the Spanish Civil War*. New York: Pantheon, 1979.

———. *Tajos: The Story of a Village on the Costa del Sol*. New York: Pantheon, 1973.

Freeman, Susan Tax. "Faith and Fashion in Spanish Religion: Notes on the Observation of Observance." *Peasant Studies* 7 (1978): 101–23.

Frigolé Reixach, Joan. "Religión y política en un pueblo murciano entre 1966–1976: la crisis del nacionalcatolicismo desde la perspectiva local." *Revista Española de Investigaciones Sociológicas* 23 (1983): 77–126.

Gaiffier, Baudouin de. *Etudes critiques d'hagiographie et d'iconologie*. Subsidia Hagiographica 43. Brussels: Societé des Bollandistes, 1967.

Gajano, Sofia Boesch, and Lucia Sebastiani, eds. *Culto dei santi, instituzioni e classi sociali in età preindustriale.* Collàna di studi storici 1. L'Aquila, Rome: L. U. Japadre, 1984.

Gallego, J. Andrés, et al. *Estudios históricos sobre la Iglesia española contemporanea.* Madrid: Biblioteca "La Ciudad de Dios," 1979.

Gallego y Burín, Antonio. *Granada. Guía artística e histórica de la ciudad.* Edited and revised by Francisco Javier Gallego Roca. Granada: Don Quijote, 1982.

García de Cortázar, Fernando. "La Nueva Historia de la Iglesia Contemporanea en España." In *Historiografía española contemporánea.* See Tuñón de Lara 1980.

García de la Torre, Fuensanta. *Estudio histórico de la hermandad del gremio de Toneleros de Sevilla.* Seville: Patronato Ricardo Canto Leal del Consejero General de Hermandades y Cofradías de la Ciudad de Sevilla, 1979.

García Sánchez, Juan Bautista. *Trotacaminos de Dios (Beato Diego José de Cádiz).* Granada: Vicepostulación del Beato Diego, 1983.

García-Nieto, María del Carmen. "Historiografía política de la guerra civil de España." In *Historiografía española contemporánea.* See Tuñón de Lara 1980.

Geary, Patrick. "Humiliation of Saints." In *Saints and their Cults.* See Wilson 1983.

Gellner, Ernest. *Muslim Society.* Cambridge: Cambridge University Press, 1981.

Georges, Robert A. "The General Concept of Legend: Some Assumptions to be Reexamined and Reassessed." In *American Folk Legend.* See Hand 1971.

Gerould, Gordon Hall. *Saints' Legends: The Types of English Literature.* Boston and New York: Houghton Mifflin, 1916.

Gilmore, David D. *Aggression and Community: Paradoxes of Andalusian Culture.* New Haven and London: Yale University Press, 1987.

——— . "Andalusian Anti-Clericalism: An Eroticized Rural Protest." *Anthropology* 8 (1983): 31–44.

——— . *The People of the Plain: Class and Community in Lower Andalusia.* New York: Columbia University Press, 1980.

——— , ed. *Honor and Shame and the Concept of Mediterranean Unity.* American Anthropological Association Special Publications 22. Washington, D.C.: American Anthropological Association, 1987.

Ginzburg, Carlo. *The Cheese and the Worms: The Cosmos of a Sixteenth-Century Miller.* Translated by John Tedeschi and Anne C. Tedeschi. New York: Penguin, 1982.

——— . *The Night Battles: Witchcraft and Agrarian Cults in the Sixteenth and Seventeenth Centuries.* Translated by John Tedeschi and Anne C. Tedeschi. Baltimore: Johns Hopkins Press, 1983.

Gironella, José María. *100 españoles y Dios*, 5th ed. Barcelona: Ediciones Nauta, 1970.

Glasner, Peter E. *The Sociology of Secularisation: A Critique of a Concept*. International Library of Sociology. London and Boston: Routledge and Kegan Paul, 1977.

Gomá, Isidro. *Por Dios y por España*. Barcelona: R. Casulleras, 1940.

Gómez-Moreno, Manuel. *Primicias históricas de San Juan de Dios ("El hombre que supo amar")*. Madrid: Provincias Españolas de la Orden Hospitalaria, 1950.

Gómez Pérez, Rafael. *Política y religión en el régimen de Franco*. Testimonio de actualidad 23. Barcelona: Dopesa, 1976.

González Caballero, Alberto. *Los capuchinos en la Península Ibérica: 400 años de la historia (1578–1978)*. Seville: Conferencia Ibérica de Capuchinos, 1985.

Goodich, Michael. *Vita Perfecta: The Ideal of Sainthood in the Thirteenth Century*. Monographien zur Geschichte des Mittelalters 25. Stuttgart: Anton Hiersemann, 1982.

Goody, Jack. *The Interface between the Written and the Oral*. Studies in Literacy, the Family, Culture, and the State. Cambridge: Cambridge University Press, 1987.

Graham, Robert. *Spain: Change of a Nation*. London: Michael Joseph, 1984.

"Granada: feligreses de San Ildefonso increparon al arzobispo por el traslado de su párroco." *El Ideal*, 19 March 1984, pp. 1 and 14.

Granatensis causa de beatificación y canonización del siervo de Dios Fray Leopoldo de Alpandeire, hermano capuchino de la provincia bética: artículos. Granada: n.p., 1961.

Granfield, Patrick. *The Limits of the Papacy*. New York: Crossroad, 1987.

Gregory, David. "The Andalusian Dispersion: Migration and Sociodemographic Change." In *The Changing Faces of Rural Spain*, edited by Joseph B. Aceves and William A. Douglas, pp. 63–96. Cambridge, Mass.: Schenkman, 1976.

Guichard, Pierre. *Al-Andalus: Estructura antropológica de una sociedad islámica en Occidente*. Breve biblioteca de reforma 16. Barcelona: Barral Editores, 1976.

Guillén, Abraham. *La "elite" del poder en España*. Montevideo: Editorial Aconcagua, 1973.

Günter, Heinrich. *Psychologie der Legende, Studien zu einer wissenschaftlichen Heiligen-Geschichte*. Freiburg: Verlag Herder, 1949.

Gurevich, Aron. *Medieval Popular Culture: Problems of Belief and Perception*. Translated by Janos M. Bak and Paul A. Hollingsworth. Cambridge Studies in Oral and Literate Culture 14. Cambridge and New York: Cambridge University Press, 1988.

Halpert, Herbert. "Supernatural Sanctions and the Legend." In *Folklore Studies in the Twentieth Century: Proceedings of the Centenary Conference of the Folklore Society,* edited by Venetia Newall, pp. 226–33. Suffolk and Totowa, N.J.: D. S. Brewer / Rowman and Littlefield, 1980.

Hand, Wayland D. "Deformity, Disease, and Physical Ailment as Divine Retribution." In *Festschrift Matthais Zender: Studien zur Volkskultur, Sprache und Landesgeschichte,* edited by Edith Ennen and Günter Wiegelmann, pp. 519–25. Bonn: L. Rohrscheid, 1972.

—————. "Status of European and American Legend Study." *Current Anthropology* 6 (1965): 439–46.

—————, ed. *American Folk Legend: A Symposium.* Publications of the UCLA Center for the Study of Comparative Folklore and Mythology, 2. Berkeley and Los Angeles: University of California Press, 1971.

Hebblethwaite, Peter. *In the Vatican.* Bethesda, Md.: Adler and Adler, 1986.

Hermet, Guy. *Les catholiques dans l'Espagne franquiste,* 2 vols. Paris: Presses de la Fondation nationale des sciences politiques, 1980–81.

Herr, Richard. *An Historical Essay on Modern Spain.* Berkeley and Los Angeles: University of California Press, 1974.

Hobsbawm, Eric, with Joan Wallach Scott. "Political Shoemakers." *Past and Present* 89 (1980): 86–114.

Hoffmann-Krayer, Eduard, and Hanns Bächtold-Stäubli. *Handworterbuch des deutschen Aberglaubens,* vol. 1. Berlin: De Gruyter, 1927.

Hølbek, Bengt. *Formal and Structural Studies of Oral Narrative: A Bibliography.* Copenhagen: Institut for Folkemindevidenskab, Kobenshavns Universitet, 1978.

Iglesias de Ussel, Julio. "Materiales para el estudio de Andalucía: selección bibliográfica." *Papers: Revista de Sociología* 16 (1981): 183–202.

Infante-Galán, Juan. *Rocío, la devoción mariana de Andalucía.* Seville: Editorial Prensa Española, 1971.

"Informe sobre la diócesis para el neuvo obispo." Granada: 1977. Mimeo.

Iribarren, Jesús, ed. *Documentos colectivos del Episcopado español (1870–1974): Presentación del cardenal Vicente Enrique Tarancón.* Biblioteca de Autores Cristianos 355. Madrid: La Editorial Católica, 1974.

Jakobson, Roman, and Petr Bogatyrev. "On the Boundary between Studies of Folklore and Literature." In *Readings in Russian Poetics: Formalist and Structuralist Views,* edited by Ladislav Matejeska and Krytstyna Pomorska, pp. 91–94. Cambridge: MIT Press, 1971.

Journal of the Folklore Institute 14, nos. 1–2 (1977).

Keller, John Esten. *Motif-Index of Mediaeval Spanish Exempla.* Knoxville: University of Tennessee Press, 1949.

Kelly, William W. "Rationalization and Nostalgia: Cultural Dynamics of a New Middle-Class Japan." *American Ethnologist* 13 (1986): 603–18.

Kemp, Eric Waldram. *Canonization and Authority in the Western Church.* Oxford Historical Series, n.s. London: Oxford University Press, 1948.

Kieckhefer, Richard, and George D. Bond, eds. *Sainthood: Its Manifestations in World Religions.* Berkeley and Los Angeles: University of California Press, 1988.

Kselman, Thomas A. *Miracles and Prophecies in Nineteenth-Century France.* New Brunswick, N.J.: Rutgers University Press, 1983.

Lannon, Frances. "The Church's Crusade against the Republic." In *Revolution and War in Spain. See* Preston 1984.

———. "Modern Spain: The Project of a National Catholicism." In *Religion and National Identity: Papers Read at the Nineteenth Summer Meeting and the Twentieth Winter Meeting of the Ecclesiastical History Society,* edited by Stuart Mews, pp. 567–90. Oxford: Basil Blackwell, 1982, for the Ecclesiastical History Society.

———. *Privilege, Persecution, and Prophecy: The Catholic Church in Spain, 1875–1975.* Oxford: Clarendon Press, 1987.

León, Angel de. *Mendigo por Dios: vida de Fray Leopoldo de Alpandeire,* 4th ed. Granada: Anel, 1987.

Lévi-Strauss, Claude. *Structural Anthropology,* 2d ed. Translated by Claire Jacobson and Brooke Grundfest Schoepf. New York: Basic Books, 1963.

———. *Tristes Tropiques: A World on the Wane.* Translated by John Russell. London: Hutchison, 1961.

Lieberman, Sima. *The Contemporary Spanish Economy: A Historical Perspective.* London: George Allen and Unwin, 1982.

Lincoln, Bruce. "Revolutionary Exhumations in Spain, July 1936." *Comparative Studies in Society and History* 27 (1985): 241–60.

Linehan, Peter. *Spanish Church and Society, 1150–1300.* London: Variorum Reprints, 1983.

Linz, Juan J., and José Cazorla Pérez. "Religiosidad y estructura social en Andalucía: la práctica religiosa." In *Problemas de estratificación social en España,* ed. José Cazorla Pérez, pp. 177–209. Madrid: Cuadernos para el Diálogo, 1973.

Lisón Tolosana, Carmelo. *Belmonte de los Caballeros: Anthropology and History in an Aragonese Community.* Princeton: Princeton University Press, 1983.

———. *Brujería, estructura social y simbolismo en Galicia.* Madrid: Akal, 1979.

————, ed. *Expresiones actuales de la cultura del pueblo*. Anales de moral social y económica 41. Madrid: Centro de Estudios Sociales del Valle de los Caídos, 1976.

————, ed. *Temas de antropología española*. Colección Manifiesto, Serie Antropología. Madrid: Akal, 1976.

Loomis, C. Grant. *White Magic: An Introduction to the Folklore of Christian Legend*. Publication 52. Cambridge: The Mediaeval Academy of America, 1948.

Luque, Enrique. "La crisis de las expresiones populares del culto religioso: examen de un caso andaluz." In *Expresiones atuales. See* Lisón Tolosana 1976.

Luque Requerey, J. *Antropología cultural andaluza: el viernes santo al sur de Córdoba*. Córdoba: Publicaciones del Monte de Piedad y Caja de Ahorros, 1980.

Lüthi, Max. *Volksmärchen und Volkssage: Zwei Grundformen erzählender Dichtung*. Bern: Francke, 1961.

————. "Aspects of the Märchen and the Legend." In *Folklore Genres. See* Ben-Amos 1976.

McKevitt, Christopher. "Suffering and Sanctity: An Anthropological Study of a Saint Cult in a Southern Italian Town." Ph.D. diss., London School of Economics and Political Science, 1989.

Maddox, Richard Frederick. "Religion, Honor, and Patronage: Culture and Power in an Andalusian Town." Ph.D. diss., Stanford University, 1986.

Maldonado, Luis. *Génesis del catolicismo popular*. Madrid: Editorial Cristiandad, 1979.

————. *Religiosidad popular*. Madrid: Editorial Cristiandad, 1975.

Marsal, Juan F. *Pensar bajo el franquismo: intelectuales y política en la generación de los años cincuenta*. Temas de historia y política contemporáneas 8. Barcelona: Ediciones Península, 1979.

Martin, David. *A General Theory of Secularization*. Explorations in Interpretative Sociology. Oxford: Basil Blackwell, 1978.

Mecklin, John M. *The Passing of the Saint: A Study of a Cultural Type*. Chicago: University of Chicago Press, 1941.

Mieder, Wolfgang. *Tradition and Innovation in Folk Literature*. Hanover, N.H.: University Press of New England, 1987.

Mintz, Jerome R. *The Anarchists of Casas Viejas*. Chicago and London: University of Chicago Press, 1982.

"Miracle." *New Catholic Encyclopedia*, vol. 9. New York: McGraw-Hill, 1967, pp. 890–94.

Mitchell, Timothy. *Violence and Piety in Spanish Folklore*. Philadelphia: University of Pennsylvania Press, 1988.

Moncada Lorenzo, Alberto. *El Opus Dei, una interpretación*. Madrid: Indice, 1974.

Montero, José Ramón. *La C.E.D.A.: el catolicismo social y político en la II República*, 2 vols. Serie historia 21, 22. Madrid: Ediciones de la Revista de Trabajo, 1977.

———. "Los católicos y el Nuevo Estado: los perfiles ideológicos de la ACNP durante la primera etapa del franquismo." In *España bajo el franquismo*, edited by Josep Fontana, pp. 100–122. Serie General Temas Hispánicos. Barcelona: Editorial Crítica, 1986.

Montero Moreno, Antonio. *Historia de la persecución religiosa en España, 1936–1939*. Madrid: Biblioteca de Autores Cristianos, 1961.

Moreno, María Angustias. *El Opus Dei*, 3d ed. Barcelona: Planeta, 1977.

Moreno Navarro, Isidoro. *La semana santa de Sevilla: conformación, mixtificación y significaciones*. Biblioteca de temas sevillanos 18. Seville: Ayuntamiento de Sevilla, 1982.

———. *Las hermandades andaluzas: una aproximación desde la antropología*. Seville: Publicaciones de la Universidad de Sevilla, 1974.

———. *Propiedad, clases sociales y hermandades en la baja Andalucía: la estructura social de un pueblo del Aljarafe*. Antropología y arqueología. Madrid: Siglo XXI, 1972.

Moule, C. F. D., ed. *Miracles: Cambridge Studies in Their Philosophy and History*. London: A. R. Mowbray, 1965.

Murphy, Michael. "Emotional Confrontations between Sevillano Fathers and Sons: Cultural Foundations and Social Consequences." *American Ethnologist* 10 (1983): 650–54.

Nebreda, Jesús. *O renacer o morir: una reflexión socio-religiosa sobre la crisis vocacional*. Madrid: Instituto Teológico de Vida Religiosa, 1974.

Nicolaisen, W. H. F. "Legends as Narrative Response." In *Perspectives on Contemporary Legend. See* Smith 1984.

Obelkevich, James, ed. *Religion and the People, 800–1700*. Chapel Hill: University of North Carolina Press, 1979.

Olsen, Alexandra Hennessey. " 'De Historiis Sanctorum': A Generic Study of Hagiography." *Genre* 13 (1980): 407–29.

Ong, Walter J. *Orality and Literacy: The Technologizing of the Word*. New Accents. London and New York: Methuen, 1980.

Orensanz, Aurelio L. *Religiosidad popular española, 1940–1965*. España en tres tiempos. Madrid: Editora Nacional, 1974.

Ortiz Nuevo, José Luís. *Pensamiento político en el cante flamenco (antología de textos desde los orígenes a 1936)*. Biblioteca de la Cultura Andaluza. Seville: Editoriales Andaluzas Unidas, 1985.

Payne, Stanley G. *The Franco Regime, 1936–1975*. Madison: University of Wisconsin Press, 1987.

———. *Spanish Catholicism: An Historical Overview*. Madison: University of Wisconsin Press, 1984.

Peeters, K. C., ed. *Tagung der "International Society for Folk-Narrative Research" in Antwerp (6.–8. Sept. 1962): Bericht und Referat.* Antwerp: Centrum voor Studie en Documentatie, 1963.

Pentikäinen, Juha. "Belief, Memorate, and Legend," translated by J. Lombardo and W. K. McNeil. *Folklore Forum* 6 (1973): 217–41.

Pérez, Ruiz. *Conchita Barrecheguren (Cincuenta años de su muerte: 1927–1977).* Granada: Gráficas del Sur, 1977.

Peristiany, J. G., ed. *Honour and Shame: The Values of Mediterranean Society.* London: Weidenfeld and Nicolson, 1965.

Petschen, Santiago. *La Iglesia en la España de Franco.* Barcelona: Sedmay, 1977.

Petzoldt, Leander, ed. *Vergleichende Sagenforschung.* Darmstadt: Wissenschaftliche Buchgesellschaft, 1969.

Pino Sabio, José, ed. *Don Andrés Manjón: vida y virtudes.* (Special issue *Revista Magisterio Avemariano* 621 [1983].)

Prat i Carós, Joan. "Estructura y conflicto en la familia pairal." *Ethnica* 6 (1973): 131–80.

———. " 'Religió popular' o experiència religiosa ordinaria?: estat de la qüestió i hipòtesis de treball." *Arxiu d'Etnografia de Catalunya* 2 (1983): 47–69.

Press, Irwin. *The City as Context: Urbanism and Behavioral Constraints in Seville.* Urbana: University of Illinois Press, 1979.

Preston, Paul. *The Coming of the Spanish Civil War: Reform, Reaction, and Revolution in the Second Republic.* London: Methuen, 1983.

———. *The Spanish Civil War, 1936–39.* London: Weidenfeld and Nicolson, 1986.

———. *The Triumph of Democracy in Spain.* London: Methuen, 1986.

———, ed. *Revolution and War in Spain, 1931–1939.* London and New York: Methuen, 1984.

Puentes, Manuel Angel. "Abuelos y nietos en la Granada de 1984." *Gazeta de Antropología* 4 (1985): 74–78.

Redfield, Robert. *Peasant Society and Culture: An Anthropological Approach to Civilization.* Chicago: University of Chicago Press, 1956.

Riegelhaupt, Joyce. "Popular Anti-Clericalism and Religiosity in Pre-1974 Portugal." In *Religion, Power, and Protest in Local Communities: The Northern Shore of the Mediterranean,* edited by Eric Wolf. Berlin: Mouton, 1984.

Rodríguez Almodóvar, Antonio. *Los cuentos maravillosos españoles.* Barcelona: Editorial Crítica, 1982.

Rodríguez Becerra, Salvador. *Guía de fiestas populares de Andalucía.* Seville: Consejería de Cultura de la Junta de Andalucía, 1982.

———. "Cultura popular y fiestas." In Michel Drain et al., *Los andaluces,* pp. 447–94. Colección Fundamentos 68. Madrid: Ediciones ISTMO, 1980.

Rodríguez Becerra, Salvador, and José María Soto. *Exvotos de Andalucía: milagros y promesas en la religiosidad popular.* Seville: Argantonio, Ediciones Andaluzas, 1980.

Röhrich, Lutz. *Sage.* Stuttgart: J. B. Metzler, 1966.

――――. *Sage und Märchen: Erzählforschung heute.* Freiburg: Herder, 1976.

Rosenfeld, Helmut. *Legende.* Stuttgart: J. B. Metzlersche Verlagsbuchhandlung, 1961.

Ruiz Rico, José. *El papel político de la Iglesia católica en la España de Franco (1936–1971).* Madrid: Tecnos, 1977.

Sánchez, José M. *Reform and Reaction: The Politico-Religious Background of the Spanish Civil War.* Chapel Hill: University of North Carolina Press, 1964.

Schiffrin, Deborah. "Tense Variation in Narrative." *Language* 57 (1981): 45–62.

Schmitt, Jean-Claude. *The Holy Greyhound: Guinefort, Healer of Children since the Thirteenth Century.* Translated by Martin Thom. Cambridge Studies in Oral and Literate Culture 6. Cambridge: Cambridge University Press, 1983.

――――, ed. *Les Saints et les stars: le texte hagiographique dans la culture populaire—études presentées a la Société d'éthnologie française, Musée des arts et traditions populaires.* Bibliothèque Beauchesne. Réligions, société, politique 10. Paris: Beauchesne, 1983.

"Se murió Fray Leopoldo, Hermano Capuchino." *El Ideal,* 10 February 1956, p. 1.

Sigal, Pierre-André. *L'homme et le miracle dans la France médiévale (XIe–XIIe siècle).* Paris: Cerf, 1985.

Slater, Candace. *Trail of Miracles: Stories from a Pilgrimage in Northeast Brazil.* Berkeley and Los Angeles: University of California Press, 1986.

Smith, Paul, ed. *Perspectives on Contemporary Legend: Proceedings of the Conference on Contemporary Legend, Sheffield, July 1982.* Cectal Conference Papers Series 4. Sheffield (England): Center for English Cultural Tradition and Language, University of Sheffield, 1984.

Stahl, Sandra Dolby. *Literary Folkloristics and the Personal Narrative.* Bloomington: Indiana University Press, 1988.

―――― (Stahl, Sandra K. D.). "The Oral Personal Narrative in Its Generic Context." *Journal of the Folklore Institute* 14, nos. 1–2 (1977): 9–30.

Tamames, Ramón. *The Spanish Economy, an Introduction,* 16th rev. ed. Translated by Darlene Marie Cervantes. London: C. Hurst and Company, 1986.

The Teachings of the Vatican Council: Complete Texts of the Constitutions, Decrees, and Declarations. Westminster, Md.: New Man Press, 1966.

Tezanos, José Félix. "Transformaciones en la estructura social española." In *Estructuras sociales y cuestión nacional en España,* edited by Francesc Hernández and Francesc Mercade. Ariel sociología. Barcelona: Ariel, 1986.

Thomas, Keith. *Religion and the Decline of Magic: Studies in Popular Beliefs in Sixteenth- and Seventeenth-Century England.* New York: Charles Scribner's Sons, 1971.

Thompson, Stith. *Motif-Index of Folk Literature: A Classification of Narrative Elements in Folk-tales, Ballads, Myths, Fables, Medieval Romances, Exempla, Fabliaux, Jest-Books, and Local Legends.* Rev. ed. 6 vols. Bloomington: Indiana University Press, 1955–1958.

Tillhagen, Carl-Herman. "Was ist eine Sage? Eine Definition und ein Vorschlag für ein europäisches Sagensystem." *Acta Ethnographica* 13 (1964): 9–17.

Titon, Jeff Todd. "The Life Story." *Journal of American Folklore* 93 (1980): 276–92.

Trinkhaus, Charles, with Heiko A. Oberman, eds. *The Pursuit of Holiness in Late Medieval and Renaissance Religion: Papers from the University of Michigan Conference.* Studies in Medieval and Reformation Thought 10. Leiden: Brill, 1974.

Tuñón de Lara, Manuel, ed. *Historiografía española contemporánea: X Coloquio del Centro de Investigaciones Hispánicas de la Universidad de Pau.—Balance y resumen.* Madrid: Siglo XXI, 1980.

Tusell Gómez, Xavier. "The Functioning of the Cacique System in Andalusia, 1890–1931." In *Politics and Society in Twentieth-Century Spain,* ed. Stanley G. Payne, pp. 1–28. Modern Scholarship on European History. New York and London: New Viewpoints, 1976.

Ullman, Joan Connelly. *The Tragic Week: A Study of Anticlericalism in Spain, 1875–1912.* Cambridge: Harvard University Press, 1968.

Utley, Francis Lee. "Oral Genres as a Bridge to Written Literature." In *Folklore Genres.* See Ben-Amos 1976, pp. 3–15.

Vásquez, Jesús María. *Realidades socio-religiosas de España.* Madrid: Editora Nacional, 1967.

"Vatican Council II." *New Catholic Encyclopedia,* vol. 14. New York: McGraw-Hill, 1967, pp. 569–72.

Vauchez, André. *La Sainteté en Occident aux derniers siècles du Moyen Age: d'après les procès de canonisation et les documents hagiographiques.* Rome: École Française de Rome, 1981.

Vida de don Andrés Manjón y Manjón: Fundador de las Escuelas del Ave-María. Alcalá de Henares: Imprenta Talleres Penitenciarios, 1946.

Viñas, Angel. "Dimensiones económicas e internacionales de la guerra civil: una presentación de la literatura reciente." In *Historiografía española contemporánea.* See Tuñón de Lara 1980.

Voragine, Jacobus de. *The Golden Legend,* translated by Granger Ryan and Helmut Ripperger. New York: Longmans, Green, 1969.

Ward, Benedicta. *Miracles and the Medieval Mind: Theory, Record, and Event, 1000–1215.* Philadelphia: University of Pennsylvania Press, 1982.

Weinstein, Donald, and Rudolph M. Bell. *Saints and Society: The Two Worlds of Western Christendom, 1000–1700.* Chicago and London: University of Chicago Press, 1982.

Wesselski, Albert. *Versuch einer Theorie des Märchens.* Prager deutsche Studien 45. Reichenberg: F. Kraus, 1931.

Whitaker, Arthur P. *Spain and Defense of the West: Ally and Liability.* New York: Frederick A. Praeger Publishers, 1962, for the Council on Foreign Relations.

Williams, Noel. "Problems in Defining Contemporary Legend." In *Perspectives on Contemporary Legend. See* Smith 1984.

Wilson, Stephen. "Cults of Saints in the Churches of Central Paris." *Comparative Studies in Society and History* 22 (1980): 548–75.

———, ed. *Saints and Their Cults: Studies in Religious Sociology, Folklore, and History.* Cambridge: Cambridge University Press, 1983.

Wolfson, Nessa. "A Feature of Performed Narrative: The Conversational Historical Present." *Language in Society* 7 (1978): 215–37.

Wyatt, Carmen Joy. "Representations of Holiness in Some Spanish Hagiographical Works: The Thirteenth through the Seventeenth Centuries." Ph.D. diss., Stanford University, 1983.

Yoder, Don. "The Saint's Legend in the Pennsylvania German Folk-Culture." In *American Folk Legend. See* Hand 1971.

Index

Compositor: BookMasters
Text: 10/13 Aldus
Display: Aldus
Printer: Braun-Brumfield
Binder: Braun-Brumfield